The BERA Guide to Decolonising the Curriculum

The BERA Guides

Critical Insights into Educational Research and Practice

About the Series

Published in partnership between the British Educational Research Association and Emerald Publishing, *The BERA Guides* are short, research-informed yet accessible introductions to key, interdisciplinary topics impacting education research and practice.

Books in the series present a summary of the research on the topic, charting how scholarly thought and practice have evolved over time, and offering critical takeaways and suggestions for future work within and beyond academia. With the guides viewed as 'primers' on each topic, the series is for use by a broad academic audience, including early career and established researchers, postgraduate students, and practitioners.

Published in the Series

The BERA Guide to Mental Health and Wellbeing in Schools: Exploring Frontline Support in Educational Research and Practice; *Edited by Michelle Jayman, Jonathan Glazzard, Anthea Rose and Aimee Quickfall*

Forthcoming in the Series

The BERA Guide to Practitioner Research: Developing Professional Knowledge in Educational Research and Practice; *Edited by Kate Mawson, Claire Tyson, Tom Perry and Joyce I-Hui Chen*

The BERA Guide to Education for Environmental Sustainability: Creating Environmentally Just Futures in Educational Research & Practice; *Edited by Elizabeth Rushton and Lynda Dunlop*

The BERA Guide to Outdoor Learning: Place-Responsive Pedagogy in Educational Research and Practice; *Edited by Lucy Sors and Ruth Unsworth*

The BERA Guide to Decolonising the Curriculum

Equity and Inclusion in Educational Research and Practice

Edited by

Marlon Lee Moncrieffe
British Educational Research Association, UK

Omolabake Fakunle
University of Edinburgh, UK

Marlies Kustatscher
University of Edinburgh, UK

Anna Olsson Rost
Manchester Metropolitan University, UK

United Kingdom – North America – Japan – India
Malaysia – China

Emerald Publishing Limited
Emerald Publishing, Floor 5, Northspring, 21–23 Wellington Street, Leeds LS1 4DL.

Editorial matter and selection © 2025 Marlon Lee Moncrieffe, Omolabake Fakunle, Marlies Kustatscher, and Anna Olsson Rost.
Individual chapters © 2025 The authors.
Published under exclusive licence by Emerald Publishing Limited.

Reprints and permissions service
Contact: www.copyright.com

No part of this book may be reproduced, stored in a retrieval system, transmitted in any form or by any means electronic, mechanical, photocopying, recording or otherwise without either the prior written permission of the publisher or a licence permitting restricted copying issued in the UK by The Copyright Licensing Agency and in the USA by The Copyright Clearance Center. Any opinions expressed in the chapters are those of the authors. Whilst Emerald makes every effort to ensure the quality and accuracy of its content, Emerald makes no representation implied or otherwise, as to the chapters' suitability and application and disclaims any warranties, express or implied, to their use.

British Library Cataloguing in Publication Data
A catalogue record for this book is available from the British Library

ISBN: 978-1-83549-147-8 (Print)
ISBN: 978-1-83549-144-7 (Online)
ISBN: 978-1-83549-146-1 (Epub)

Contents

About the Editors ix

About the Contributors xi

INTRODUCTION

Chapter 1 – Decolonising the Curriculum: Fostering
Praxis for Equity and Inclusion 3
Marlon Lee Moncrieffe, Omolabake Fakunle, Marlies Kustatscher and Anna Olsson Rost

EARLY CHILDHOOD AND PRIMARY EDUCATION – INTRODUCTION

Chapter 2 – Decolonising and Diversifying Primary School
Curriculum Knowledge: Enacting Theory in Practice
and Pedagogy 19
Hannah Tyreman, Lisa-Maria Muller and Marlon Lee Moncrieffe

Chapter 3 – The Primary Curriculum for Religious Education
in Northern Ireland: Making a Case for Epistemic Justice 31
Rebecca Loader, Erika Jiménez, Joanne Hughes and Aisling O'Boyle

Chapter 4 – Decolonising Early Childhood Education:
Disrupting Professional Discourses 41
Chandrika Devarakonda and Marlies Kustatscher

Chapter 5 – Decolonial Education Through Solidarities:
Anti-racism Learning in Early Childhood Education
and Care in Canada 51
Zuhra Abawi and Rachel Berman

Chapter 6 – Decolonising Knowledge of the Parent-Practitioner Relationship in Early Childhood Practice Through Reflective Intercultural Teaching and Learning Interventions 61
Lesleann Whiteman

Chapter 7 – Decolonising the Curriculum: A Comparative Case-study of Black Learner and Educator Perspective Experiences from London (UK) and Johannesburg (South Africa) 71
Omena Osivwemu

EARLY CHILDHOOD AND PRIMARY EDUCATION – SUMMARY

SECONDARY AND TERTIARY EDUCATION – INTRODUCTION

Chapter 8 – Diversifying the History Curriculum in England: A Slow (R)evolution 91
Katharine Burn, Richard Harris and Joseph Smith

Chapter 9 – Challenging Dominant Narratives: Centring Historically Underserved Voices to Create New Enquiries for the History Classroom 103
Dan Lyndon-Cohen

Chapter 10 – A Professional Development Model for the Teaching of British Empire, Migration, and Belonging 111
Abigail Branford and Jason Todd

Chapter 11 – Decolonisation in Further Education: Engaging Diverse Students in the Delivery of a Decolonised Curriculum for A Level Biology in the Heart of the Former Empire 121
Samantha Hughes and Neil Hart

Chapter 12 – Decolonising Language Teaching: More Than a Box-ticking Exercise 131
Christina Richardson, Jane Jones and Tanya Linaker

Chapter 13 – HEADSUP: Using Deliberate Reflexive Practice
to Strengthen Decolonial Thinking and Action   141
Balqis Mohammed, Anna Olsson Rost and Karen Pashby

SECONDARY AND TERTIARY EDUCATION – SUMMARY

HIGHER EDUCATION – INTRODUCTION

Chapter 14 – Creating the Anti-racism Framework to Transform
the Curriculum for Student Teachers in England   159
Heather Jane Smith and Vini Lander

Chapter 15 – Decolonial Praxis in Wales: Reflections on
Research, Policy, and Anti-racist Action   169
Susan Davis and Jeremiah Adebolajo Olusola

Chapter 16 – Decolonising the Curriculum in Higher Education:
Introducing a Practice-informed Framework from Two Non-white
Academics in a UK University   177
Farah Akbar and Omolabake Fakunle

Chapter 17 – Relationality, Plurilingualism, and Place:
Language Education in Higher Education in
Northern Ireland   187
Mel M. Engman

Chapter 18 – 'Hunting' for a Black Feminist Decolonial
'Archive' at a Predominantly White University   197
Sahar D. Sattarzadeh

Chapter 19 – Decolonising Teaching and Research: A Student
Buddying Programme Between Burundi and the UK   211
*Louise Taylor, Jill Childs, Susan Muchiri, Naomi King,
Diana Wanjagi and Frankii Charles*

HIGHER EDUCATION – SUMMARY

CONCLUSION

Chapter 20 – What Are the Next Steps to Advancing Equity and Inclusion in Teaching and Learning Through Decolonial Educational Research and Practice? 225
Marlon Lee Moncrieffe, Omolabake Fakunle, Marlies Kustatscher and Anna Olsson Rost

Glossary 233

Index 235

About the Editors

Marlon Lee Moncrieffe is President of the British Educational Research Association. He teaches in primary school education and higher education. His international award-winning interdisciplinary action research and his academic and non-academic publications are framed by decolonial theories for critical thinking on educational policy, pedagogy, curriculum and culture, history, and sport.

Omolabake Fakunle is Chancellor's Fellow, Director of Equality, Diversity and Inclusion, and Decolonisation Lead, Curriculum Transformation Project at the University of Edinburgh. Her award-winning research, teaching, and consultancy focus on inclusivity in internationalisation, employability, and decoloniality. She is keenly interested in the intersection of research, educational policy, and practice.

Marlies Kustatscher is a Senior Lecturer in Childhood Studies at the University of Edinburgh. She is a Co-convenor of the Race and Inclusivity in Global Education Network and a Member of the Childhood and Youth Studies Research Group. Her research interests include childhood and intersectionality and participatory arts-based methodologies.

Anna Olsson Rost is a Senior Lecturer on the PGCE Secondary (history) programme at Manchester Metropolitan University. Her main research field is the history of education, but her research interests also include 'hidden histories' and teacher education and learning – with a particular focus on decolonial and anti-racist pedagogies and curricula.

About the Contributors

Zuhra Abawi is an Assistant Professor of Education at Niagara University. Her work focuses on how discourses of race, equity, and identity are negotiated, mediated, and socialised in education. Her most recent co-edited collection is *Enacting Antiracist and Activist Pedagogies in Teacher Education: Canadian Perspectives*, Canadian Scholars Press.

Farah Akbar is a Lecturer in Language Education. Her interest lies in the areas of language learning and teaching especially in evaluation and design of instructional materials, assessment literacy, language identity, community building at higher institutions – all underpinned by the notion of equality, diversity, and inclusion.

Rachel Berman is a Professor in the School of Early Childhood Studies at Toronto Metropolitan University. Her teaching and research focus on 'race' in early childhood settings. Her work has appeared in the *International Critical Childhood Policy Studies Journal*, the *Journal of Childhood Studies*, and *Children & Society*, among others.

Abigail Branford works as a Post-doctoral Research Assistant on the Oxford-UCL 'portrait of the teaching of Empire Migration and Belonging'. Her recently submitted doctoral research explored how the British Empire is understood by students in secondary schools in England. More broadly, she is interested in the role of educational institutions in postcolonial knowledge production.

Katharine Burn is an Associate Professor of Education at the University of Oxford. She is the PGCE Course Director, and her research focuses both on history education in school and on teachers' professional learning at all career stages. She is particularly interested in how teachers learn through engagement in and with research.

Frankii Charles is a Registered Social Worker, Lecturer, and Former Social Work Student at Oxford Brookes University, UK, where she co-led a student discussion and advisory group for students from the Global Ethnic Majority to reform curricula.

Jill Childs is Senior Fellow of the Higher Education Academy. Her work on anti-racism has won a number of national awards, including Silver Social Worker of the Year Awards for University of the Year (2022), and she was Team Leader for the Collaborative Award for Teaching Excellence by Advance HE (2022).

Susan Davis is Reader in Diversity, Equity, and Inclusion in Education at Cardiff Metropolitan University. She is also the Professional Doctorate/EdD Pathway Leader. On the Welsh Government DARPL programme (Darpl.org), she is Research Lead. Her research interests are around quiet, shy, and anxious learners and DEI.

Chandrika Devarakonda is an Associate Professor at the University of Chester. Her teaching, research, and publications focus on inclusion and diversity in early childhood. She is the Chair for social justice, equity, and diversity for the Research Development Communities in the Association for Teacher Education in Europe.

Mel M. Engman is a Senior Lecturer at Queen's University Belfast, where she teaches on a wide range of topics related to language, education, and power. Her research advocates for the maintenance and reclamation of indigenous languages, and it examines human-land relations, bilingual family learning, and anticolonial approaches to language education.

Omolabake Fakunle is Chancellor's Fellow, Director of Equality, Diversity, and Inclusion, and Decolonisation Lead, Curriculum Transformation Project at the University of Edinburgh. Her award-winning research, teaching, and consultancy focus on inclusivity in internationalisation, employability, and decoloniality. She is keenly interested in the intersection of research, educational policy, and practice.

Richard Harris is a Professor of Education at the University of Reading. They taught history in schools for 16 years and have been training history teachers for over 20 years. Their research covers different aspects of history education, including young people's engagement with the curriculum, and history teachers' decision-making.

Neil Hart is a Teacher of Biology and Environmental Science A levels at City and Islington College, London. He has an MA in Education Policy and Practice from the UCL IOE and has published on critical race theory and Prevent Duty. He has research interests in social and environmental justice in schools.

Joanne Hughes is Professor of Education and Director of the Centre for Shared Education at Queen's University Belfast, where she holds a UNESCO Chair in Shared Education for Peacebuilding and Social Justice. Her research addresses the role of education in divided societies, intergroup relations, and equality in education.

Samantha Hughes is the Subject Lead for Biology at City and Islington College, London. She is part of the teaching and learning network, with a focus on writing to learn. She also works consulting in developing specifications in Biology-related subjects.

Erika Jiménez is a Leverhulme Early Career Fellow at the School of Law, Queen's University Belfast, where her work explores how Golani youth deploy human rights in their struggle against the forgotten occupation. She is interested in decolonial approaches to human rights, human rights education, and childhood research.

Jane Jones was for many years Head of MFL Education. She has published widely on all aspects of language teaching, learning, and assessment. Her research interests include formative assessment practices, relationships and health education, teacher and pupil wellbeing, and the promotion of students as researchers and agents of change.

Naomi King is a Researcher in Psychology at Oxford Brookes University, UK, specialising in Applied Social Psychology. Her work investigates contemporary topics with real-world implications for social change.

Marlies Kustatscher is a Senior Lecturer in Childhood Studies at the University of Edinburgh. She is a Co-convenor of the Race and Inclusivity in Global Education Network and a Member of the Childhood and Youth Studies Research Group. Her research interests include childhood and intersectionality and participatory arts-based methodologies.

Vini Lander is Professor of Race and Education and Director of the Centre for Race, Education, and Decoloniality at Leeds Beckett University, UK. Her research deploys critical race theory to examine race inequalities in teacher education examining teachers' attitudes to race and the lived experiences of teacher educators of colour.

Tanya Linaker has been the Team Leader for Slavonic and Middle Eastern Languages at King's Language Centre since 2016. She has also led the Centre in all Equality, Diversity, and Inclusion matters, including curriculum decolonising. Her research interests include educational leadership and language teacher identity construction.

Rebecca Loader is a Senior Research Fellow at the School of Social Sciences, Education, and Social Work at Queen's University Belfast. Her interests are in education and peacebuilding, migration, and social justice. During 2021–2023, she was the Lead Investigator of a study examining education among minority ethnic and migrant groups in Northern Ireland.

Dan Lyndon-Cohen is the Director of the Schools History Project and Lead Practitioner for Humanities at Park View School, Tottenham. He is the author of many publications for schools, on multicultural and migration histories. He has also worked as a Consultant for the Imperial War Museum, National Portrait Gallery, and BBC Bitesize.

Balqis Mohammed is a PhD Student at Manchester Metropolitan University, and her research interests lie in the fields of decolonial studies, Black studies, and social justice in education.

Marlon Lee Moncrieffe is President of the British Educational Research Association. He teaches in primary school education and higher education. His international award-winning interdisciplinary action research and his academic and non-academic publications are framed by decolonial theories for critical thinking on educational policy, pedagogy, curriculum and culture, history, and sport.

Susan Muchiri is the Head of Department of Social Work and Community Development at Hope Africa university. Her contribution on decolonisation has been recognised by the Collaborative Award for Teaching Excellence by Advance HE (2022).

Lisa-Maria Muller is Head of Research at the Chartered College of Teaching, where she works on improving the links between research, policy, and practice. A Former MFL Teacher with experience in Austria and England and Post-doctoral Researcher at the Universities of Cambridge and York, she is passionate about systematically capturing and sharing teacher expertise.

Aisling O'Boyle is a Senior Lecturer in Education at Queen's University Belfast, where she directs the Centre for Language

Education Research. Her research interests are in the fields of English Language learning and teaching, including school- and community-based approaches to English Language learning for migrant children and families.

Jeremiah Adebolajo Olusola is DARPL's Post-doctoral Research Fellow at Cardiff Metropolitan University. Alongside this Welsh Government funded Fellowship, he is undertaking a research project with the British Library's Research and Development Team, aimed at improving EDI in postgraduate development. His research interests surround British multiculturalism, race, Islamic epistemology, and religious conversion.

Omena Osivwemu is a Primary School Educator, School Governor, Sociologist, Humanities Leader, Mentor to Black Early Career Teachers, and a Black History Consultant. She creates EdTech resources, writes blog articles on diverse curricula, and provides consultancy to educational publishers. Passionate about social justice, she frequently speaks on diversity and decoloniality in education.

Karen Pashby teaches undergraduates and postgraduates in the School of Childhood, Youth, and Education Studies. A Former Secondary School Educator (in Canada and Brazil) and experienced Teacher Educator, her research draws on postcolonial and decolonial theoretical resources to identify productive pedagogical tensions in education for global citizenship in 'multicultural contexts'.

Christina Richardson has worked as a Teacher Educator for modern languages for over two decades. Her research interests are inclusive education, more specifically supporting ethnolinguistically minoritised pupils, and those with special educational needs and disabilities in mainstream education and decolonising the curriculum. She is Editor-in-Chief of *NALDIC's EAL Journal*.

Anna Olsson Rost is a Senior Lecturer on the PGCE Secondary (history) programme at Manchester Metropolitan University.

Her main research field is the history of education, but her research interests also include 'hidden histories' and teacher education and leaning – with a particular focus on decolonial and anti-racist pedagogies and curricula.

Sahar D. Sattarzadeh is a daughter of Azeri, Iranian, Kurdish, and Persian refugee settlers. She writes, researches, and teaches about critical comparative global ethnic, racial, and Indigenous communities and the (in)justices and (in)equities they transform and reimagine within the context of higher education, knowledge systems, activism, and human rights.

Heather Jane Smith is Professor of Race and Language Equality in Education at Newcastle University. She is a Critical Race Theory Scholar. Her research includes critical analyses of education policy, racism in ITE, and translanguaging as an emancipatory pedagogy for multilingual pupils. She is Co-author of the anti-racism framework for ITE/T.

Joseph Smith is a Lecturer in Education at the University of Stirling. His research concerns the framing of history curricula, the identity of history teachers, and the ways in which the two intersect. He taught history in schools for nine years and has published on both history and education for general and academic audiences.

Louise Taylor, PhD, is a Professor of Education and Student Experience at Oxford Brookes University. Her pedagogic innovation and leadership applies psychological theory to contemporary issues in higher education, including decolonisation. She is a National Teaching Fellow and Principal Fellow of Advance HE.

Jason Todd is a Departmental Lecturer in Education at the University of Oxford, where he also currently leads on the PGCE history programme. He is the Principal Investigator on a joint Oxford-UCL three-year research project, 'A portrait of the teaching of Empire, Migration and Belonging in English Secondary Schools', investigating both students' and teachers' learning.

Hannah Tyreman is a Curriculum Designer, Writer, Walker, Reader, and Wonderer. Previously an English Teacher and Manager in FE colleges, she now designs professional development for teachers. She is an advisory board member for the Paul Hamlyn Foundation Teacher Development Fund, and she also maintains the BAMEed Network's website.

Diana Wanjagi is an Associate Lecturer and Former Social Work Student at Oxford Brookes University, UK, where she co-led a student discussion and advisory group for students from the Global Ethnic Majority to reform curricula.

Lesleann Whiteman is a Senior Lecturer in Early Childhood at the School of Education, University of Brighton, UK. Her research examines how the content of early childhood degree courses prepares students to identify gaps in their knowledge on anti-discriminatory practices with diverse families in advancing parent–practitioner relationships.

INTRODUCTION

CHAPTER 1

Decolonising the Curriculum: Fostering Praxis for Equity and Inclusion

Marlon Lee Moncrieffe[a], Omolabake Fakunle[b], Marlies Kustatscher[b] and Anna Olsson Rost[c]

[a]British Educational Research Association, UK
[b]University of Edinburgh, UK
[c]Manchester Metropolitan University, UK

Welcome, readers, to the *BERA Guide to Decolonising the Curriculum: Equity and Inclusion in Educational Research and Practice*. The motivation of this BERA guide is to share examples of impactful decolonial research-informed teaching and learning in early childhood education and care, primary education, secondary and tertiary education, and higher education so that this praxis can be fostered more widely. The chapters in this guide offer insight into a broad range of decolonial theories, and methodological approaches applied in research for teaching and learning through expert early childhood practitioners, primary and secondary school teachers, further and higher education lecturers, educational consultants, teacher-educators, and experienced academic researchers. This unique collective of contributors shares research from across the four UK nations of England, Scotland, Wales, and Northern Ireland and through international comparative educational contexts and perspectives from the USA, Canada, Burundi, Trinidad and Tobago, and South Africa.

Background

In the introduction to this BERA guide, it is important to recognise the power of public activism in championing racial, social, and educational justice. The Black Lives Matter anti-racism public protests of 2020 in the UK, raised awareness and support for a decolonised national history curriculum (Moncrieffe, 2020; Moncrieffe & Harris, 2020; Weale et al., 2020), and influenced multiple public petitions to UK Parliament demanding government accountability, debate, and action for change (see Moncrieffe, 2023). For example, 'Teach Britain's colonial past as part of the UK's compulsory curriculum' was supported by 268,722 signatories (UK Government and Parliament Petitions, 2020). Before these events, in 2014, the call for a decolonised education had been raised to public attention by students at the University College London through their 'Why is my Curriculum White Campaign?' (Peters, 2015). Outside of the UK, public activism with aims to decolonise education had been occurring in settler colonial states such as Canada and South Africa. The 'Idle No More' movement led by indigenous peoples across Canada challenged the federal conservative government, in demanding education for the revitalisation of indigenous peoples through awareness and empowerment (Tupper, 2014). In South Africa, students at the University of Cape triggered the 'Rhodes Must Fall' movement in 2015, leading to wider movements across South Africa to decolonise education (Hlophe, 2015). This wave of influence was captured by the decolonising movement led by students at the University of Oxford in the UK (Chantiluke et al., 2018; Sabaratnam, 2017). Here, student complaints and demands pointed to what Peters (2015, p. 641) described as 'the lack of awareness that the curriculum is comprised of "White ideas" by "White authors" and is a result of colonialism that has normalised Whiteness and made Blackness invisible'.

What Is Meant by 'Decolonising the Curriculum'?

Modern society is based upon the hierarchies of Eurocentrism in which the creation of anti-Blackness is essential (Andrews,

2018) to maintaining the European (white) projection of its own self-image above all others (Moncrieffe, 2020). Where curriculum for teaching and learning is an official selection that structures knowledge in ways that privilege a particular construction of knowledge and the history of knowledge (Peters, 2015) such as Eurocentrism, Anglocentrism, and whiteness, then to decolonise the curriculum is to expose, disrupt, and dismantle the ongoing processes of western (neo) colonialism and the uncritical cultural reproduction of epistemic power that is fuelled by racism (Moncrieffe, 2020, 2022; Le Grange, 2023). To decolonise a curriculum as such is an anti-racist venture. Bhambra et al. (2018, p. 1) provide a succinct two-step definition of decolonising as:

> *thinking about the world which takes colonialism, empire, and racism as its empirical and discursive objects of study; it re-situates these phenomena as key shaping forces of the contemporary world, in a context where their role has been systematically effaced from view. Second, it purports to offer alternative ways of thinking about the world and alternative forms of political praxis.*

This relates closely to Arshad's (2020) definition of decolonising education as being:

> *an approach involving a critical analysis of how colonial forms of knowledge, pedagogical strategies and research methodologies have shaped what we know, what we recognise, and how we reward such knowledge accordingly.* (Arshad, 2020)

According to Walsh and Mignolo (2018, p. 381), 'decoloniality' is 'neither a field of study, nor a discipline, but a way of being in the world, interrogating the structures of knowledge and of knowing that have thrown us'. Thus, while the motivations in education to decolonise colonialism, empire, and racism in the curriculum may stem from the same origins of oppression, the route to achieving this outcome comes by different pathways due to the 'heterogeneity of viewpoints, approaches, political projects, and normative concerns' (Bhambra et al., 2018, p. 1).

Arresting Epistemic Violence

This BERA guide presents a broad range of pathways of creativity taken in action to decolonise the curriculum, sharing on the impact achieved in this through several definitions, interpretations, aims, and research strategies. A significant action of motivation to transform education opportunities for all, for the better, given by contributors across this BERA guide is through disrupting and arresting the epistemic violence (Moncrieffe, 2020; Spivak, 1999) of anti-Blackness produced by educational policies, curriculum guidance aims, and contents dominated by whiteness across all educational phases. In talking about whiteness, this BERA guide does not point to white people, but to the social and educational ideologies which empower people racialised as white over other people (Peters, 2015; Pirbhai-Illich et al., 2023). Thus, the target of this disrupting and arresting of epistemic violence is also aimed at innate and often unconscious cultural and knowledge biases brought to education by uncritical practitioners during curriculum teaching and learning processes (Harris, 2013; Lander, 2011, 2014; Moncrieffe, 2020). The rich evidence generated by this BERA guide through the data, testimonies, and the arguments given across the chapters shows that by applying decolonial thinking in pursuit of equity and inclusion in education, this can heighten opportunities in knowledge acquisition through a broader and generally neglected range of non-Eurocentric epistemologies, thus advancing teaching and learning for all as epistemic justice. To a greater extent, this BERA guide sees decolonisation operating synchronously as anti-racist action, particularly when tackled at the intersection of universities and schools (Le Grange, 2023). Decolonising the curriculum and anti-racist pedagogy can strengthen continued professional development, where practitioner training in developing equity and inclusion of marginalised knowledges can be taught for implementation. Fostering decolonial praxis in teacher practitioners can be the route to this goal.

Fostering Decolonial Praxis

Freire (1996, p. 52) discusses praxis as 'reflection and action upon the world in order to transform it'. Praxis is given by this

BERA guide as an enlightened route to conceptualising practice (Crouch & Pearce, 2013, p. 40). Praxis is the conscious and intentional approach to research, teaching, and learning through theories and lenses of decoloniality, applied in analysis and critique of coloniality. Decolonial praxis, therefore, makes visible, opens up, and advances radically distinct perspectives and positionalities that can displace Western rationality as the only framework of knowledge (Walsh & Mignolo, 2018). In aiming to foster decolonial praxis that is potent and transformative, this BERA guide provides critical and theoretically informed research, teaching, and learning for challenging and decentring the dominant focus in education given to Eurocentrism, Anglocentrism, and whiteness. Aligned to educational values of equity and inclusion, the decolonial praxis shared in this BERA guide means that attention to knowledge acquisition and educational development comes by the rich value of 'alternative' or non-white, non-Anglocentric, and non-Eurocentric cultural ways of knowing and being. The educational challenge in this means unlearning the taken-for-granted ways by which we in the contemporary Western world come to know, understand, and perceive reality through the influence of formal educational institutions, the state, religious institutions, and the media and through informal influences such as families, communities, and public opinion. Decolonial praxis manifested by contributors to this BERA guide offers broad examples of critical unlearning for re-learning in aiming for the genuine conveyance of equity and inclusion in teaching and learning.

Equity and Inclusion

In relation to decoloniality, equity is the starting point for devising strategies and initiatives for inclusion in practice. This approach recognises the impact of historical injustices on current-day manifestations of inequalities pertaining to ethnic and racial differences. To mitigate these structural disadvantages, there is a need to recognise that people have different starting points and needs. This differentiates equity from equality, which assumes that everyone should be treated equally. It is important to restate that the conflation of equality and equity merits a rethink, as the former remains a term used by educational institutions in describing their inclusion policy, which includes racial inclusiveness. While recognising the importance of nomenclature, the enactment of equity and inclusion goes beyond words, and this BERA guide highlights some of the challenges faced in different national and global contexts in embedding in equitable practice to foster inclusion. The main challenge echoes the construct of pedagogy of discomfort (Zembylas, 2015). This BERA guide goes further with examples of decolonial praxis that demonstrates teachers' reflexivity on their positionality as they seek to foster equity and inclusion in practice. This alludes to the potential benefits inherent in an inclusive internationalised classroom where staff and students from different cultural backgrounds have opportunities to learn together (Fakunle et al., 2022), as a microcosm of the global society where equity and inclusion remain a worthy goal, and work in progress.

Objective and Aims

The objective of this BERA guide is to present examples of impactful decolonial research-informed teaching and learning in early childhood and primary education, secondary and tertiary education, and higher education so that decolonial praxis can be fostered more widely and further advanced. The key aims of the guide are to:

- Provide an overview of action being taken to decolonise the curriculum across key phases of compulsory and non-compulsory education in the UK.
- Provide contextual international comparative approaches to decolonising the curriculum.
- Share a wide range of decolonial theories and methodological approaches for decolonising the curriculum.
- Provide insights on the positive impact generated by teaching and learning a decolonised curriculum.
- Share on next steps for advancing decolonial praxis across key phases of compulsory and non-compulsory education.

The Contents

This BERA guide is shaped by three sections of research-informed practice, broadly reflecting three distinct arenas of education across the life course:

1. Early childhood education and care and primary school education.
2. Secondary school education and tertiary education.
3. Higher education.

Each section begins with an *Introduction*, sharing key themes and challenges within that phase of education in teaching and learning. By sharing short insights of the chapters, the introduction invites reflections on current practices and discourses around decolonising the curriculum. Each section concludes with a *Summary*, for recapping key messages and offering *reflective questions*. These are given to foster reflective discussion among educators and researchers and can be used for preparing lectures and seminars and for feeding into writing and research by stimulating critical reflective thinking around what decolonising the curriculum can look like in educational practice, policy, and research. *Further recommended reading* is also provided.

The *six chapters in each section* provide situated case studies, examples, and practical applications of how educators can work towards decolonising the curriculum in their own practice and settings. While there are many underlying commonalities around how this can be done, and what the challenges are, there are also distinct features within each section:

Early childhood education and care and primary school education: the chapters in this section are informed by evaluations of continued and advanced professional development programmes; by qualitative research with children, families, educators, and students; by policy and curriculum analysis; and by reflective practitioner research. In centring the youngest members of society, multiple chapters in this section draw critical attention to how children and childhoods are constructed and how this shapes our educational systems and practices – for example, whether children are seen as empty vessels to be filled with knowledge, as incomplete, developing beings, or as capable social actors who coproduce their education and need to be actively involved in processes of decolonisation. The primary school education chapters make the case for improving curricula (such as of British history, or of religious education) by diversifying taken-for-granted knowledges, for increasing intercultural competencies among practitioners, for addressing and challenging hegemonic whiteness in professions and practices, and for strengthening relationships with diverse groups of children, families, and communities.

Secondary school education and tertiary education: the chapters in this section draw on diverse research methods, such as survey research, multimodal and creative research practices, and training programme evaluations. These highlight, in particular, the potential of action research and reflective practice to develop and embed decolonial approaches in education. This section also draws attention to the importance of decolonising science subjects, such as biology, by complementing and enhancing accepted, taken-for-granted subject knowledges with critical socio-scientific historical narratives. This is aided by educators engaging in critical and subversive thinking which goes beyond 'traditional' approaches and considers who is under-served by our current practices and systems.

Higher education (HE): contributions in this section utilise survey research, reflective practice, teaching observations and evaluations, archival research, and participatory and creative research to make the case embedding decolonisation processes in educational policy and practice. Chapters in this section draw attention to the role of policy in aiding (or hindering) processes of decolonisation in the curriculum in initial teacher education and internationalised HE delivery. They highlight the importance of critically interrogating knowledge claims and epistemic power dynamics. This includes challenging the hegemonic role of English language in international higher education, as well as of the written word, in order to move beyond a Eurocentric gaze.

A broad range of educational expertise is provided across this unique collective of chapters for showing decolonial praxis. The breadth offered is a key strength of this BERA guide, but it is also acknowledged that this presents challenges, since the contextualised accounts given cannot easily be generalised across all of the phases of education covered. Similarly, the examples of international case studies, and the richer insights and comparables of best practice that this provides, is a strength of this collection. However, the sample of international case studies could be broader and more prominent to provide a more significant sample of contrasts and comparisons.

While all the four UK nations are well represented in this BERA guide, these are not equally exemplified in all sections of the book. However, the uniformed structure of the chapters given in this BERA guide provides the opportunity to share and compare rationales, methodologies, analyses, and findings. Furthermore, the impact and next steps sections in each chapter are designed to offer further ideas in the development of this work, where existing ideas and practices can be built upon.

References

Andrews, K. (2018). *Back to black: Retelling black radicalism for the 21st century.* Zed Books.

Arshad, R. (2020, September 7). Decolonising and initial teacher education. *CERES Blog.* https://www.ceres.education.ed.ac.uk/2020/08/19/decolonising-and-initial-teacher-education/

Bhambra, G. K., Gebrial, D., & Nişancıoğlu, K. (2018). *Decolonising the university.* Pluto Press.

Chantiluke, R., Kwomba, B., & Athinangamso, N. (2018). *Rhodes must fall: The struggle to decolonise the racist heart of empire.* Zed Books.

Crouch, C., & Pearce, J. (2013). *Doing research in design.* Bloomsbury Publishing.

Fakunle, O., Kalinga, C., & Lewis, V. (2022). Internationalization and decolonization in UK higher education: Are we there yet? *International Higher Education, 110,* 1–3. https://ejournals.bc.edu/index.php/ihe/article/view/14993

Freire, P. (1996). *Pedagogy of the oppressed (revised) (first published in 1968)* (Vol. 356, pp. 357–358). Continuum.

Harris, R. (2013). The place of diversity within history and the challenge of policy and curriculum. *Oxford Review of Education, 39*(3), 400–419.

Hlophe, W. (2015, April 1). HLOPHE: Rhodes must fall everywhere. *Yale Daily News*. http://yaledailynews.com/blog/2015/04/01/rhodes-must-fall-everywhere/

Lander, V. (2011). Race, culture, and all that: An exploration of the perspectives of White secondary student teachers about race equality issues in their initial teacher education. *Race Ethnicity and Education, 14*(3), 351–364. https://doi.org.10.1080/13613324.2010.543389

Lander, V. (2014). Initial teacher education: The practice of whiteness. In R. Race & V. Lander (Eds.), *Advancing race and ethnicity in education* (pp. 93–110). Palgrave Macmillan.

Le Grange, L. (2023). Decolonisation and anti-racism: Challenges and opportunities for (teacher) education. *The Curriculum Journal, 34*(1), 8–21. https://doi.org/10.1002/curj.193

Moncrieffe. M. L. (2020). *Decolonising the history curriculum: Eurocentrism and primary schooling*. Palgrave MacMillan.

Moncrieffe, M. L. (2022). Why decolonising curriculum knowledge? In M. L. Moncrieffe (Ed.), *Decolonising curriculum knowledge: International perspectives and interdisciplinary approaches* (pp. 1–14). Palgrave Macmillan. https://doi.org/10.1007/978-3-031-13623-8_1

Moncrieffe, M. L. (2023). *Examining challenges and possibilities in the objective of a decolonized education*. Oxford Research Encyclopaedia of Education. https://oxfordre.com/education/display/10.1093/acrefore/9780190264093.001.0001/acrefore-9780190264093-e-1863

Moncrieffe, M., & Harris, R. (2020). Repositioning curriculum teaching and learning through Black-British history. *Research Intelligence, 144*, 14–15.

Peters, M. A. (2015). Why is my curriculum white? *Educational Philosophy and Theory, 47*, 641–646. https://doi.org/10.1080/00131857.2015.1037227

Pirbhai-Illich, F., Martin, F., & Pete, S. (2023). *Decolonizing educational relationships: Practical approaches for higher and teacher education*. Emerald Publishing Limited.

Sabaratnam, M. (2017). *Decolonising intervention: International statebuilding in Mozambique*. Rowman & Littlefield International.

Spivak, G. C. (1999). *A critique of postcolonial reason: Toward a history of the vanishing present*. Harvard University Press.

Tupper, J. (2014). Social media and the idle no more movement: Citizenship, activism and dissent in Canada. *Journal of Social Science Education, 13*(4), 87–94.

UK Government and Parliament Petitions. (2020). *Teach Britain's colonial past as part of the UK's compulsory curriculum*. https://petition.parliament.uk/petitions/324092 London: UK Government and Parliament

Walsh, C. E., & Mignolo, W. D. (2018). *On decoloniality concepts, analysis, praxis* (p. 304). Duke University Press.

Weale, S., Bakare, L., & Mir, S. (2020, June 8). Calls grow for Black history to be taught to all English school pupils. *The Guardian*. https://www.theguardian.com/education/2020/jun/08/calls-mount-for-black-history-to-be-taught-to-all-uk-school-pupils

Zembylas, M. (2015). 'Pedagogy of discomfort' and its ethical implications: The tensions of ethical violence in social justice education. *Ethics and Education*, *10*(2), 163–174. https://doi.org.10.1080/17449642.2015.1039274

EARLY CHILDHOOD AND PRIMARY EDUCATION – INTRODUCTION

This section provides guidance and insight on leading approaches to decolonial praxis emerging through a range of broad foci: reframing the teaching and learning of British history in the primary school curriculum for better sense of connection and belonging for all learners; exposing the marginalising effects on primary school students by the one-dimensional teaching and learning of religious education in the primary school; arresting the normalcy of whiteness and lack of attention given to racism in early childhood education and care spaces; raising attention to reflexive professional intercultural engagements in parent–practitioners relationships; and leading with Black student learner voices in co-producing knowledge for sharing experiences of curriculum engagement and possible advancements. These diverse research areas and approaches taken in generating evidence-informed knowledge have produced some common themes in practice, in impact, and in discussion of next steps in advancing decolonial praxis:

1. *Continued and advanced professional development (CAAPD)*. Decolonising educational curricula requires fundamental changes to how we think about and enact education in our contemporary societies. All chapters in this section speak to the need for robust professional dialogue through coherent continued advanced professional development as exemplified in the research given by *Tyreman et al.* (Chapter 2). This shows how a refined collation of leading evidenced-informed research in the field can provide CAAPD for supporting practitioners with decolonising and diversifying the curriculum in meaningful ways. *Abawi and Berman* (Chapter 5) in their research

contribution also place strong emphasis on CAAPD initiatives that include grassroot perspectives, voices, and lived experiences of children, families, and communities as vital to pre-service education. This, in turn, emphasises a culturally responsive pedagogy.

2. *Culturally responsive pedagogy (CRP)*. An asset-based approach which requires educators to centre the children they work with; to be knowledgeable about their own, their pupils' and other cultures; and to embed this knowledge in their resources and practices. This goes beyond tokenistic and superficial practices of 'celebrating diversity'. For example, *Loader et al.* (Chapter 3) illuminate the detrimental marginalising effects of a narrow one-dimensional Eurocentric curriculum design in practice on minority group children and, in sharing on this, argue how richer educational opportunities for all will come by the use and application of substantive subject content and knowledge, giving teaching, and learning through the plurality of worldviews. Developing CRP is also advocated by *Whiteman* (Chapter 6) in research which guides towards calling for formal assessments in early-childhood placement-learning university teaching modules, where student-practitioners should demonstrate their professional understanding and competencies in applying CRP to their intercultural professional engagements. Similarly, *Osivwemu's* (Chapter 7) research guides on placing emphasis on Black student learners sharing the leadership of curriculum innovation in co-production of knowledge with their teachers in shaping the cultural relevance of curriculum that they are learning from. Such approaches to reframed curriculum design and renewed pedagogy give new challenges for some practitioners who may require support with transformative thinking for action.

3. *Critically reflexive research-informed practitioners.* Reflexivity and research-informed practice are essential vehicles in driving this transformation. All the chapters in this section speak to the advanced approach in

pedagogy enabled by the practitioners' commitment to reflexive practice. For example, *Devarakonda and Kustatscher* (Chapter 4) offer valuable insights and guidance in this, by sharing their implementation of a 'model of diversity' typology used with their early childhood students in supporting critical reflexivity. This is enabling a greater awareness of their power and positionality as educators to challenge structural injustices by providing equity in education for their learners through decolonial practice.

CHAPTER 2

Decolonising and Diversifying Primary School Curriculum Knowledge: Enacting Theory in Practice and Pedagogy

Hannah Tyreman[a], Lisa-Maria Muller[b] and Marlon Lee Moncrieffe[c]

[a]Teacher Development Trust, UK
[b]Chartered College of Teaching, UK
[c]British Educational Research Association, UK

ABSTRACT

Decolonising the curriculum has been increasingly discussed in education, particularly following the Black Lives Matter anti-racism protests in 2020. This chapter presents how teachers in UK primary schools are approaching curriculum-making through decolonial lenses. With a focus on teaching and learning about race, cultural diversity, and British history in primary school education, the authors refer to key examples of teacher education research which has argued over the years for decolonising and diversifying curriculum knowledge. The authors relate these arguments to evaluate data from online learning modules on this topic created by the Chartered College of Teaching. Findings show that when provided with robust continuous professional development (CPD), teachers grow in confidence in seeing and challenging the limitations of knowledge centred by the Eurocentric discourses of the primary national curriculum. Adopting decolonial lenses for critical curriculum thinking enables teachers to plan and implement approaches to pedagogies framed by a diversification of knowledge in curriculum-making.

Keywords: decolonising; diversifying; evidence-informed education; continuous professional development; curriculum

Research Context

Since 2020, the Covid-19 pandemic and the Black Lives Matter movement have highlighted well-established gender, racial, and socioeconomic disparities in UK society (Blundell et al., 2022; Nazroo & Becares, 2021). The focus on racial disparities has seen a drive towards decolonising and diversifying the curriculum, resulting in new and increased dialogue among teachers and school leaders.

The Chartered College of Teaching, the professional body for teachers in the UK, recognised that this well-intentioned dialogue needed to be supported towards effective and evidence-informed action. Acknowledging the importance of CPD to support high-quality practice, especially in this area (Moncrieffe, 2020; Moncrieffe & Harris, 2020), we produced six online learning modules exploring two key questions:

1. How is the decolonisation and diversification of curriculum and pedagogy being interpreted and enacted by teachers today?
2. How might CPD support teachers embarking on this work?

We acknowledged that these online learning modules would be a starting point for this work rather than the conclusion, serving as a source of initial reflection, and a catalyst for further development and action both for the sector and for us as a professional body. This chapter reports the findings from our development and evaluation of the modules.

Literature

A British discourse on race and cultural diversity in education began to evolve in the 1960s in response to the growing population of immigrants (Modood & May, 2001). Regarding this and the calls for decolonisation of education and curriculum knowledge, Black parents began to set up supplementary schools for their children, to counter the inequities they faced in learning through a Eurocentric curriculum discourse (Chantiluke, 2018) justified by Coard's (1971) report on how the West Indian child is made 'educationally sub-normal' in the British school system.

By the 1980s, contending educational theories of multicultural and antiracist education severely fractured the educational discourse (Gilroy, 1987; Modood & May, 2001). A shift to a focus on British history as central to teaching and learning about race and cultural diversity came when the New Labour Government (1997–2010) sought to advance notions of citizenship through students' exploration of 'Britishness' (Ajegbo et al., 2007). However, this proposed route to advancing learning was overtaken in 2010 by the Conservative/Liberal Democrat coalition government's implementation of a British history master narrative (Department for Education, 2013) for curriculum teaching and learning.

In critically examining this through teacher education research, Moncrieffe (2020) argues that the aims and contents of the national curriculum (Department for Education, 2013) are framed by a regressive approach to the acquisition of historical knowledge that can serve to reinforce a superior white British culture and world view, where 'white' becomes the norm to which other 'races' stand apart.

Even before this argument, Nichol and Harnett's (2011) research highlighted how primary school teachers showed grave concerns about the lack of government direction and guidance that would help them engage pupils in their classrooms with more diverse and multicultural perspectives of British history. Harris (2013) argued that the past is inherently diverse, so the national curriculum ought to reflect this.

Evidence-informed research for primary school teacher education aiming to advance possibilities for learning about race and cultural diversity through past and present British histories has been pioneered over the years by the Runnymede Trust (e.g. Alexander et al., 2015). The argument given by proponents of decolonising and diversifying curriculum knowledge is for teachers to apply critical curriculum thinking to decentre the privilege given to epistemic 'whiteness' in the aims and contents of the curriculum (Moncrieffe & Harris, 2020), thereby supporting efforts to dismantle racism and oppression (Milne, 2019).

Objective and Methods

Since initial teacher training and early career support may not adequately prepare teachers for decolonising and diversifying the curriculum in the UK, the Chartered College of Teaching's vision was that these online modules would begin to build teachers' capacity and knowledge, as framed by Moncrieffe (2020):

> *teachers should be empowered to be able to engage in questions and debate on the 'what' and the 'why' of curriculum implementation in their teaching and learning. Not simply to become 'curriculum makers', but to become reflexive 'critical curriculum thinkers' that actively evaluate the educational worth of given curriculum aims and contents, so that their future practice can become engaged, anti-racist and decolonial.* (p. 87)

In view of this, our objectives were to provide support for teachers in the form of professional development in designing and implementing rich and challenging curricula that would also broaden and deepen students' knowledge and develop their skills in critical thinking.

The online modules of our design combined key evidence from leading research in the field of decolonising the curriculum, with meaningful models of curriculum pedagogy and practice from various education contexts, subjects, and phases.

A rigorous process of peer reviewing ensured that selected written case studies would support our aims and teachers' learning. In our leading on how a decolonised curriculum can be coherent and rigorous in advancing teachers' professional development, we populated the modules of learning with key literature and teaching resources selected and utilised to foster belonging for all involved in curriculum teaching and learning.

In testing the online modules of learning before their launch, we consulted with four teachers and academics who have leadership experience and expertise in decolonising and diversifying curriculum. This peer review of the online modules of learning enabled us to increase their quality before their publication in Spring 2022.

The impact of the online module of learning content on teachers' understanding of key concepts for decolonising and diversifying the curriculum for implementation in their contexts was assessed using pre- and post-learning surveys, complemented by one-on-one online interviews.

Analysis and Findings

499 teachers and school leaders (participants) completed at least one of the six modules with 45 completing all six. The number to have completed pre- and post-learning surveys is provided in Table 2.1. These contained open and closed questions, the latter using a Likert-scale (1 = strongly agree, 5 = strongly disagree). Participants who completed all six modules were invited for interview and five were accepted.

Motivation and Knowledge Levels Before Undertaking the Modules

Data showed that it was both teachers working in diverse settings and those working in predominantly white British schools who engaged in the modules. Participants recognised the need to expand their knowledge and expose their students to a wider range of knowledge and experiences, particularly in homogeneous school contexts:

> It's a very white area, and our school is very white. And I'm really conscious of that. [...] I just wanted to make sure that I have more understanding of it. (Primary School Leader)

Table 2.1. Response Rates for Pre- and Post-module Surveys.

	Pre-survey	Module 1	Module 2	Module 3	Module 4	Module 5	Module 6
Respondents	181	113	71	63	57	48	43

Knowledge levels prior to the online learning were relatively high, with 40% of participants rating their existing knowledge of decolonising and diversifying the curriculum as *developing*, meaning that they had been engaging in ongoing learning on the topic, reflecting critically on it, and had begun making changes to practice. Despite these relatively high ratings before starting the modules, there remained obvious learning potential as only 6% of participants indicated that all their teaching decisions were grounded in diversifying and decolonising the curriculum and 17% of participants indicated a *rudimentary* knowledge of the topic, suggesting that they only had a basic understanding of some key terms (see Fig. 2.1).

Participants seemed less confident in implementing their knowledge with 36% having no idea where to start and the 21% who had begun implementing initial steps declaring a lack of confidence in them, highlighting the need for continued professional development that supports teachers in taking assured actions towards curriculum change (see Fig. 2.2).

Module 1 – Defining Decolonisation

This module addressed the challenges of defining what it means to decolonise and diversify the curriculum. Overall, participants stated that the module supported them to define key terms in

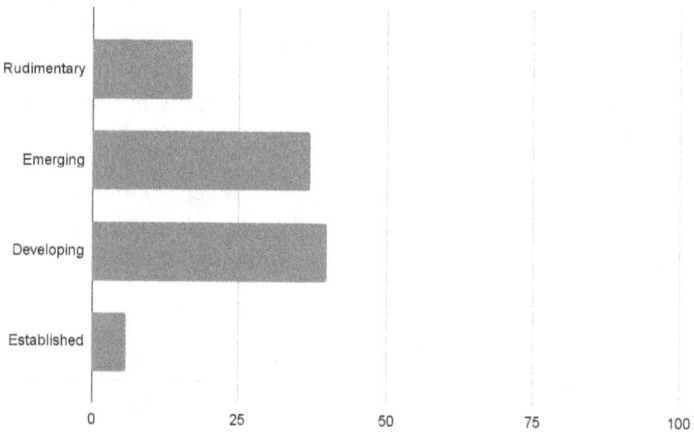

Fig. 2.1. Self-reported Knowledge of Decolonising and Diversifying the Curriculum (Pre-survey).

relation to defining the curriculum (average rating = 1.48) and to identify key barriers to this work (1.69):

> [J]ust the definition at the start of the difference between the two [diversifying and decolonising] was really useful. (Primary school leader)

However, participants' confidence with implementing their new learning was relatively low (1.88), suggesting that more work is needed for this.

Module 2 – Knowing Our Histories

This module addressed the multiplicity of British histories and their influence on the curriculum. Average ratings indicate a positive impact on participants' understanding of the multiplicity of British histories (1.55) and why deep knowledge of these matters to their pupils (1.47). Again, participants' confidence in implementing their learning was lower on average (1.80), but one example from an interview shows how this learning can be implemented as part of staff continued professional development:

> I took the reading list and the videos and all of that, and then I compiled an Inset, that I delivered to the staff just to start to open their eyes a little bit about

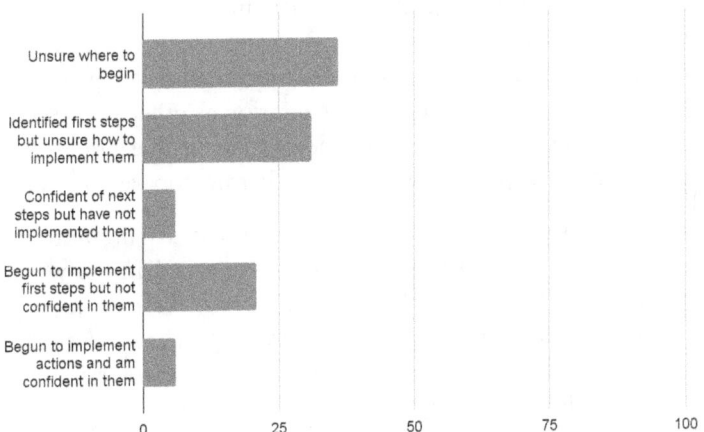

Fig. 2.2. Actions Taken Towards Decolonising and Diversifying the Curriculum (Pre-survey).

some different aspects and different perspectives and things that we could change. (Primary school leader)

Module 3 – Why Decolonise and Diversify the Curriculum

This module addressed the reasons why schools do and might choose to undertake this work. Average ratings indicated a positive impact on participants' understanding of *why* this work is important (1.57) and what it could look like (1.65), but there was continued uncertainty about implementation (1.84). One interview participant also highlighted the need to take time to reflect on what schools are already doing and what part of their work needs to improve:

> *The team I work in needs to stop and take time to reflect on and review our progress, and really assess whether indeed we are making progress, and how we move forwards.* (Learning participant)

Module 4 – Approaches to Decolonising and Diversifying the Curriculum

This module addressed what decolonising and diversifying the curriculum might look like in practice across a range of settings. This module's increased focus on practical application had a positive impact on participants' confidence levels, which improved from Modules 1–3 to an average of 1.75. This highlights the need for continued professional development to include explicit models for implementation as otherwise, teachers may struggle to mobilise their new learning. One interviewee explained the impact of the course on her practice as follows:

> *The most impactful moment for me was delving into the different approaches to decolonising and diversifying the curriculum. Understanding how these principles can be practically applied to my specific teaching context has been truly eye-opening and empowering.* (Module participant)

Another participant also mentioned how changes to the curriculum, school display boards, and inclusive messaging in their setting had already led to a diversification in student applications and intake.

Module 5 – Belonging in Literature

This module addressed how to make literature and resource choices that foster belonging for all pupils. Average ratings show that teachers' understanding of how literature can create a sense of belonging for students increased because of taking the course (1.54).

This module's continued focus on practical support for implementation resulted in the highest confidence ratings for implementation (1.60) and a concrete understanding of which steps they can take next to implement change (1.60), which is also supported by a comment from an interview participant:

> *The course deepened my understanding of how diverse and inclusive texts can positively impact students' identities and experiences in the classroom.* (Module participant)

Module 6 – Conversations About Race

This module addressed how to become more confident and effective in conversations about race.

Participants' understanding of how to conduct effective conversations about race increased because of this module (1.53) and they felt confident in their ability to apply their learning to their practice (1.70) though confidence levels were slightly lower here than for the previous module.

Overall, the post-learning surveys indicate that the continued professional development had a positive impact on teachers' understanding of key concepts relating to decolonising and diversifying the curriculum and that confidence with implementation can be increased with explicit focus on modelling and exemplifying practice.

Strengths and Limitations

The strength of this work lies within its applied nature and the close collaboration between research and practice. The combination of research, tools, and case studies meant that teachers and school leaders experienced a wide range of views and perspectives, which seems especially important in the context of this work. For example, one respondent said:

> *The case studies as they gave clear guidance whilst encouraging professional judgement.* (Learning participant)

A limitation to acknowledge from this study lies within the response rate. Only 181 of the 499 participants responded to the pre-survey and the post-survey received 395 responses across all modules. While this is a good response rate for an opt-in survey, not all views have been collected, what has been obtained is self-reported, and participants with positive experiences may be over-represented.

Results also highlight the need for continued work in this space and that while a course such as this one can present an important first step, learning is never completed and teachers as well as school leaders will require additional training and support with implementation.

Finally, the very nature and title of this course (Decolonising and Diversifying the Curriculum) implies a self-selection bias in that teachers and leaders who were already interested in the topic of the course were more likely to enrol in it, so we know less about its potential impact on those who may be less interested in the topic.

Impact and Next Steps

Ultimately, the findings suggest that online continued professional development, like this set of modules, that combines best examples of evidenced-informed research and practice, holds the potential to support teachers towards decolonising and diversifying the curriculum in meaningful ways.

- Going forward, there will be a need to update resources and expand case studies to further exemplify decolonising and diversifying curriculum work as it is enacted in schools.

- Continuing to share the course and resources through our and others' networks to increase reach and engagement will be important.

- Given that work to decolonise and diversify the curriculum does not exist in isolation but is closely connected to the setting and leadership culture within which the curriculum resides, The Chartered College of Teaching has developed a follow-on course focusing on the creation of inclusive school cultures. This includes modules on supporting staff and students containing diverse lived experiences, ranging from LGBTQ+ colleagues, teachers on parental leave, and individuals with disabilities.

References

Ajegbo, K., Kiwan, D., & Sharma, S. (2007). *Curriculum, diversity & citizenship*. Department for Education and Skills. http://www.educationengland.org.uk/documents/pdfs/2007-ajegbo-report-citizenship.pdf

Alexander, C., Weekes-Bernard, D., & Chatterji, J. (2015). *History lessons: Teaching diversity in and through the history national curriculum*. Runnymede.

Blundell, R., Dias, M., Cribb, J., Joyce, R., Waters, T., Wernham, T., & Xu, X. (2022, January 4). *Inequality and the Covid crisis in the United Kingdom*. Institute for Fiscal Studies. https://ifs.org.uk/publications/inequality-and-covid-crisis-united-kingdom

Chantiluke, R. (2018). British values' and decolonial resistance in the classroom. In R. Chantiluke, B. Kwomba, & N. Athinangamso (Eds.), *Rhodes must fall: The struggle to decolonise the racist heart of empire* (pp. 285–308). Zed Books.

Coard, B. (1971). *How the West Indian child is made educationally subnormal in the British school system: The scandal of the Black child in schools in Britain*. New Beacon Books.

Department for Education. (2013, July). History programmes of study: Key stages 1 and 2; National curriculum in England. In *The national curriculum in Britain framework document* (pp. 1–5).

Gilroy, P. (1987). *"There ain't no Black in the Union Jack": The cultural politics of race and nation*. Hutchinson.

Harris, R. (2013). The place of diversity within history and the challenge of policy and curriculum. *Oxford Review of Education, 39*(3), 400–419.

Milne, A. (2019, March 29). *White supremacy in our classrooms*. https://www.annmilne.co.nz/blog/white-supremacy-in-our-classrooms

Modood, T., & May, S. (2001). Multiculturalism and education in Britain: An internally contested debate. *International Journal of Educational Research, 35*(3), 305–317.

Moncrieffe, M. L. (2020). *Decolonising the history curriculum: Eurocentrism in primary school education*. Palgrave Macmillan.

Moncrieffe, M. L., & Harris, R. (2020). Repositioning curriculum teaching and learning through Black-British history. In S. Gorard (Ed.), *Research intelligence* (Issue 144, pp. 14–15). British Educational Research Association.

Nazroo, J., & Becares, L. (2021). *Ethnic inequalities in COVID-19 mortality: A consequence of persistent racism*. Runnymede Trust. https://www.runnymedetrust.org/publications/ethnic-inequalities-in-covid-19-mortality-a-consequence-of-persistent-racism

Nichol, J., & Harnett, P. (2011). History teaching in Britain and British national history curriculum, past, present and into the future. *International Journal of History Learning, Teaching and Research*, *10*(1), 106–119.

CHAPTER 3

The Primary Curriculum for Religious Education in Northern Ireland: Making a Case for Epistemic Justice

Rebecca Loader, Erika Jiménez, Joanne Hughes and Aisling O'Boyle

Queen's University Belfast, UK

ABSTRACT

Religious education (RE) in Northern Ireland (NI) is taught according to the Core Syllabus produced by representatives of the region's four main Christian churches and, at primary level, is exclusively Christian in content. In this chapter, the authors apply the lens of epistemic injustice to examine the implications of this given an increasingly diverse society and pupil population. Drawing on a recent study of educational experiences among minority ethnic and migrant groups, the authors suggest that the primary RE curriculum may perpetuate epistemic injustice in three ways: (1) by impeding children from minority faith traditions from sharing their experiences in a way meaningful to their peers; (2) by reducing the resources available to children to make sense of encounters with other religious traditions; and (3) through a lack of appropriate alternative arrangements for pupils whose parents withdraw their children from RE. The authors conclude with recommendations to increase epistemic justice within the primary RE curriculum.

Keywords: Northern Ireland; religious education; epistemic injustice; hermeneutical injustice; primary curriculum

Research Context

While NI has long been home to ethnic minority communities, the decades since the 1998 Belfast/Good Friday Agreement have seen substantial inward migration. This, combined with growing secularism in society, has resulted in the proportion of children from 'other' (i.e. neither Catholic nor Protestant) or no religious background almost trebling from 8% in 2002/03 to 20% in 2022/23 (DENI, 2023).

Despite this increasing religious diversity, as well as a curriculum aspiration to foster 'mutual understanding in the local and global community' (CCEA, 2007, p. 2), the NI Core Syllabus for RE remains largely Christian in content. Designed by a Working Group comprising representatives of the four main Christian Churches – Catholic, Presbyterian, Church of Ireland, and Methodist – the curriculum was considered an 'ecumenical achievement' when it was issued in 1993 (Armstrong, 2009, p. 297) but received some criticism for its mono-religious orientation (Barnes, 2002). A revised syllabus, issued in 2007, includes a requirement to teach two 'world religions' at Key Stage 3, but remains exclusively Christian at primary level, as reflected in its three learning objectives: 'the Revelation of God', 'the Christian Church', and '[Christian] Morality' (DENI, 2007). This chapter considers the implications of this exclusive focus, particularly for children from other religious traditions.

Literature

Arguments justifying or critiquing the curricular focus on Christianity often centre around the types of knowledge that are deemed important – for example, knowledge of Christianity in a society in which it remains dominant, or knowledge of different religious traditions in the context of increasing religious diversity (Barnes, 2002; Nelson, 2019). Questions of what knowledge is valued and particularly how knowledge transmission processes perpetuate social inequalities are central to Fricker's (2007) work on epistemic injustice, which she defines as 'consisting, most fundamentally, in a wrong done to someone specifically in their capacity as a knower' (p. 1). Fricker defines two forms of epistemic injustice: 'testimonial injustice', where a speaker is accorded reduced credibility on account of identity bias; and 'hermeneutical injustice', whereby a lacuna in the collective interpretive resources impedes a person's ability to make sense of their social experiences. The latter is particularly pertinent to our analysis.

Within education, scholars have suggested that children are at particular risk of hermeneutical marginalisation as they lack power in decisions about what they learn and, thus, the knowledge they receive to interpret the world (McNulty & Henning, 2019). Members of racially minoritised groups are also at risk as they are under-represented in knowledge construction processes, including curriculum development (Omodan, 2023). Where such marginalisation constitutes injustice – that is, Fricker (2007) argues, where absences in the collective hermeneutical resources are 'harmful but also wrongful, whether because discriminatory or because otherwise unfair' (p. 151) – the impacts can be substantial. In education, these include the devaluation and erasure of minority histories, philosophies, and cultural perspectives (Omodan, 2023), and lack of opportunity to explore and engage with alternative knowledges and worldviews – outcomes antithetical to contemporary decolonisation movements, which seek to interrogate and challenge the primacy of Western knowledge systems. This marginalisation, in turn, can impede a subject's ability to express their experiences intelligibly, thereby reducing their intellectual confidence (Omodan, 2023).

Objective and Methods

The research that forms the basis of this chapter was conducted as part of a two-year study examining the educational experiences of minority ethnic groups in NI, funded by the Nuffield Foundation (Loader et al., 2023). Involving participation from children, parents, and educational and policy stakeholders, the study represents the most substantial piece of research to date exploring perspectives on schooling among, and for, minority ethnic and migrant families in the region.

An objective of the research was to examine how the curriculum is responding both to an increasingly multicultural pupil population and to wider calls for the decolonisation and diversification of knowledge. This has received limited attention in educational research in NI to date, which has more commonly focused on the representation of British/Protestant/Unionist and Irish/Catholic/Nationalist perspectives and traditions in the curriculum. Thus, the study provided a means to address this omission.

The research comprised three phases, the first involving analysis of relevant regional and school-level policy, including the curriculum for Key Stage 2 and Key Stage 3, and available educational data. The second phase comprised interviews with children (aged 9–15) from minority ethnic and migrant backgrounds across NI and their parent(s)/carer(s) to explore their experiences of education. In total, 62 children and 53 parents were interviewed, typically in their home or a community venue. Interviews with children were based around a creative task for which materials were provided. The third phase involved interviews and focus groups with 43 individuals working in educational policy and delivery, including teachers, and community organisations that support minority ethnic and migrant populations. Ethical approval for this research was received from the departmental ethics committee at the authors' institution. In this chapter, we draw principally on curriculum analysis and relevant interview data to reflect on the provision of RE at primary level.

Analysis and Findings

The Core Syllabus at Key Stage 2 includes an objective to 'develop an awareness, knowledge, understanding and appreciation of the key Christian teachings' (DENI, 2007, p. 13); in comparison, pupils need only become 'aware of and have respect for differing cultures and faiths' as a manifestation of 'Christian moral principles' (DENI, 2007, p. 19). In this way, the curriculum establishes Christianity as normative within the school and society and 'communicates a message that certain knowledge systems are superior or more valid than others' (Omodan, 2023, p. 4). This may marginalise those from minority traditions directly, through the exclusion of their experience from the curriculum, and indirectly, by fostering an educational and social climate in which these traditions lack value, as the following participant recognised:

> I think we should have a fundamental review of collective worship and religious education in schools ... It must be welcoming to all, even if you don't have any ethnic minorities in your school. And I think that's the misconception. 'Oh, we don't have any ethnic minorities in this school. It doesn't matter therefore that we only do this.' Yes, it does. Because you're giving a message to the young people who are in your school. You're actually devaluing everything else. (Stakeholder)

Interviews also revealed that, for those teachers who wished to acknowledge diverse beliefs and religions beyond Christianity, there was only enough space to do this in a fragmentary way, typically through teaching about individual festivals such as Diwali and Eid. This serves to reinforce a religious hierarchy as, while Christianity is taught as an integrated belief system, other traditions are not afforded similar epistemic status or coherence.

Through this marginalisation of other religious traditions, we suggest that the Core Syllabus may perpetuate epistemic injustice in three ways, first by impeding children from faiths other than Christianity from sharing their social experiences in a way meaningful to both them and their peers. As the current curriculum provides only the concepts and language of Christianity to communicate religious experience, children from other faith traditions may find that the available hermeneutical resources offer 'at best ill-fitting meanings to draw on in the effort to render [their social experiences] intelligible' to others (Fricker, 2007, p. 148). The hegemony of Christianity is such that children may find themselves having to 'translate' their experiences into terms familiar from Christian teaching.

Second, by limiting teaching about the range of religions and beliefs in NI, the curriculum reduces the hermeneutical resources available to all children to make sense of their encounters with faiths or belief systems of which they are not members. This may be considered an injustice against children in their capacity as knowers, given their lack of influence over the curriculum that maintains their ignorance. Moreover, in the absence of such information, children may rely on what hermeneutical resources are available to evaluate other religious traditions. Due to the marginalisation of members of minority faiths, such resources are 'unduly influenced by more hermeneutically powerful groups' (Fricker, 2007, p. 155) and may portray non-Christian religious traditions unfavourably, particularly Islam (see Ahmed & Matthes, 2017). This, in turn, can precipitate the development of negative attitudes towards these faiths among children, as one mother described:

> *Some of them, the boys in [my son's] school, were telling about terrorists, that Muslim represents terrorism ... So, I think that awareness is very important. Telling people what is, for example, the real Islam. What do Muslims do, real Muslims, what our values are, what we believe in. Because it's so prevalent, that Islam is a religion of killing ... I remember he said that in first year and second year.* (Mother, Indian ethnic group)

This participant reports that children had formulated prejudiced views of Islam by the time of their first year of post-primary school when 'world religions' are first introduced in the curriculum. This was also the experience of teachers interviewed by Nelson and Yang (2022), who reported that such attitudes could subsequently inhibit pupils' willingness to learn about other faiths. The interviewee's reference, above, to the association of Muslims with terrorism illustrates, furthermore, how the available hermeneutic resources also shape perceptions of faith group members, such that the latter can be 'socially constituted as ... something they are not, and which it is against their interests to be seen to be' (Fricker, 2007, p. 168). This constitutes a further example of hermeneutic injustice – one that might be diminished by the earlier teaching of religions other than Christianity.

Third, where parents do not wish their children to participate in exclusively Christian RE, the only alternative, which is to withdraw the child from all RE teaching, may entrench epistemic inequalities. Like Richardson et al. (2013), we found that provision for pupils withdrawn from RE is often inequitable and lacks a defined educational purpose, with reported activities including drawing or using an iPad. Several participants also stated that withdrawn pupils remained in the classroom where RE was taught: as one child described, 'the lesson is for

Christianity so we Muslim students have to stay at the back'. These examples suggest that RE at primary level risks perpetuating epistemic injustice both by failing to provide teaching of equal educational value to pupils from other faith traditions (and none) and by failing to respect parents' decisions that their child *not* be exposed to certain knowledge.

Strengths and Limitations

A key strength of this research is the inclusion of the perspectives of children, parents, and educational, policy, and community stakeholders among the participant group, permitting the exploration of multiple perspectives concerning practice in RE. The principal limitation is that, as data were collected as part of a larger project which prioritised ethnic rather than religious diversity in the selection criteria, some faith traditions were under-represented in the sample. A more focused research project, with purposive sampling to maximise participation from participants from a range of faith backgrounds, would provide further insight into variations in experience.

Impact and Next Steps

Following a judicial review in 2022, the High Court ruled that the RE curriculum for state-controlled primary schools in NI 'is not conveyed in an objective, critical and pluralist manner' and is, thus, unlawful according to the European Convention on Human Rights (JR87, Re Application for Judicial Review (Rev1) [2022], p. 23). A subsequent Court of Appeal ruling in April 2024 upheld the original judgement regarding the lack of objectivity, criticality and pluralism in the RE curriculum, but argued that this did not constitute a breach of the ECHR due to the 'unqualified statutory right' of parents to withdraw their children from RE (JR87, Re Application for Judicial Review [2024] NICA 34, p. 37). This ruling noted, further, that the Department of Education was 'clearly minded to consider a refresh to the NI curriculum' that would take account of 'the complexion and changing needs of our modern society' (pp. 37–38). Based on this research, we make the following recommendations to ensure that any refreshed curriculum is both human rights-compliant and epistemically just:

- Include members and adherents of major world religions and worldviews alongside Christian representatives on the working group responsible for drafting a revised syllabus.
- De-centre Christianity within the primary curriculum to allow for more substantive content on other religions and worldviews.
- Encourage the teaching of religious plurality as a priority in schools with limited religious diversity.
- Require schools to provide alternative activities of educational value for pupils whose parents exercise their right to withdraw them from RE.

References

Ahmed, S., & Matthes, J. (2017). Media representation of Muslims and Islam from 2000 to 2015: A meta-analysis. *International Communication Gazette*, 79(3), 219–244. https://doi.org/10.1177/1748048516656305

Armstrong, D. (2009). Religious education and the law in Northern Ireland's controlled schools. *Irish Educational Studies*, 28(3), 297–313. https://doi.org/10.1080/03323310903335401

Barnes, L. P. (2002). World religions and the Northern Ireland Curriculum. *Journal of Beliefs and Values*, 23(1), 19–32. https://doi.org/10.1080/13617670220125647

CCEA. (2007). *The Northern Ireland curriculum: Primary*. CCEA. https://ccea.org.uk/downloads/docs/ccea-asset/Curriculum/The%20Northern%20Ireland%20Curriculum%20-%20Primary.pdf

DENI. (2023). *Pupil enrolment by school management type 2000/01 to 2022/23*. Department of Education (Northern Ireland). https://www.education-ni.gov.uk/publications/school-enrolments-northern-ireland-summary-data

DENI. (2007). *Core Syllabus for religious education*. Department of Education (Northern Ireland). https://www.education-ni.gov.uk/sites/default/files/publications/de/religious-education-core-syllabus-english-version.pdf

Fricker, M. (2007). *Epistemic injustice: Power and the ethics of knowing*. Oxford University Press. https://doi.org/10.1093/acprof:oso/9780198237907.001.0001

JR87, Re Application for Judicial Review (Rev1) [2022].
JR87, Re Application for Judicial Review [2024] NICA 34.
Loader, R., Jiménez, E., O'Boyle, A., & Hughes, J. (2023). *Experiences of education among minority ethnic groups in Northern Ireland*. Queen's University Belfast. https://www.qub.ac.uk/public-engagement/Filestore/PubAffFiles/Filetoupload,1862560,en.pdf
McNulty, L., & Henning, L. (2019). Children's epistemic rights and hermeneutical marginalisation in schools. In T. Feldges (Ed.), *Philosophy and the study of education: New perspectives on a complex relationship* (pp. 54–64). Routledge.
Nelson, J. (2019). Meaning-making in religious education: A critical discourse analysis of RE departments' web pages. *British Journal of Religious Education, 41*(1), 90–104. https://doi.org/10.1080/01416 200.2017.1324757
Nelson, J., & Yang, Y. (2022). World religions in religious education in Northern Ireland: A policy implementation analysis using strategic action field theory. *Religion and Education, 49*(1), 61–81. https://doi.org/10.1080/15507394.2021.2009303
Omodan, B. I. (2023). Unveiling epistemic injustice in education: A critical analysis of alternative approaches. *Social Sciences and Humanities Open, 8*(1), 1–8. https://doi.org/10.1016/j.ssaho.2023.100699
Richardson, N., Niens, U., Mawhinney, A., & Chiba, Y. (2013). Opting out or opting in? Conscience clauses, minority belief communities and the possibility of inclusive religious education in Northern Ireland. *British Journal of Religious Education, 35*(3), 236–250. https://doi.org/10.1080/01416200.2012.750595

CHAPTER 4

Decolonising Early Childhood Education: Disrupting Professional Discourses

Chandrika Devarakonda[a] and Marlies Kustatscher[b]

[a]University of Chester, UK
[b]University of Edinburgh, UK

ABSTRACT

In this chapter, we share our reflections on decolonising early childhood education in our respective contexts of England and Scotland and the implications for early childhood practitioners. The foundations of early childhood education have traditionally been shaped by white, male, Global North perspectives that position young children as 'innocent' and unknowledgeable, as defined by developmental discourses and milestones, and as sites of economic investment within neoliberal politics. We challenge the relevance of these ideas in diverse and evolving contexts. We provide some suggestions on how early childhood practitioners can work towards decolonising early childhood education by unlearning prejudiced assumptions, and by relearning new perspectives in disrupting hegemonic whiteness, and advocating for structural and institutional change.

Keywords: early childhood education; decolonisation; unlearning; hegemonic whiteness; early childhood practitioners

Research Context

Prompted by the Black Lives Matter anti-racist protests of 2020 across the world, educational institutions in the United Kingdom have been seen to engage with questions of how to decolonise their curricula, practices, and systems (see Moncrieffe, 2019a, 2019b, 2020a, 2020b, 2021). Scholars in early childhood education for some time have called for the decolonisation of curriculum knowledge and the reconceptualization of practice to provide equitable learning opportunities for minority-ethnic group children (see Cannella & Viruru, 2004; Soto & Swadener, 2002). But these calls have yet to manifest in policy and practice.

In England, there is a noticeable absence of reference to race and ethnicity within early childhood education policy (Tembo, 2021). Around 10% of the early years workforce consists of Black, Asian, and other Minority Ethnic groups (Department for Education, 2022). These figures link to data given by The Newly Qualified Teacher Survey (Department for Education, 2018) which highlighted declining levels of teachers' confidence in supporting learners from minority ethnic and EAL backgrounds. While the early childhood curriculum [in England: Early Years Foundation Stage (Department for Education, 2014), in Scotland: the Curriculum for Excellence (Education Scotland, 2019) and Realising the Ambition: Being Me (Education Scotland, 2020)] is fluid and not prescriptive, it is argued that there is a need to bring in awareness and knowledge more explicitly about non-Western contexts and processes of marginalisation (Devarakonda, 2021a, 2021b).

In Scotland, a policy rhetoric around anti-racism and decolonisation has been developing in recent years. This can be seen through the Scottish Government's Anti-Racism in Education Programme (2023) which promotes guidance on how to embed race equality and anti-racism in education. This guidance explicitly includes those working in early childhood education. However, just 1% of the early years workforce in Scotland belong to minority ethnic groups, compared to 4% of the overall Scottish workforce (Skills Development Scotland, 2019), and research on decolonising early childhood education in Scotland is scarce. There is a knowledge gap which needs to be bridged for incorporating decolonial principles into everyday professional practice (Tembo & Bateson, 2022).

Literature

We understand decolonisation as the undoing of historical and ongoing processes of colonisation and the material, economic, political, intellectual, and emotional reversal of colonial injustices (Moncrieffe, 2022). This goes beyond reframing our educational institutions as more inclusive or celebrating diversity. Decolonising early childhood education does not simply constitute an add-on to existing curricula and practices. It is important to consider the foundations, purposes, and assumptions of early childhood education today, to meaningfully consider what decolonisation involves.

Burman (2018) argues that the dominant concept of early childhood education has been shaped by predominantly white, male thinkers from the Global North. This is rooted in developmental psychology which tends to inscribe normative (racialized, gendered, classed, ableist, etc.) ideas onto all children, while often pathologizing those who do not fit these norms (Burman, 2018). Against this concern, and with a view towards delivering epistemic justice for all children in teaching and learning, decolonising early childhood education requires an onto-epistemological shift (Pérez & Saavedra, 2017). This means a need to resist taken-for-granted Eurocentric epistemes about best practice which are framed by colonial and capitalist power relations, expressed, for example, through standardised tests and their deterministic, universalising assumptions (Cannella & Viruru, 2004).

Objectives and Methods

Decolonising early childhood education challenges Eurocentric assumptions about what early childhood education is, and what and who it is for. Early childhood practitioners are encouraged to orientate their approaches to learning and care to a critical position of dismantling, reconceptualising, and rebuilding professional knowledge for their reapplication in practice. We offer our reflections on this process by asking the question:

> *How can we work towards decolonising early childhood education, with practitioner students, in our contexts?*

We position ourselves not as experts, but as learners, unlearners, and relearners (Devarakonda, 2021a, 2021b) seeking to advance the broader scholarly and practice movement in this field.

We draw on our experiences of teaching early childhood practitioner cohorts in our respective white dominated UK university settings and give reflective analysis to research projects which we have been involved in.[1] We are coming to these insights from different ethnic identities and social positionalities: Chandrika as an Asian, multilingual woman and mother, born and educated in India and living in England for over 30 years; Marlies as a white, middle-class woman, born and socialised in a multilingual region of Italy and living in Scotland for 15 years. While a full exploration of our positionalities and the impact of these on our reasons for engaging in this study are beyond the scope of this chapter, we are mindful in disclosing how our ethnic identities and positionalities direct us to interrogate from these perspectives the relations of power in early childhood education, teaching, and learning.

To disrupt professional discourses with our dominant white student-practitioner cohorts of early childhood education undergraduate students, in our teaching, we shared the Model of Awareness of Diversity (see Fig. 4.1), developed by Devarakonda (2021a, 2021b). This provided contrasting views on the heterogeneous nature of 'diversity'.

We each applied this framework in our professional contexts to encourage our student practitioners to identify stereotypes and prejudices which could affect the shape and direction of their perspectives in practice. We recognised that this could be a huge challenge to our students, in asking them to reflect on prejudice, to recognise this, to unlearn this, and to conceptualise transformative approaches to practice that could respond proactively and positively to the broader diversity of children and families they work with.

	Known by self	Unknown by self
Known by others	Open and free (stereotypes and prejudices) – what we do know is open and flexible to adapt to new information	Blind spot – you are prejudiced and do not necessarily believe you are prejudiced
	Visible diversity – what is politically correct, attitudes to diverse populations	Religious diversity, minority ethnic groups, EAL, Gypsy, Roma, and traveller families
		Perceived by others – especially the members of diverse communities
Unknown by others	Façade or mask (hidden) – you are prejudiced, but do not like to admit to your prejudices because they are not acceptable	Unknown by self and others – you do not know that you hold some stereotypes because it is unconscious
	Attitudes towards specific groups – Gypsy, Roma and traveller families, minority ethnic groups, specific religions	Invisible diversity – ingrained by society, lack of awareness
		Perceived by others – especially the members of diverse communities

Fig. 4.1. Model of Awareness of Diversity.

Sources: Devarakonda (2021a, 2021b).

Analysis and Findings

Our practice experiences and our research have shown that there is a tendency among white early childhood student practitioners to position themselves as 'colourblind', that is as claiming not to 'see' race and, thus, not to engage in racist actions (Tembo, 2021). The concern here is that in turning a blind eye to race and racisms as colour-blindness in practice, this merely stands in for whiteness as the normative standard (Tembo, 2021). Whiteness is encapsulated in (often unnamed) social practices that define the social world and is based on collective and deliberate ignorance and avoidance to acknowledge the conditions for the re-production of racism (Mills in Emejulu, 2016). Richardson (2019) suggests that early childhood practitioners need a 'safe space' to reflect openly and without blame to consider complex processes of racialisation and discrimination in early childhood. In facilitating this through our use of the 'Model of Awareness of Diversity' with early childhood student practitioners, we saw that they tended to locate racism 'elsewhere', or wanted to ensure that they would not be judged or reprimanded if they 'accidentally' or 'unintentionally' say 'something racist' (Kustatscher, 2020).

It is impossible to take seriously the call for decolonising early childhood education without assuming a position of action and disruption. Early childhood educational spaces must be recognised as politicised spaces, where allyship and solidarity are required to challenge Eurocentric developmentalist discourses that marginalise non-white bodies (Abawi, 2022). For the dominant white practitioner early years workforce across England and Scotland, this needs to begin from a willing position of critical self-reflexivity and self-education about the colonial, capitalist and patriarchal power relations which shape early childhood education today.

Decolonial practice, thus, must be ongoing and involve a continuous critical analysis of place (work context), practices (pedagogy), and personal and professional identities (self). Our teaching interventions as decolonial praxis have shown us that this multifaceted critical analysis requires ongoing commitment by early childhood student practitioners so that reconceptualised and transformed practice becomes innate. As Cannella and Viruru (2004, p. 93) write:

> *Decolonial practice must be emergent while at the same time planned, must be individual while at the same time community-based, must recognise dominant discourses while at the same time turning them upside down.*

Strengths and Limitations

Although our teaching and research have encouraged critical reflexive practice in early childhood practitioners through a 'Model of Awareness of Diversity' template, we recognise several challenges with bringing decolonising praxis into early childhood education. One barrier is the political culture of 'pushback', such as in the form of increasingly right-wing policy discourses in England (e.g. the curtailment of educational curricula by targeting the teaching of critical race theory) (see Breen & Meer, 2019). A perhaps subtler form of pushback against racial justice is to locate white supremacy as an ideology related to 'fringe elements' of society, while being reluctant to engage in deconstructing white hegemony engrained in the mainstream. For early childhood education, such taken-for-granted discourses of whiteness mean that the inequitable conceptual framework of power remains unrecognised and unchallenged. Tokenistic 'diversity' actions, rooted in a lack of understanding or commitment to an anti-racist agenda, are another barrier to genuine transformations in practice (Devarakonda, 2021a, 2021b).

Impact and Next Steps

A significant uptake and implementation of this reconceptualised approach to practice across early childhood educational sites is required for meaningful impact on young children's lives. In advancing decolonial praxis in early childhood education, we see the important next steps for action as the following:

- Moving beyond professional discourses of celebrating diversity and being inclusive in re-imagining a decolonial early childhood education.
- Early childhood practitioners' critical engagement with and deconstruction of curricula.
- Wider recognition by the early childhood education workforce that decolonising the curriculum and challenging engrained assumptions and prejudices is part of realising children's rights.
- Further research across England and Scotland, illuminating the challenges faced by early childhood practitioners in decolonising the curriculum, and supporting them with remedies.

- Deeper policy support towards a decolonial early childhood education, located within broader efforts to acknowledge and address England's and Scotland's colonial histories and their ongoing effects.

Note

1. Chandrika: Practices of Diversity with Undergraduate Teacher Training Programmes (funded by University of Chester). Marlies: Froebelian Futures project, funded by Froebel Trust UK, Cuál es la verdad? (What is the Truth?) Project, funded by AHRC GCRF Changing the Story.

References

Abawi, Z. (2022). Decolonising early childhood curricula: A Canadian perspective. In M. L. Moncrieffe (Ed.), *Decolonising curriculum knowledge: International perspectives and interdisciplinary approaches*. Palgrave Macmillan. https://doi.org/10.1007/978-3-031-13623-8_8

Breen, D., & Meer, N. (2019). Securing whiteness?: Critical race theory (CRT) and the securitization of Muslims in education. *Identities*, 26(5), 595–613. https://doi.org/10.1080/1070289X.2019.1589981

Burman, E. (2018). *Fanon, education, action: Child as method*. Routledge.

Cannella, G. S., & Viruru, R. (2004). *Childhood and postcolonization: Power, education, and contemporary practice*. Routledge. https://doi.org/10.4324/9780203463536

Department for Education. (2014). *Early years foundation stage*. Retrieved February 2, 2024, from https://www.gov.uk/government/publications/early-years-foundation-stage-framework

Department for Education. (2018). *Newly qualified teachers (NQTs): Annual survey 2017*. Retrieved November 10, 2023, from https://www.gov.uk/government/publications/newly-qualified-teachers-nqts-annual-survey-2017

Department for Education. (2022). *Childcare and early years provider survey*. Retrieved November 10, 2023, from https://explore-education-statistics.service.gov.uk/find-statistics/childcare-and-early-years-provider-survey/2022#dataBlock-8efa3b23-6fbf-4e00-a306-a435d18d92ba-tables

Devarakonda, C. (2021a). *Decolonising and diversifying the early years curriculum*. Retrieved November 10, 2023, from https://my.chartered.

college/early-childhood-hub/decolonising-and-diversifying-the-early-years-curriculum.

Devarakonda, C. (2021b). *Promoting inclusion and diversity in early years settings.* Jessica Kingsley.

Education Scotland. (2019). *Curriculum for excellence.* Retrieved February 2, 2024, from https://education.gov.scot/curriculum-for-excellence/about-curriculum-for-excellence

Education Scotland. (2020). *Realising the ambition: Being me.* Retrieved February 2, 2024, from https://education.gov.scot/media/3bjpr3wa/realisingtheambition.pdf

Emejulu, A. (2016). *The centre of a Whirlwind: Watching whiteness work.* Verso Books. Retrieved November 10, 2023, from https://www.versobooks.com/blogs/2934-the-centre-of-a-whirlwind-watching-whiteness-work

Kustatscher, M. (2020). Disrupting hegemonic whiteness in the higher education. classroom. *CERES/RACE.ED Blog.* Retrieved January 9, 2024, from https://www.race.ed.ac.uk/disrupting-hegemonic-whiteness-in-the-higher-education-classroom

Moncrieffe, M. L. (Ed.). (2019a, July). *Decolonising the curriculum: Teaching and learning about race equality* (Issue 1). University of Brighton.

Moncrieffe, M. L. (Ed.). (2019b, December). *Decolonising the curriculum: Teaching and learning about race equality* (Issue 2). University of Brighton.

Moncrieffe, M. L. (2020a). #BlackLivesMatter in education. *BERA Blog.* Retrieved December 15, 2023, from https://www.bera.ac.uk/blog/blacklivesmatter-in-education

Moncrieffe, M. L. (Ed.). (2020b, July). *Decolonising the curriculum: Teaching and learning about race equality* (Issue 3). University of Brighton.

Moncrieffe, M. L. (Ed.). (2021, May). *Decolonising the curriculum: Teaching and learning about race equality.* University of Brighton.

Moncrieffe, M. L. (2022). Why decolonising curriculum knowledge? In M. L. Moncrieffe (Ed.), *Decolonising curriculum knowledge: International perspectives and interdisciplinary approaches* (pp. 1–14). Palgrave Macmillan. https://doi.org/10.1007/978-3-031-13623-8_1

Pérez, M. S., & Saavedra, C. M. (2017). A call for onto-epistemological diversity in early childhood education and care. *Review of Research in Education, 41*(1), 1–29. https://doi.org/10.3102/0091732X16688621

Richardson, A. (2019). Beyond colour-blindness in early childhood settings. In M. L. Moncrieffe (Ed.), *Decolonising the curriculum: Teaching and learning about race equality* (Issue 2). University of Brighton.

Scottish Government. (2023). *Anti-racism in education programme*. Retrieved January 10, 2024, from https://www.gov.scot/publications/anti-racism-in-education-programme-factsheet.

Skills Development Scotland. (2019). *Achieving diversity in the Scottish early learning and childcare workforce*. Retrieved November 10, 2023, from https://www.skillsdevelopmentscotland.co.uk/media/46248/achieving-diversity-in-the-elc-workplace_final.pdf

Soto, L. D., & Swadener, B. B. (2002). Toward liberatory early childhood theory, research and praxis: Decolonizing a field. *Contemporary Issues in Early Childhood*, 3(1), 38–66.

Tembo, S. (2021). 'Hang on, she just used that word like it's totally easy': Encountering ordinary racial affects in early childhood education and care. *Ethnicities*, 21(5), 875–892. https://doi.org/10.1177/1468796820963960

Tembo, S., & Bateson, S. (2022). Liminal relationalities: On collaborative writing with/in and against race in the study of early childhood. *International Journal of Qualitative Studies in Education*, 37(2), 530–544. https://doi.org/10.1080/09518398.2022.2061738

CHAPTER 5

Decolonial Education Through Solidarities: Anti-racism Learning in Early Childhood Education and Care in Canada

Zuhra Abawi[a] and Rachel Berman[b]

[a]Niagara University Ontario, Canada
[b]Toronto Metropolitan University, Canada

ABSTRACT

This work takes a decolonial and, specifically, an antiracist approach to thinking about teaching and learning in Early Childhood Education and Care (ECEC) within the settler-colonial Canadian context, a context in which Euro-centric developmentalist narratives predominate. To address this situation, a team of academics, along with the College of Early Childhood Educators and the Association of Early Childhood Educators Ontario, carried out antiracist professional learning with the early childhood sector in Ontario, Canada. Four two-hour sequential on-line sessions were offered. Three hundred professionals participated. This knowledge transfer initiative focused on sharing information and providing a platform for educators to ask questions, learn, and unpack their own positionalities in challenging race and racism in early learning pedagogies and curriculum. Pre- and post-session surveys were distributed, the results of which are discussed in this chapter. Strengths and weaknesses of this initiative are considered, along with impact and next steps.

Keywords: early childhood education and care; western developmentalism; Canada; anti-racism; professional development

Research Context

This work takes an antiracism approach to thinking about, teaching, and learning in Early Childhood Education and Care (ECEC) within the settler-colonial Canadian context (Escayg et al., 2017; Pacini-Ketchabaw & Berikoff, 2008). Canada is often discursively constructed as kinder, benevolently multicultural, and less racist than our southern neighbour, the United States (Maynard, 2017). However, this narrative is problematic in perpetuating the past and ongoing legacies of brutality, including the systematic genocide of Indigenous people, Canada's history of slavery, and ongoing anti-Black racism, as well as widespread inequities between racialised and white Canadians (Colour of Poverty, 2019; Maynard, 2017; Truth and Reconciliation Commission, 2015; United Way, 2019). Although Canada prides itself on its demographic diversity, the ECEC field is largely premised upon objective, developmentalist, neutral, race-less, apolitical, and ahistorical constructions of children and childhood that pathologise difference and non-conformity (Davies et al., 2022). Such pathologisation and deficit perspectives seek to further depict a reductionary perspective of Black, Indigenous, and other racialised children and families (Nxumalo & Pacini-Ketchabaw, 2023). This dominant reductionary developmentalist framework portrays young children as 'racially innocent' and incapable of engaging in understandings of race and identity (Escayg, 2020). These pedagogical norms perpetuate practices of exclusion against such communities through the marginalisation of other ways of knowing as well as lived experiences of Black, Indigenous, and other racialised children and families (Brady, 2022; Ineese-Nash, 2020).

Educational policy within the context of settler-colonial states, in this case Canada, has long been weaponised as part of the country's brutal settler-colonial project, notably the commissioning of residential schools, segregated schooling, and racist child welfare practices that continue to disenfranchise Black and Indigenous communities (Abawi, 2022).

The decolonial research interventions shared in this chapter were conceived to counter what we identify as racist Western developmentalist paradigms for ECEC education in Canada. These interventions were empowered by decolonial epistemologies, and anti-racist approaches for curricula and pedagogy. The findings from our research give illumination to the deficiencies of formal anti-racist education in pre-service education programmes. We provide next step approaches for advancing the awareness of ECEC educators in applying anti-racism in their curriculum design and professional practice.

Literature

Through the Western developmentalism epistemic norms submerging ECEC, young children are conceptualised as incapable of discussing and engaging in encounters and entanglements of race and identity (Berman et al., 2022; Brown et al., 2010; Escayg et al., 2017; MacNevin & Berman, 2017; Pacini-Ketchabaw & Berikoff, 2008). Developmentalism is widely rooted in the lived experiences of white, *cis*-gendered, able-bodied, middle-class white children and their families, thus privileging whiteness (Abawi, 2021; Abawi & Berman, 2019). Reconceptualist scholarship, which remains on the margins of the field, offers multidisciplinary theoretical approaches, including critical race theory, anti-racism, and decolonialism to disrupt Western theoretical underpinnings of children and childhoods. Despite widespread claims that young children are incapable of noticing or negotiating in racial socialisations, extant literature suggests that young children actively participate in meaning-making encounters associated with race (Berman et al., 2017; Brown et al., 2010; Iannacci & Whitty, 2009; MacNaughton & Davis, 2009). Furthermore, young children demonstrate positive and negative associations with their own race as well as other races (Escayg, 2019; Xiao et al., 2017). Additionally, several studies have pointed to positive dispositions towards whiteness among both white and Black children (Berman et al., 2017, 2022; Escayg et al., 2017; MacNevin & Berman, 2017). As such, young children are both aware of race and, indeed, may reinforce racialised hierarchies through interactions such as play and relationships with other children (Escayg, 2020; MacNevin & Berman, 2017). By omitting discussions and pedagogies that centre race and positive racial self-awareness, educators effectively perpetuate whiteness as the status quo, often ignoring or minimising racist encounters. This colourblind approach on the part of majority white, female educators, demonstrates significant gaps in education and training concerning antiracism that are informed by the hegemony of white privilege and ontologies of whiteness (Brasche, 2022; Miller & Harris, 2018; Picower, 2009). Many educators enter the profession without antiracism education and training, and as such uphold whiteness (Abawi, 2021; Berman et al., 2022). Anti-Black practices in the ECE field in Canada must be addressed (Kissi & Ewan, 2023).

Objectives and Methods

There has been a proliferation of anti-racism training and professional development initiatives across both corporate and educational institutions following the public screening of the Black man George Floyd being murdered by police in Minneapolis, USA, in May 2020. In our conversations with faculty, students, and in considering our past research projects, we found that many pre-service and in-service educators were not only unaware of decolonial education, but that many had also never learned about the realities of racism in Canada. The absence of these narratives in their professional education speaks to the predominance of Eurocentric developmentalism in pre-service education programmes as well as professional learning initiatives. As such, we, along with a group of colleagues, and the College of Early Childhood Educators (the regulatory body for ECEs in the province) and the Association of ECEs Ontario (a professional body) applied for grant funding to offer antiracism and decolonial professional learning to early childhood educators across Ontario. The project became known as *Give Race Its Place: An Antiracism Knowledge Sharing Initiative for Early Childhood Educators.* We received funding through the Social Sciences and Humanities Research Council. The project sought to unpick educator understandings of race, racial awareness, and hierarchies in early learning contexts, to fill gaps through our proposed professional learning workshops. Our research project focused on providing a platform for educators to ask questions, learn, and unpack their own positionalities in challenging the presence of race and racism in early learning pedagogies and curriculum.

Four consecutive three-hour online workshops were facilitated over a two-week period in the summer of 2021, with more than 300 attendees (although attendance fluctuated over the four sessions). The inter-active sessions were carried out by members of the research team who also provided a plethora of educational resources and a private reflection document after each session.

Before and after the sessions occurred, the research team distributed surveys to participants. Pre-session surveys were used to gauge participant understandings of anti-racism, colonialism, and social location. This allowed the research team to understand what participants hoped to gain from the professional learning initiative. Post-session surveys enabled evaluative feedback to be collected on the sessions, with particular attention to key learnings, potential impact on practice, how educational resources shared may provide understanding of anti-Black racism in Canada and ECEC, and what could be improved in teaching and learning in any future sessions. These evaluation activities did not require a formal review.

Analysis and Findings

Pre-session survey responses suggested that the majority of the 218 respondents had not received any anti-racism education in their pre-service degree or diploma programmes (72.5%), while more reported receiving such training after they began work in the field (52%). About half reported consulting resources that combat anti-Black racism. Most participants stated that they were aware of their positionalities and intersecting identities and how such identities and biases might impact practice (69%).

The post-session survey data revealed that most of the 66 respondents found the knowledge significantly impactful to their understanding and professional practice. However, at the same time, emerging themes that came from the responses included: the prevalence of colour-blindness and affinities to Western developmentalism in that participants felt children were too young to have such discussions. As well, while the team was aware that it takes time to shift practice and that learning and unlearning is a process, many respondents deflected to 'bias-free approaches' (treating everyone the same, a form of colour-blindness) rather than naming and acknowledging differences to promote antiracism. Some participant responses were also aligned with Canadian narratives of celebratory multiculturalism, which effectively centres on food and clothing, rather than unpacking racialised power structures that have real and often devastating consequences for Black, Indigenous, and other racialised children and families. The team found that responses pertaining specifically to anti-Black racism were focused on the resources provided rather than how anti-Black racism might be named, challenged, and dismantled.

Finally, as anticipated, there was resistance to acknowledging whiteness and white privilege. This was evident in at least two of the post-survey responses, and in the live chat that was moderated throughout sessions, which were all led by Black women (Berman et al., 2022).

Strengths and Limitations

Further work is needed for early childhood practitioners to move away from a reliance on Eurocentric developmental narratives. Yet the project held many strengths, such as offering a platform for professional learning on anti-racism, especially pertaining to anti-Black racism for early childhood educators, many of whom had never had such learning opportunities.

Some of the feedback received will be helpful for moving forward, such as the need to tailor our sessions to meet the needs of participants for advancing on their anti-racism learning. As noted, the participants in this research ranged from having limited anti-racism knowledge while others had more experience.

Our training sessions challenged participant dispositions and called out and called in problematic normalised assumptions in practice such as colour-blindness and neutrality. Although the sessions were designed sequentially, some participants did not attend each session and this often was disruptive to the flow of the workshops, and this fact was noted in the post-session feedback. As one respondent wrote: 'I think folks that missed the first week were not able to full grasp content'. Certificates of training completion were provided to those who attended.

Impact and Next Steps

We see that this work remains extremely important to the sector for carving out new ontologies, possibilities, solidarities, and sites of resistance in ECEC across Canada, as the population continues to grow in ethnic diversity. Our suggested next steps in this research:

- The normalcy of whiteness and lack of attention to racism in ECEC spaces needs to be continually challenged, unpacked, and dismantled, not as a single event or even a series of workshops, but as an ongoing commitment to antiracism.
- Professional development initiatives are important, but they are clearly not enough; antiracist and decolonial perspectives and practices must be infused throughout pre-service education.
- Professional development programmes to include grassroot perspectives, voices and lived experiences of children, families, and communities.

References

Abawi, Z. (2021). Privileging power: Early childhood educators, teachers, and racial socialization in full day kindergarten. *Journal of Childhood Studies*, 46(1), 1–12.

Abawi, Z. (2022). Decolonising early childhood curricula: A Canadian perspective. In M. L. Moncrieffe (Ed.), *Decolonising curriculum knowledge: International perspectives and interdisciplinary approaches* (pp. 115–126). Palgrave Macmillan. https://doi.org/10.1007/978-3-031-13623-8_8

Abawi, Z., & Berman, R. (2019). Politicizing early childhood education and care in Ontario: Race, identity and belonging. *Journal of Curriculum, Teaching, Learning and Leadership in Education*, 4(2), 3–13.

Berman, R., Abawi, Z., Haile, F., Daniel, B. J., Butler, A., Escayg, K. A., & Royer, N. (2022). Give race it's place: An antiracism knowledge sharing initiative for early childhood educators in Ontario. *eceLINK Journal*, 6(1), 42–54.

Berman, R., Daniel, B. J., Butler, A., MacNevin, M., & Royer, N. (2017). Nothing or almost nothing to report: Early childhood educators and discursive constructions of colourblindness. *International Critical Childhood Policy Studies Journal*, 6(1), 52–65. https://journals.sfu.ca/iccps/index.php/childhoods/article/view/45

Brady, J. (2022). Exploring the role of Black feminist thought in pre-service early childhood education: On the possibilities of embedded transformative change. *Contemporary Issues in Early Childhood*, 23(4), 392–407.

Brasche, M. K. (2022). *White blindness: An investigation into teacher whiteness and racial ignorance* [Unpublished doctoral dissertation]. University of South Carolina. https://scholarcommons.sc.edu/cgi/viewcontent.cgi?article=7898&context=etd

Brown, S., Souto-Manning, M., & Tropp Laman, T. (2010). Seeing the strange in the familiar: Unpacking racialized practices in early childhood settings. *Race Ethnicity and Education*, 13(4), 513–532. https://doi.org/10.1080/13613324.2010.519957

Colour of Poverty. (2019). *Factsheets*. https://colourofpoverty.ca/fact-sheets/

Davies, A., Karmiris, M., & Berman, R. (2022). Contesting the hegemony of developmentalism in pre-service early childhood education and care: Critical discourses and new directions. *Contemporary Issues in Early Childhood*, 23(4), 371–375.

Escayg, K. (2019). "Who's got the power?": A critical examination of the anti-bias curriculum. *International Journal of Childcare and Education Policy*, 13(6), 1–18. https://ijccep.springeropen.com/articles/10.1186/s40723-019-0062-9

Escayg, K. (2020). Anti-racism in US early childhood education: Foundational principles. *Sociology Compass*, 14(4), 1–15.

Escayg, K. A., Berman, R., & Royer, N. (2017). Canadian children and race: Toward an antiracism analysis. *Journal of Childhood Studies*, 42(2), 10–21.

Iannacci, L., & Whitty, P. (Eds.). (2009). *Early childhood curricula: Reconceptualist perspectives* (pp. 143–165). Brush Education Inc.

Ineese-Nash, N. (2020). Disability as a colonial construct: The missing discourse of culture in conceptualizations of disabled Indigenous children. *Canadian Journal of Disability Studies*, 9(3), 28–51.

Kissi, E., & Ewan, A. (2023). The erasure of Blackness and shortcomings within the Early Learning and care sector in Canada: Recommendations for a way forward. *Journal of Childhood Studies*, 48(3), 33–47.

MacNaughton, G., & Davis, K. (2009). Discourses of "race" in early childhood: From cognition to power. In G. MacNaughton & K. Davis (Eds.), *Race and early childhood education: An international approach to identity, policies, and pedagogy* (pp. 17–30). Palgrave Macmillan.

MacNevin, M., & Berman, R. (2017). The Black baby doll doesn't fit-the disconnect between childhood diversity policy, early childhood educator practice, and children's play. *Early Childhood Development and Care, 187*(5–6), 827–839.

Maynard, R. (2017). *Policing Black lives: State violence in Canada from slavery to the present.* Fernwood Publishing.

Miller, L. A., & Harris, V. W. (2018). I can't be racist – I teach in an urban school, and I'm a nice white lady! *World Journal of Education, 8*(3), 1–11.

Nxumalo, F., & Pacini-Ketchabaw, V. (2023). Centering Black life in Canadian early childhood education. *Gender and Education, 35*(2), 186–198. https://doi.org/10.1080/09540253.2022.2050680

Pacini-Ketchabaw, V., & Berikoff, A. (2008). The politics of difference and diversity: From young children's violence to creative power expressions. *Contemporary Issues in Early Childhood Education, 9*(3), 256264.

Picower, B. (2009). The unexamined Whiteness of teaching: How White teachers maintain and enact dominant racial ideologies. *Race Ethnicity and Education, 12*(2), 197–215. https://doi.org/10.1080/13613320902995475

Statistics Canada. (2016). *Immigration and ethnocultural diversity: Key results from the 2016 census.* https://www150.statcan.gc.ca/n1/daily-quotidien/171025/dq171025b-eng.htm

Truth and Reconciliation Commission of Canada. (2015). *Truth & reconciliation: Calls to action.* https://nctr.ca/records/reports/

United Way. (2019). *Rebalancing the opportunity equation.* chrome-extension://efaidnbmnnnibpcajpcglclefindmkaj/https://www.unitedwaygt.org/wp-content/uploads/2021/10/2019_OE_fullreport_FINAL-1.pdf

Xiao, N. G., Quinn, P. C., Shaoying, L., Ge, L., Piscalis, O., & Lee, K. (2017). Older but not younger infants associate their own race faces with happy music and other-race faces with sad music. *Developmental Science, 21*(2), 1–10.

CHAPTER 6

Decolonising Knowledge of the Parent–Practitioner Relationship in Early Childhood Practice Through Reflective Intercultural Teaching and Learning Interventions

Lesleann Whiteman

University of Brighton, UK

ABSTRACT

This chapter draws on the author's pedagogical intervention with graduates who observed that, while studying on their early childhood degree courses, they learnt the value of establishing relationships with families; however, they found in the modules of teaching and learning limited practical strategies for work with families categorised within the Black Asian Minority Ethnic (BAME) context in the UK. Their concerns are with seeking to understand the root causes of social-economic challenges impacting upon families from ethnically diverse minority groups, cultures different to their own majority ethnic group backgrounds, and how they can provide support through their teaching and learning approaches. This chapter discusses how the inclusion of module activities provides students with opportunities to deconstruct anti-discriminatory practices within the BAME parent–practitioner relationship.

Keywords: early childhood students; relationships; families; reflection; intercultural teaching; learning

Research Context

In this chapter, I share my research interest and pedagogical interventions concerning parent–practitioner relationships between parents of diverse minority ethnic groups and early childhood students, set in the English context of my work as a Senior Lecturer at UK Higher Education Institution (HEI).

International Comparative Perspectives

I conducted a comparative critical review of course content that focused on parent involvement taught in early childhood degree courses at two universities: one in England and another in Trinidad and Tobago. I analysed the teaching approaches used to prepare students to identify gaps in their knowledge on anti-discriminatory practices, and the influence of such knowledge on narratives used to develop parent–practitioner relationships.

From an English context, and in my critical review of the early childhood degree course that I teach on, 9 out of 16 module contents explore the concept of parent partnership within topics such as inclusive engagement strategies, expression of a genuine concern for parents' lived experiences, and the valuing of parenting practices. However, these topics are parts of varied modules rather than one specific module focused on developing parent–practitioner relationships. Although a module – 'working with families in early childhood contexts' – explores how poverty and inequality impact on the family dynamic and care of children, the content is theoretical rather than a 'how to approach'. Herein lies the concern of graduates from this course on the development of their confidence and competency to engage with diverse parents. Within the professional placement module, a two-hour lecture and seminar session is devoted to students critically examining specific questions related to the development of the parent–practitioner relationship. This session explored five questions to help students reflect upon the parent–practitioner relationship. The question (*what are the gaps in your own knowledge and understanding of diversity and anti-discriminatory practice with parents/families?*) identified gaps in students' knowledge and understanding of anti-discriminatory practice with parents, and this led to my critical review of the early childhood education curriculum in this context.

In my experience as an early childhood teacher trainer within the tertiary context in Trinidad and Tobago, I have led early childhood students in taking an active role in advocating for young children and their families. One university early childhood degree course that I previously managed applied the module of learning 'Working with Families and Communities'. The topics within this module were specifically chosen for students to be aware of societal issues which influence the family dynamics and diverse needs of Caribbean families, and the possible influence of these social and cultural issues on the parent–practitioner relationship.

Advancing Intercultural Learning

In reflecting on the working in families modular content from my previous teacher training experience in Trinidad and Tobago, I critically reviewed the content of modules and assessment framework within the early childhood degree courses in my English context, in considering a pedagogical intervention that could be used to advance skills and competencies that early childhood students could apply in reflecting upon their interactions with BAME parents. Campbell (2023, pp. 102–113) in Thompson and Simmons (2023) in her discussion on 'cultural approaches to parenting' reminds us that the content of early childhood degree courses is rooted within the philosophical theories of white middle-class men which highlights to early childhood students that valuable knowledge comes from this demographic. Which may also suggest that the curriculum of early childhood degree courses may work against the concept of a decolonised curriculum in UK HEI. Within parent–practitioner relationships of intercultural engagement, this may mean that students from an English context are left without any specific pedagogy on how to navigate the challenges and teachable experiences they would encounter from working with BAME parents. For example, Harper and Pelletier's (2010) research highlighted that language barriers may hinder EAL parents from communicating with practitioners about their children's needs as compared to English-speaking parents. Furthermore, Appleby et al. (2023, pp. 153–162, in Owen & Barnes, 2023) in her discussion on 'working with parents, carers and families in the early years' claims that if these language barriers are not sensitively navigated by practitioners the parents may feel that their voices are powerless within the early years setting and by extension the parent–practitioner relationship.

Therefore, I believe students of early childhood studies from an English context need pedagogical support to critically examine their professional and personal identities in seeking to deconstruct any found innate concepts of otherness and normalcy in their interactions with parents from ethnic and cultural groups from their own. I saw that my conception of an intercultural teaching, learning, and assessment framework could support early childhood students in the English context in developing a conscious awareness of power and privilege and an enhancement of their confidence when partnering with BAME parents. This collaborative approach would require a relationship founded on mutual respect, trust, and an understanding of cultural parenting practices.

Literature

The *Birth to 5 Matters* (2021, pp. 28–29) 'parents as partners' guidance emphasises the need for practitioners to be aware of their biases when engaging with parents by respecting their lived cultural experiences. Such a reflective approach implies time is allocated for staff to meet and discuss how to solve issues of inclusion, equality, and equity encountered by children and families. Additionally, when staff have allotted time within their busy schedule to reflect on their practice, they can use that opportunity to deconstruct their biases about parents from diverse ethnic minorities. Such guidance for challenging the issues of equality and equity, via a reflective paradigm for practitioners, and a strengths-based approach for families, creates the foundation for both practitioners and parents to transform the parent–practitioner relationship. The 'parents as partners' guidance is constructed around the theme of attentive listening by practitioners to parents, which is supported with relevant examples of how to demonstrate to parents their views and opinions about their lived experiences and their children's development are valued and acknowledged (Birth to 5 Matters 2021, pp. 28–29). For example, the guidance advises practitioners to use a level of engagement that best suits the needs of parents, to be open, and willing to work with diverse minority ethnic group family types, and such practices should be underpinned within the philosophical framework and management of the early years setting.

The *Birth to 5 Matters* (2021, pp. 28–29) 'parents as partners' guidance appears as practical and implementable within varied early childhood contexts, by considering the inclusion of time for practitioners to meet as a team reflecting on their biases. Reflective practice provides staff with an opportunity to monitor the narratives used in the parent partnership policies, in considering equality and equity for BAME parents. Likewise, Campbell (2023, in Thompson & Simmons, 2023) believes that early years' practitioners have a responsibility to ensure their interactions with intercultural parents are genuine rather than cosmetic to avoid the perpetuation of stereotypical western views about diverse cultural parenting practices. It seems that the *Birth to 5 Matters* (2021) guidance promotes a reflective and decolonised approach in comparison to *Development Matters* (Department for Education, 2021) which although is non-statutory curriculum guidance for the early years foundation stage (EYFS) appears to be framed by deficit narratives of parents' inability to provide stimulating learning home environments which can influence and perpetuate the power imbalance between parents and practitioners.

The *Birth to 5 Matters* (2021, pp. 28–29) 'parents as partners' guidance is grounded within the theoretical framework of transformational learning. Mezirow (1990) discusses transformational learning theory as an idea that people can adjust their thinking based on added information which helps to evaluate past ideas. Simply stated, learning new perspectives while questioning one's previous assumptions (Rix, 2018). In the context of the parent–practitioner relationship between an early childhood practitioner from an English context and BAME parents, such a transformed relationship will provide valuable opportunities for embedded perspectives and behaviours around the caring of young children to be re-evaluated.

Objectives and Methods

While reviewing student feedback for a seminar activity used for the working in partnership session, I observed their feedback emphasised the need to be provided with practical strategies for developing a parent-practitioner relationship, which they learnt while on placement instead of from the module content. Based on student feedback, I designed a teaching module entitled 'Genuine Parent-Teacher Relationships with Parents from Diverse Ethnicities'. This sought to provide early childhood students with an opportunity to deconstruct and rebuild their knowledge about the cultural and societal contexts of the parent–practitioner relationship.

At the 2022 World Forum Early Childhood Conference, my presentation entitled: *Genuine Parent–Teacher Relationship – Realism or a Myth?* I sought feedback from international early childhood practitioners on the level of preparedness focused within early childhood courses to support students' competency to develop intercultural parent–practitioner relationships with their assigned families. The three main questions guiding my presentation were:

1. Are we truly teaching early childhood students to engage in genuine parent–practitioner relationships?
2. Are we falling short in our early childhood teacher education programmes?
3. What should we do to bridge the gap between theory and practice?

Working in small groups, I asked the 25 participants to share their experiences of working with parents from ethnically diverse minority group cultures and answer the four questions

1. What is your definition of the intercultural parent-teacher relationship? What life experiences contributed to your definition?
2. In your opinion what ethical issues would early childhood practitioners encounter when developing a genuine relationship with an ethnically diverse minority group of parents?
3. From your perspective how can early childhood practitioners navigate safeguarding and child protection policies and legislations to develop a trusting relationship with parents from ethnically diverse minority group cultures?
4. Do you believe your conscious and unconscious biases about engaging with families from different cultures influence your ability to develop genuine parent–teacher relationships? Why or why not?

Fig. 6.1. Questions Answered by Participants.

listed in Fig. 6.1 with the aim of modifying my proposed module content.

Analysis and Findings

Based on the feedback I received from the conference participants (see Fig. 6.2), I revised the learning outcomes and the topics to be covered in the teaching module 'Genuine Parent-Teacher Relationships with Parents from Diverse Ethnicities'. The revised learning outcomes were a blend of theoretical academic debates on parent–teacher relationships, and the practical approaches like using an empowerment narrative when communicating with parents verbally to engage in a trusting relationship with parents from diverse minority group cultures.

The content of the teaching and learning module included an underlying theme of reflection on the practitioners' beliefs and attitudes of families from diverse cultures. To understand the significance of cultural parenting beliefs the module content sought to challenge the narratives used by the media to perpetuate the societal stereotypes of diverse minority families. The themes (see Fig. 6.3) were all framed within the context of trust and transparency within the parent–practitioner relationship.

In connecting to these successful strategies, Bolton (2010) discusses the power created in professional practice given

1. 'Have to know your community, translated materials, policies and procedures aligned with families served, offer resources in a safe way'
2. Family engagement strategies like 'Frequent check-ins and trust building activities to welcome families "in" the setting'
3. 'Regular parenting meetings – share education and perspectives to help parents and understand "school" culture'

Fig. 6.2. Participants' Successful Strategies for Developing a Trusting Parent–Practitioner Relationship.

1. 'Important to embrace everyone's culture and learn about cultures, balance cultural activity, help families feel comfortable and familiar, parent opportunities to interact with each other and support children'
2. 'Different cultures have different perspectives- some will share, others are private, do we know our own cultures and how to share with parents'?
3. 'We all have unconscious bias-influence of our personal and larger cultures, we need to learn cultural differences, also be open to learning and discussion, less impact – if know what biases we hold'
4. 'Head-start regulations – to have parents in leadership roles – organically address some of these challenges, system leadership and policy has to support engaging practices – not just at individual level'

Fig. 6.3. Participants' Successful Strategies for Reflection on Their Parent–Practitioner Relationship.

through reflection and in challenging the influence of stereotypes and the uncritical formation of bias. Likewise Hamilton (2021, p. 36) in her discussion on the portrayal of minority and marginalised groups by the British media, advocates for early childhood students to continually question, challenge, and reflect upon their own 'knowledge and value base'. This is because Hamilton (2021) believes students should learn to identify how stereotypes and prejudices about minority families may contribute to their conscious and unconscious biases.

Strengths and Limitations

The inability to pilot the module's effectiveness in bridging the gap between theory and practice is a notable research limitation

1. Common ethical issues that may arise when working with parents from diverse cultures
2. Defining parent-practitioner relationships is inextricably linked to one's personal as well as professional identity as an educator
3. Safeguarding policies should not be a hindrance to the facilitation of a trusting parent and practitioner relationship
4. Being a life-long learner means being open to learning about diverse cultural beliefs about parenting by understanding the differences and embracing the similarities

Fig. 6.4. Specific Topics to Be Covered When Teaching About the Parent–Practitioner Relationship.

to this intervention. Nevertheless, the feedback obtained from the participants highlighted specific topics (see Fig. 6.4) for early childhood teacher-educators to consider when teaching about the parent–practitioner relationship with parents from diverse minority ethnic groups.

Impact and Next Steps

The analysis of the participant's responses shows that by using a reflective pedagogical approach, early childhood students can feel more aware of their professional practices with BAME parents by using an empowerment narrative which addresses issues of equality and equity. Likewise, for early childhood education and care degree courses, it is paramount to ensure that students of the English context identify and critically deconstruct what may be the root causes of bias in any future parent–practitioner relationship that they may have with BAME families. New collaborative efforts between practitioners and early childhood academia must seek to bridge the gap between theory and practice in advancing these efforts:

- Formal assessments for placement-learning modules which require students to support a BAME family while on placement and their experiences documented in a critical reflective piece of writing.
- A collaborative effort among practitioners, early childhood students, and academia for writing and publishing

a practical guide on developing parent–practitioner relationships with BAME families.

- Funding and accreditation to pilot the new module (Genuine Parent–Practitioner Relationships with Parents from Diverse Ethnicities) with early childhood practitioners across England.

References

Appleby, M. (2023). Working with parents, carers, and families in the early years. In K. Owen & C. Barnes (Eds.), *Family relationships in the early years* (pp. 154–162). Sage Publications.

Bolton, G. (2010). *Reflective practice: Writing and professional development* (2nd ed.). Sage Publications.

Campbell, H. (2023). Cultural approaches to parenting. In P. Thompson & H. Simmons (Eds.), *Partnership with parents in early childhood today*. Sage Publications.

Department for Education. (2021). *Development Matters, non-statutory curriculum guidance for the early years' foundation stage*. www.gov.uk/government/publications

Early Years Coalition. (2021). *Birth to 5 Matters, non-statutory guidance for the early years' foundation stage*. www.birthto5matters.org.uk

Hamilton, P. (2021). *Diversity and marginalisation in childhood a guide for inclusive thinking 0-11*. Sage Publications.

Harper, S. N., & Pelletier, J. (2010). Parent involvement in early childhood: A comparison of English language learners and English first language families. *International Journal of Early Years Education*, 18(2), 123–141.

Knowles, A. (2021). Partnerships. In I. Palaiologou (Ed.), *The early years foundation stage, theory, and practice* (pp. 329–341) (4th ed.). Sage Publications.

Mezirow, J. (1990). *Fostering critical reflection adulthood: A guide to transformative [Database][Mismatch] and emancipatory learning*. Jossey-Bass.

Rix, J. (2018). Thinking about a community of provision. In K. Stafford & L. Chamberlain (Eds.), *Learning & teaching around the world: Comparative and international studies in primary education* (pp. 37–43). Routledge.

CHAPTER 7

Decolonising the Curriculum: A Comparative Case-study of Black Learner and Educator Perspectives and Experience from London (UK) and Johannesburg (South Africa)

Omena Osivwemu

University College London, UK

ABSTRACT

Black university student protests calling for decolonising the curriculum in South Africa in 2015 and the Black Lives Matter movement sweeping across the UK in 2020 have brought attention to the need for anti-racist and decolonial education and practice in schools. Drawing on critical pedagogy and decolonial discourse, this research analyses conceptualisations of decolonising the curriculum and anti-racist pedagogy through Black learner and educator understandings from a London primary school and educator perspectives in Johannesburg. Empirical data collected from a learner focus group, field journal, and educator interviews showed key themes for informing best practice as belonging, identity and community knowledge, cultural relevance, critical thinking, and consciousness raising. Findings from this research suggested shared educator understandings of 'decolonising the curriculum' and evidence of decolonial practice. While Black learners' critique raised considerations for progression of 'soft reform' to more 'radical' transformation.

Keywords: decolonising; curriculum; anti-racism; Black learners; praxis

Research Context

This chapter presents research which examined perceptions of decolonising the curriculum in school in London and Johannesburg and privileged dialogue with Black learners and decolonial educators. Having identified white-centric epistemic dominance in the aims and contents of the English National Primary Curriculum (DfE, 2014; Kadiwal & Moghli, 2021; Moncrieffe, 2020; Morreira et al., 2020), the research sought to gain insight into educator and Black learner perspectives on 'decolonising the curriculum'. This colonial epistemic dominance had also been identified in the English literature and historical perspectives taught within the CAPS curriculum in Johannesburg (DFBE, 2021). This research sought to compare and contextualise Black learner and educator experiences of the curriculum in a London (UK) setting, with Johannesburg (South African) educator conceptualisations as propagators in decolonial discourse and practice (Agherdien et al., 2022).

Literature

The research is grounded in the theories of Paolo Freire's 'pedagogy of the oppressed' (1998) and Gloria Ladson-Billings' 'culturally relevant pedagogy' (2014). Central was Freire's notion of a pedagogy *of* the oppressed, rather than *for* the oppressed (1998). Freire (1998) advocates for resistance via politicisation of the marginalised through humanising, liberatory pedagogy, contesting the 'banking concept' of education which positions learners as empty vessels.

This research applied the lens of Ladson-Billings' (2014) theory of a culturally relevant pedagogy, which centres racially marginalised learners focusing on the cultural and community knowledges they hold. It is argued that, in applying culturally relevant pedagogies, teachers commit to 'cultural competence (rather than) cultural assimilation or eradication, and sociopolitical consciousness rather than school-based tasks that have no beyond-school application' (Ladson-Billings, 2014, p. 76).

Connecting with bell hooks' (1984) notion of 'teaching to transgress', Mignolo's (2011, in Kadiwal et al., 2021, p.8).) notion of decolonisation relates to subversive curricula 'addressing interrelated systems of hegemonic control, such as patriarchy, racism, knowledge …, all of which are concepts that underpin colonial institutional structures'. Colonial 'Western rationality as the only framework and possibility of existence, analysis and thought' (Walsh, 2018, p. 17) is disrupted and elite white, Eurocentric and male knowledge production and validation processes are decentred (Collins, 2009; Molefe, 2016, in Kadiwal et al., 2021; Morreira et al., 2020). Decolonial praxis is to subvert the epistemic and social power dynamics at play in classrooms (Morreira et al., 2020) enabling space for recognition, co-production, and critical thinking (Freire, 1998; hooks, 1994; Ladson-Billings, 2014). As is proposed through 'revolutionary approaches' such as Afrocentric education (Perryman-Clark, 2013), *ubuntu* (Knaus et al., 2022; Sekudu, 2019), or a Black radical paradigm (Andrews in Moncrieffe, 2020).

Scholars identify education's role in maintaining structural oppression (Knaus et al., 2022) in South Africa. They point to the colonial epistemic dominance of the 'White Eurocentric curriculum' (Morreira et al., 2020) and teaching models reflective of the banking concept of education (Freire, 1998). Sekudu (2019) states that the #FeesMustFall movement of 2015 illuminated the inadequacies of 'White Eurocentric curricula' serving indigenous (Black) South Africans.

From a UK perspective, decolonising the curriculum requires challenge to colonial legacies, decentring the totality of white-Britishness (Moncrieffe, 2020) in creating a 'route to epistemic innovation' for critical educators and learners to 'dismantle (societal) racism and oppression' (Moncrieffe, 2020, p. 3). This requires a commitment to reflexive 'critical curriculum thinking' (Moncrieffe, 2020) in educators and learners through collaborative knowledge production and consciousness raising, thus enacting social justice in education.

Moncrieffe (2020) and Arday (2021) frame Black-British histories as an opportunity to widen learners' knowledge base and teachers' professional capabilities to engage a greater range of learners. They advance Black-British history as *essential* knowledge 'that provides the contextual and historical backdrop to how generations of Black people ... have shaped constructions of Britishness' (Arday, 2021, p. 16), and richer critical pedagogical orientations in examining historical *cross-cultural encounters* (Moncrieffe, 2020, 2014), where Britons have reckoned with ethnic and cultural difference.

Objectives and Methods

In recognising education as a practice for transgression (hooks, 1994), this research acknowledged the colonial roots of research (Ndlovu-Gatsheni, 2017). The privileges of the 'knower'/researcher were disrupted to place participants as 'knowers' and critics of their social realities (Parson, 2019) alongside the researcher. Within an interpretative paradigm (Mahabeer, 2020), this research sought to make meaning of educator and Black learner perceptions through a case study (Candappa, 2017) comparative research conducted in one London and one Johannesburg primary school, drawing on further South African educator perspectives to highlight the glocality of decolonial education.

Acknowledging the gap that Morreira et al. (2020) identify between theory and practice, a key objective of this research was to analyse conceptualisations of decolonising the curriculum and critical pedagogy. Built from a comparison of Black learner and educator voice on decolonising the curriculum, this research aimed to contribute to decolonial discourse situated in primary school and share experience (Freire, 1998; Mahabeer, 2020) of subversive decolonial practice to further transform educator praxis.

This research applied multiple methods of data collection: four semi-structured educator interviews, a focus group with seven self-identifying upper Key Stage two (KS2) Black learners, and reflections from research field notes collated during a one-month research trip hosted by a Johannesburg university and including a primary school visit. Schultz et al. (2018, in Kadiwal et al., 2021, p.10).) affirm it is 'a transformation effort to produce knowledge with and from, rather than about' the marginalised (in Kadiwal et al., 2021, p. 10). Hence, new knowledge was co-produced with learners and decolonial educators (Ladson-Billings, 2014) through humanising dialogue in response to the following questions:

1. What does it mean to 'decolonise the curriculum'?
2. To what extent can schools decolonise the curriculum?
3. How do Black learners experience the curriculum?

The research design and methods conducted with children were informed by Mcgillicuddy and Devine's (2020) framework for research: the *facilitation of voice through dialogue*, rather than plundering information. hooks (in Collins, 2009, p. 279) considers this 'humanising speech – one that challenges and resists domination'. Furthermore, the authenticity and knowingness of speech was honoured when rich data was collated and analysed into the following themes:

- Belonging, identity, and community;
- Co-production and community knowledges;
- Cultural relevance;
- Critical thinking and consciousness raising.

Analysis and Findings

Educator Understandings and Practice

In both London and Johannesburg, educators shared understandings on the purpose of education as social justice through transformation and liberation, reaching beyond inclusivity or 'add on' tokenism. Decolonial practice was evident in a variety of approaches to epistemic innovation. For example, through the incorporation of intersectional community lived experience and critical thinking in curricula as:

reflective of historical injustices. (UK Educator)

To critiquing notions of 'Modern Foreign Languages' in the British context:

> *languages are languages... there's like a hierarchy of languages and these are the 'beneficial' ones ....* (UK Educator)

Decolonial curricula and practice evident in the London case study fit within Moncrieffe's conceptualisation of the 'radical approach' (2020), defined as an embedded and sustained approach to teaching and learning. Wherein, basic assumptions of Eurocentrism in curriculum and validated knowledges shift from a white-British vantage point, to include histories, experience and knowledges of marginalised peoples. The curriculum offer was 'transformative critical, multicultural education' (May & Sleeter, in Moncrieffe, 2020) stemming from decolonial transformation in teaching and learning driven by senior and curriculum leaders; acknowledged in this setting as a continuous ongoing project.

In the Johannesburg case-study context, two to four languages were taught in schools including the nine indigenous languages, depending on the area's demographics. Johannesburg educators reflected on their positionality and power dynamics in the classroom, emphasising the necessity to recognise learners as a whole-being with knowledges, histories, and cultures:

> *[...] in the way we engage ... to bring in ... not just the voices of the underprivileged ... bring in student agency acknowledging ... the whole person, bring value, valuing not just the opinions, but the insights.* (South African Educator)

Finally, educators referenced practice that facilitated the co-production of knowledge through collaborative dialogue and sharing of experience (Ladson-Billings, 2014). Namely space for critical conversations on 'race' and racism with school communities, including a primary parent and teacher group and secondary consciousness-raising discussion forums, which centred the lives of racially marginalised parents and students, giving power to:

> *decolonise the relationships we have with our community.* (UK Educator)

Learner Perceptions

Overall, Black learners' had a negative perception of schooling, associated with boredom, labour, and containment. Although, learners identified multiple curriculum areas where Black cultures, histories, and knowledges were taught in the London case such as history, PSHE, and english. Black learners highlighted the lack of diversity of knowledge offered, and the negativity of the Black histories taught. As is exemplified here:

> *I don't like history because almost everyone said its mostly ... white people that we learn about, not really Black ... all we learn about is Black people getting colonised or like segregation in America.* (UK Learner)

Seemingly, here the learner experience of the curriculum aligned with Freire's (1998) banking concept of education described as:

> *sitting down and trying to cram it (knowledge) into your heads.* (UK Learner)

Strong opposition to traditional, formal methods of teaching was expressed, while suggested alternatives related to Ladson-Billings' (2014) notion of a culturally relevant pedagogy drawing on youth culture:

> *I'd rather do things like something that makes Maths fun or like we mix it up a little ... you can like learn Maths and like learn a rap ... make music.* (UK Learner)

Finally, much learner-led dialogue focused on recognition of Black History Month, or lack thereof, and the perception of racism in school and society. One learner contended that responsibility for reducing Black histories to a month lay with society rather than schools:

> *I think it's just Britain needs to work on the impact of being racist and making our months fair because we only have one month.* (UK Learner)

It was concluded that to intentionally move from 'soft reform' (Kadiwal et al., 2021) or a 'radical approach', to a 'revolutionary approach' to decolonising (Moncrieffe, 2020, p. 3):

- Learners should be consulted throughout curriculum innovation, basing adaptations on the shifting demographics of a setting, ensuring the co-production of knowledge, cultural relevance of curriculum, and recognition of the fluidity of pedagogy and knowledge (Ladson-Billings, 2014).
- Black learners demonstrated socio-political consciousness and developing critical thinking in the London case: central features of decolonial curriculum/practice.
- British educators considered time constraints and knowledge as barriers to 'revolutionary' reform, requiring the upskilling of staff to embody a greater understanding of criticality, rather than a lack of will.
- Yet, South African educators voiced a lack of will from colleagues, institutions, and, in some instances, wider community: emphasising the need for institutional and community wide solidarity with decolonising projects, as reform cannot exist in isolation (Kadiwal et al., 2021).

Overall, educator conceptualisations aligned with learner perceptions, while illuminating the complexity of decolonising, and the continuous, reflexive journey of curriculum transformation, even when it is more diverse and critical than the standard offer.

Strengths and Limitations

Due to the researcher's dual role and lived experience as a Black woman teacher–researcher, conducting data collection was experienced as positive process of collaborative dialogue. Participants were equal knowers in relationship with the researcher. Similarly, given the relationship of trust, prior learning, and conversation with learners, participants expressed candidly, particularly pertaining to issues of 'race' and racism.

Yet, tensions while occupying the 'insider-outsider' role (Parson, 2019) also posed limitations. For instance, the role as teacher prevailed in relation to learners during the focus group, and the relative racialisation of the researcher was contested in South Africa, being identified as 'coloured' rather than Black.

Imperatively, subsequent ethical dilemmas were recorded in the field journal and examined alongside data analysis; as Gordon (in Parson, 2019, p. 22) argues, 'the identity of the researcher and the researched is part of every study, and examining it makes the work richer and more comprehensible'.

Given the research focus on comparative singular case studies, the data offered limited generalisability. However, rather than generalise populations, this research sought to draw inferences from the particular case, informed by theory (Candappa, 2017). Thus, a small sample allowed for greater individual voice and 'thick' descriptive data aligning with the research aims and approach (Parson, 2019).

Impact and Next Steps

The aim of the research was met in illuminating transgressive decolonial practice and educator perceptions of decolonising the curriculum in schools. Black learner voice was given space to share and co-produce knowledge of curriculum engagement and possible advancements. This informed the research conclusions for moving praxis forwards. Proposed next steps in advancing this research include:

- To develop practitioners' decolonial praxis.
- To share findings of this research on learner voice and practice with educators across schools.
- To continue contributing to discourse surrounding anti-racism and decoloniality in education.
- To pursue opportunities for further research in this field and related topics such as the impact of racial trauma on children's behaviour.

References

Agherdien, N., Puillay, R., Dube, N., & Masinga, P. (2022). What does decolonising education mean to us? Educator reflections. *Scholarship of Teaching and Learning in the South*, 6(1), 55–78.

Arday, J. (2021). *The Black Curriculum: Black British history in the national curriculum report*. The Black Curriculum. https://theblackcurriculum.com/research-review

Candappa, M. (2017). Case studies. In J. Swain (Ed.), *Designing research in education concepts and methodologies* (pp. 197–216). Sage.

Collins, P. H. (2009). *Black feminist thought: Knowledge, consciousness, and the politics of empowerment*. Routledge.

DFBE. (2021). *Curriculum Assessment Policy Statements (CAPS)*. Department of Basic Education. https://www.education.gov.za/Curriculum/CurriculumAssessmentPolicyStatements(CAPS).aspx

DFE. (2014). *The national curriculum in England-framework document*. assets.publishing.service.gov.uk/government/uploads/system/uploads/attachment_data/file/381344/Master_final_national_curriculum_28_Nov.pdf

Freire, P. (1998). *Pedagogy of freedom: Ethics, democracy, and civic courage*. Rowman and Littlefield Publishers, Inc.

hooks, b. (1994). *Teaching to transgress: Education as the practice of freedom*. Routledge.

Kadiwal, L., & Moghli, M. (2021). Decolonising the curriculum beyond the surge: Conceptualisation, positionality, and conduct. *London Review of Education*, 19(1), 1–16.

Knaus, C., Mino, T., & Seroto, J. (2022). *Decolonising African higher education: Practitioner perspectives from across the continent*. Routledge.

Ladson-Billings, G. (2014). Culturally Relevant Pedagogy 2.0: a.k.a. the Remix. *Harvard Educational Review*, 84(1), 74–84. https://meridian.allenpress.com/her/article-abstract/84/1/74/32149/Culturally-Relevant-Pedagogy-2-0-a-k-a-the-Remix?redirectedFrom=fulltext

Mahabeer, P. (2020). Decolonising the school curriculum in South Africa: Black women teachers' perspectives. *Third World Thematics: A TWQ Journal*, 5(1–2), 97–119. https://doi.org/10.1080/23802014.2020.1762510

Mcgillicuddy, D., & Devine, D. (2020). You feel ashamed that you are not in the higher group – Children's psychosocial response to ability grouping in primary school. *British Educational Research Journal*, 46(3), 553–573.

Moncrieffe, M. L. (2014). Reconceptualising mass migration within the primary school history curriculum master narrative for a broader sense of connection and belonging to England and English History. In E. Haplin, A. Hunter, K. Murji, A. Ozerdem, R. Race,

S. Robinson & M. Demir (Eds.), *Academic workshop proceedings: Sense of belonging in a diverse Britain* (pp. 191–206). Dialogue Society.

Moncrieffe, M. L. (2020). *Decolonising the history curriculum: Eurocentrism and primary schooling*. Palgrave MacMillan.

Morreira, S., Luckett, K., Kumalo, S. H., & Ramgotra, M. (2020). Confronting the complexities of decolonising curricula and pedagogy in higher education. *Third World Thematics: A TWQ Journal, 5*(1–2), 1–18.

Ndlovu-Gatsheni, S. (2017). *Decolonising research methodology must include undoing its dirty history*. The Conversation. https://theconversation.com/decolonising-research-methodology-must-include-undoing-its-dirty-history-83912

Parson, L. (2019). Considering positionality: The ethics of conducting research with marginalised groups. In K. K. Strunk & L. A. Lock (Eds.), *Research methods for social justice and equity in education* (pp. 15–32). Palgrave Macmillan.

Perryman-Clark, S. (2013). *Afrocentric teacher-research: Rethinking appropriateness and inclusion*. Peter Lang.

Sekudu, J. (2019). Ubuntu. In A. van Breda & J. Sekudu (Eds.), *Theories for decolonial social work practice* (pp. 105–119). Oxford University Press South Africa.

Walsh, C. (2018). The decolonial for: Resurgences, shifts and movements. In W. Mignolo & C. Walsh (Eds.), *On decoloniality: Concepts, analytics, praxis* (pp. 15–32). Duke University Press.

EARLY CHILDHOOD AND PRIMARY EDUCATION – SUMMARY

The research given by these chapters share on how decolonial praxis has been enacted by epistemological disruption to dominant curriculum frameworks and dominant pedagogical approaches. The evidence-informed research shared in this section has guided on how these critical and disruptive processes can build for equity in education.

Advancing decolonial praxis in early childhood education and in primary school education requires the continuation of high-quality evidence-informed decolonial research which exemplifies best practices. It is important that any such research is sensitive to, and challenges, the broader epistemic politics of how knowledge comes to be constructed, valued, and utilised. Critical reflexive practice applied to engaging with curriculum and in pedagogy across early childhood and primary school educational sites has a genuine and meaningful impact on young children's learning opportunities. Such practice celebrates the diversity of children's communication, both in terms of children's non-verbal forms of expression and in terms of different languages spoken in children's families and communities. Continued and advanced professional development that combines the best examples of evidenced-informed research and practice will support critical reflective practitioners in their commitment to decolonising and diversifying the curriculum for achieving equity in education.

Reflective Questions

1. What may be the key cultural challenges for the critical reflexive practitioner in aiming to decolonise the curriculum?

2. How can these key cultural challenges be mitigated?

3. How can professional development programmes and teaching resources for decolonising the curriculum in early childhood education and primary school education better include grassroot perspectives, voices and lived experiences of children, families, and communities?

Recommended Reading

Abawi, Z. (2022). Decolonising early childhood curricula: A Canadian perspective. In M. L. Moncrieffe (Ed.), *Decolonising curriculum knowledge: International perspectives and interdisciplinary approaches* (pp. 115–126). Palgrave Macmillan. https://doi.org/10.1007/978-3-031-13623-8_8

Cannella, G. S., & Viruru, R. (2004). *Childhood and postcolonization: Power, education, and contemporary practice*. Psychology Press.

Kustatscher, M., Calderón, E., Tisdall, E. K. M., Evanko, W. A., & Gomez Serna, J. M. (2022). Decolonising participatory methods with children and young people in international research collaborations: Reflections from a participatory arts-based project with Afrocolombian and indigenous young people in Colombia. In M. L. Moncrieffe (Ed.), *Decolonising curriculum knowledge: International perspectives and interdisciplinary approaches* (pp. 15–34). Palgrave Macmillan. https://doi.org/10.1007/978-3-031-13623-8_2

Kustatscher, M., & Konstantoni, K. (2023). Intersectional perspectives on childhood. In K. Tisdall, J. Davis, D. Fry, K. Konstantoni, M. Kustatscher, C. Maternowska, & L. Weiner (Eds.), *Critical childhood studies: Global perspectives* (1 ed., p. 149). Bloomsbury Academic.

Ladson-Billings, G. (2014). Culturally relevant pedagogy 2.0: a.k.a. the remix. *Harvard Educational Review*, 84(1), pp. 74–84. https://meridian.allenpress.com/her/article-abstract/84/1/74/32149/Culturally-Relevant-Pedagogy-2-0-a-k-a-the-Remix?redirectedFrom=fulltext

Loader, R., Jiménez, E., O'Boyle, A., & Hughes, J. (2023). Experiences of education among minority ethnic groups in Northern Ireland. Queen's University Belfast. https://www.qub.ac.uk/public-engagement/FileStore/PubAffFiles/Filetoupload,1862560,en.pdf

Moncrieffe, M. L. (2020). *Decolonising the history curriculum: Eurocentrism and primary schooling*. Palgrave MacMillan.

Moncrieffe, M. L. (2022). Why decolonising curriculum knowledge?. In M. L. Moncrieffe (Ed.), *Decolonising curriculum knowledge: International perspectives & interdisciplinary approaches* (pp. 1–14). Palgrave Macmillan. https://doi.org/10.1007/978-3-031-13623-8_1

Moncrieffe, M. L. (2023). *Examining challenges and possibilities in the objective of a decolonized education.* Oxford Research Encyclopaedia of Education. https://oxfordre.com/education/display/10.1093/acrefore/9780190264093.001.0001/acrefore-9780190264093-e-1863

Nxumalo, F., & Brown, C. P. (Eds.). (2019). *Disrupting and countering deficits in early childhood education.* Routledge.

Pérez, M. S., & Saavedra, C. M. (2017). A call for onto-epistemological diversity in early childhood education and care: Centering Global South conceptualizations of childhoods. *Review of Research in Education*, 41(1), 1–29. https://doi.org/10.3102/0091732X16688621

Souto-Manning, M., & Rabadi-Raol, A. (2018). (Re)Centering quality in early childhood education: Toward intersectional justice for minoritized children. *Review of Research in Education*, 42(1), 203–225. https://doi.org/10.3102/0091732X18759550

Varga, D. (2011). Look–normal: The colonized child of developmental science. *History of Psychology*, 14(2), 137–157. https://doi.org/10.1037/a0021775

SECONDARY AND TERTIARY EDUCATION – INTRODUCTION

This section of chapters offers a range of practical approaches as well as insights in regard to decolonial approaches in secondary and tertiary education. The first chapter starts with a wider perspective of history teachers' views and practices regarding diversifying and decolonising curricula. The two subsequent chapters provide examples of how individual practitioners have developed their approaches in the subjects of history and English, and also highlight the role that that continued and advanced professional development (CAAPD) can play in developing teachers' thinking and practice. Such CAAPD is revealed to be very important for preservice teachers, who demonstrate the development of their thinking through reflective practice when using specifically designed resources. Similarly, in the chapter that follows, modern foreign language (MFL) preservice teachers engaged in decolonial thinking through arts-based research methods and were found to develop a critical and activist mindset in their developmental activities. The chapter given on tertiary biology shows this as a broadly colonised subject. Practitioners are shown to reposition the discipline within a socio-scientific context to introduce a critical lens to students. The final chapter in this section places emphasis on action research, highlighting the importance of reflective practice. Some noteworthy and recurring themes are identified across the chapters:

1. *Action research and reflexive practice* as distinctive approaches to decolonial teaching and learning can be observed where *Richardson et al.* (Chapter 12) apply this in their study with MFL preservice teachers and Post Graduate Certificate in Education (PGCE) lecturer colleagues. Similarly, *Hughes and Hart* (Chapter 11) share and reflect on these themes of practice in their work to introduce their students to socio-scientific thinking in biology, while

Lyndon-Cohen's (Chapter 9) contributions illustrate the approaches taken within the history classroom. The action research and reflexive practice shared provides insight and guidance to decolonial practice emphasised by collaboration and coproduction of knowledge. For example, *Richardson et al.* (Chapter 12) in their use of arts-based methods discuss how their research participants become the coproducers of knowledge. A similar theme can be found in *Lyndon-Cohen's* (Chapter 9) presentation of young history students who undertook their own research interviews and developed their own banks of knowledge from this.

2. *Subject and disciplinary knowledge* is closely intertwined with the necessary critical thinking for decolonising curricula and practice. *Lyndon-Cohen* (Chapter 9) demonstrates this by the bespoke design of historical enquiries in relation to who the underserved narratives belong to, where to find them (procedural knowledge), and how to encourage students to engage with these. *Mohammed et al.* (Chapter 13) share how discussions among preservice history teachers were firmly framed within their knowledge of the discipline, and how to work with historical sources in the classroom, even though the pre-created resource itself was non-subject specific. Both *Richardson et al.* (Chapter 12) and *Hughes and Hart* (Chapter 11) challenge the nature and traditional perspectives of subject and disciplinary knowledge. This is illustrated by the very different considerations and perspectives accounted for in their writing. It is noteworthy that, in all the chapters in this section, the critical scrutiny of subject and disciplinary knowledge appears to provide an essential starting point or 'way in' for developing decolonial praxis.

3. *Subversive thinking and action* – or at the very least, a commitment to go beyond the traditional way of delivering subject teaching and learning in the context of the highly regulated and performative education sector in England. All samples of research in this section exemplify the greater value in this critical teaching and learning approach with students and colleagues. *Burn et al.* (Chapter 8) point to the

differences between practitioners, and therefore, the need for diverse learning experiences in the students that they teach. *Lyndon-Cohen* (Chapter 9) and *Hughes and Hart* (Chapter 11) share how taking the initiative within their subject departments raises awareness and the profile in the value of decolonial teaching and learning. *Richardson et al.* (Chapter 12) illustrate not only how their teaching and learning is implemented by their subversive initiative, but also how the outcomes are personalised in the way in which the mindset of the preservice teachers were transformed to that of activists. Finally, subversive thinking and action against curricula norms beyond the traditional way of delivering subject teaching and learning can be seen where both *Mohammed et al.* (Chapter 13) and *Branford and Todd* (Chapter 10) give importance in their research insights to the development of individual insight and re-education among teachers and preservice teachers for their ability to decolonise their practices.

CHAPTER 8

Diversifying the History Curriculum in England: A Slow (R)evolution

Katharine Burn[a], Richard Harris[b] and Joseph Smith[c]

[a]*University of Oxford, UK*
[b]*University of Reading, UK*
[c]*University of Stirling, UK*

ABSTRACT

This chapter provides a context for other case-study chapters in this volume that explore in more depth steps taken to provide a decolonised perspective in the history curriculum. The chapter first provides a brief overview of developments in recent years towards diversifying the history curriculum. It then focuses specifically on two surveys conducted by the Historical Association in 2019 and 2021, examining how history teachers have responded to more recent calls both to diversify and (from some) to decolonise the curriculum. As the surveys only provide self-reported data about any changes made (rather than allowing direct observation of teachers' practice), it is not possible to determine whether a genuinely decolonised approach is being adopted. There are, nonetheless, clear indications that small but significant steps are being taken in many school contexts to diversify curriculum content, seeking to address both an overwhelming Anglo-centric bias and a narrow conception of what constitutes 'British history'.

Keywords: diversifying; decolonising; history curriculum; secondary curriculum, curricular choices

Research Context

Fifteen years ago, the introduction of a new national curriculum for history (QCA, 2007) appeared to offer considerable encouragement to teachers' initiatives to diversify the content that they were teaching at Key Stage 3 (KS3). The Ajegbo Report into citizenship education, commissioned by the government in response to the 'homegrown' terrorist bombings of July 2005, had called for the addition of a new strand to the citizenship curriculum, 'Identity and diversity: living together in the UK' (Ajegbo et al., 2007, p. 12), recommending that it should be linked to more inclusive teaching of British history. The history curriculum that followed included a thematic unit on 'the impact of the movement and settlement to, from and within the British Isles' as well as an explicit injunction to teach about 'the British Empire and its impact in Britain and overseas, the slave trade, resistance and decolonisation' (QCA, 2007, p. 115).

These reforms proved short-lived, with the Coalition Government that came to power in 2010 immediately declaring its intention to restore a more traditional approach. The first draft of a new national curriculum, shared for consultation in February 2013 (Department for Education, 2013a), was widely condemned in terms which suggested that teachers were deeply committed to a less Anglo-centric, more diverse approach (Harris & Burn, 2016) and so strong was this opposition that the final version reframed virtually all the detailed content as optional elements (Department for Education, 2013b). Nonetheless, the government's emphasis on 'knowledge-rich' curricula meant that schools appeared to eschew opportunities to look at topics such as the transatlantic trade in enslaved people from a new perspective (including pre-colonial African history, of legacies of the trade, or decolonisation), persisting instead with more familiar approaches based on the 'triangular trade'. Those schools that wished to do so were able to retain a KS3 thematic unit on migration, but few appeared to persevere with the kind of content choices that their complaints about the draft national curriculum had implied (Harris & Reynolds, 2018).

Literature

Over the next few years, individuals and campaigning groups made regular calls for the teaching of more diverse history, with new demands from some for a decolonised approach (see Alexander & Weekes-Bernard, 2017; Haydn, 2014; Mohamud & Whitburn, 2016). While the terms are sometimes used as though they are interchangeable, there is an important difference between them. For Moncrieffe and Harris (2020, p. 15) 'Diversifying is simply adding different content. Decolonising goes deeper than that: it requires an awareness of "white privilege" and an appreciation that mindsets have created institutional structures that favour the white majority'. Decolonising the curriculum is a reflexive process that involves explicit acknowledgement of the colonial power relationships that have served to privilege certain forms of knowledge and seeks to adjust 'those power relations in real and significant ways' (Decolonise Keele Network, 2018).

Important curriculum initiatives such as *Our Migration Story* (Runnymede Trust, 2016) sought to provide teachers with appropriate curriculum resources to begin to make changes. Yet their impact was essentially limited, as reflected in the findings of the Royal Historical Society's report on *Race, Ethnicity, and Diversity* (Atkinson et al., 2018), which drew attention both to the continued narrowness of the school curriculum and to the under-representation of Black and Minority Ethnic students studying history.

It was in this context, following the concerns raised by the Royal Historical Society (RHS), that the Historical Association used its 2019 survey of history teachers in England (Burn & Harris, 2019) to ask about their perceptions of the subject's take-up. Around one-fifth of the 278 schools that responded acknowledged that students from certain ethnic backgrounds, particularly Chinese, Asian, Black, and Roma students, were either 'somewhat' or 'significantly' under-represented among those opting for history at General Certificate of Education (GCSE) level. At A-level, the proportion of teachers reporting such under-representation was closer to a third. However, very few teachers took the opportunity to offer any explanation for this pattern. Those that were prepared to do so merely reported that Chinese and Asian students were more likely to take STEM subjects (i.e., science, technology, engineering or maths), skirting round any issues of curriculum content.

Where respondents claimed some success in persuading students from minoritised backgrounds to continue with history beyond KS3, they were encouraged to suggest reasons for their success. Just 15 chose to do so – focusing, in part, on the quality of teaching and, in part, on efforts to make history relevant to students' lives through content choices that reflected a more inclusive curriculum.

The 2019 survey also asked about any curriculum changes made during the past two years, specifically in response to the RHS report or, more generally, to improve the representation of a diverse past. Around a third of schools claimed to have made such a change. While the most common adaptation was to ensure that KS3 students learned more about the history of Africa than the devasting impact of Britain's forced transportation of millions of enslaved people, there was considerable variety among the responses. These included emphases on the study of India, China, and the Middle East, as well as a deliberate focus on Black British history.

These survey results suggest that even before George Floyd's murder in May 2020 and the resultant surge in support for the Black Lives Matter anti-racism movement, some significant – but relatively small steps – were being taken by teachers in England to create a more diverse and inclusive curriculum. Nonetheless, the galvanising effect of the Black Lives Matter anti-racism protests was profound, especially when combined with the effects of school closures in response to the Covid-19 pandemic. The sudden increase in online lectures and seminars, giving teachers direct access to historians' expertise, enabled teachers not merely to call for more Black history and greater cultural diversity in the curriculum – as they did in the series of petitions which forced a parliamentary debate on the subject in June 2021 (Petitions Committee, 2021) – but also to create and share new schemes of work.

Objectives and Methods

With only an anecdotal awareness of the extent of these changes, the Historical Association decided to use its 2021 survey to identify the kinds of previously marginalised histories now being taught and to determine what proportion of schools had recently taken action to make their curriculum more inclusive (Burn & Harris, 2021). We worked with Claire Alexander and Sundeep Linder (regular academic partners of the Runnymede Trust) to devise questions related to five of the most likely topic areas, asking both about their inclusion within the KS3 curriculum and the amount of time allocated to them. We also sought to elicit teachers' motivation for making changes, along with reflections on barriers encountered or valued forms of support.

Invitations to participate were sent directly to secondary teacher members of the association, and the survey was widely advertised via social media. Responses were received from 316 history teachers in England, working in 286 different contexts (including 214 state-funded, non-selective schools). In terms of the ethnic mix of their students, 11% of the schools were categorised as having a majority 'Black or other minority ethnic population' and 73% as having a majority white population, with the remaining 16% more evenly split.

Analysis and Findings

Teaching of Specific Topics

Reports of the extent to which schools were teaching five designated topics were analysed in relation to various factors including school type and the ethnic background of both the student population and the teacher. While space constraints preclude the full presentation of this analysis, the extent to which each topic was being taught is shown in Table 8.1.

Teaching about the *transatlantic trade in enslaved people* had clearly achieved a secure place within the KS3 curriculum, with at least 90% of all state-maintained schools teaching not just about the development of the 'triangular trade' and 'the experiences of enslaved peoples' but also about 'forms of resistance or rebellion by enslaved peoples' as well as other forms of opposition. Nonetheless, only 13% of respondents reported including any consideration of the 'legacies' of that trade.

Teaching about the *history of the British Empire* also appeared similarly secure, with 82% of schools teaching at least

Table 8.1. The Extent to Which Schools Reported Teaching Particular Topics.

Specific Topic	Percentage of Schools Teaching This Topic Within KS3 (n = 286)			
	In *Some* Way	As a Dedicated Topic	Just One or Two Lessons	Not at All
Transatlantic Slave Trade	98%	86%	12%	2%
British Empire	97%	82%	15%	3%
Black & Asian British History	81%	57%	24%	19%
History of a non-European society (independently of relations to Britain/Europe)	73%	42%	31%	27%
Migration to Britain	73%	40%	33%	27%

one specific unit devoted to it. There were only seven schools (all with majority white populations) in which students could complete their compulsory study of history without having learned anything about the British Empire. However, the periods most commonly taught were the 18th and 19th centuries (especially the latter), with a much smaller proportion choosing to tackle 20th-century decolonisation.

Black and Asian British history featured in some way in the KS3 curriculum of 81% of schools although most commonly with only one or two lessons allocated to it. The ethnic mix of the student population seems significant here, with 36% of those with a majority Black and Minority Ethnic (BAME) population devoting a series of lessons to Black and Asian British history, compared with 23% of more evenly mixed schools and just 18% of schools with a majority white population.

Although 73% of schools reported allocating at least one or two lessons to teaching about the *history of a non-European nation*, less than half of all schools (42%) made it the focus of designated topic. It is also notable that schools with a majority white population were less likely to include a specific unit devoted to the history of non-European nations (38%) than schools with a majority BAME population or an even mix of students from different backgrounds (57%).

The possible continued influence of the Ajegbo Report (Ajegbo et al., 2007) and the 2008 national curriculum (Department for Education, 2013b) can be seen in that some aspects of the history of *migration* to Britain were taught by 73% of respondents' schools. Although encouraging, the impression conveyed by this curriculum focus may not be entirely helpful, since the period most often taught was the 20th century, perhaps tending to obscure the diversity of British society in earlier centuries.

Recent Curriculum Changes and the Stimulus for Them

While the impression given by the range of content being taught at KS3 is, thus, not entirely positive, there was a very clear contrast to the 2019 data in terms of the proportion of schools that had begun to make changes to improve their representation of the diversity of the past. In 2021, the vast majority of schools reported having made 'some' (35%) or 'considerable' (48%) change in the previous two years. Although there was little variation in these proportions depending on the nature of the school population, it is perhaps notable that the 4% of schools which reported no change at all had majority white populations.

Among those who had introduced changes, the most important barriers encountered were reported to be lack of money for resources and lack of time. As Fig. 8.1 reveals, other prominent obstacles cited were insufficient subject knowledge and a lack of training or access to resources.

Fig. 8.2 reveals that in combatting these barriers, the main sources of support were found in teachers' own engagement

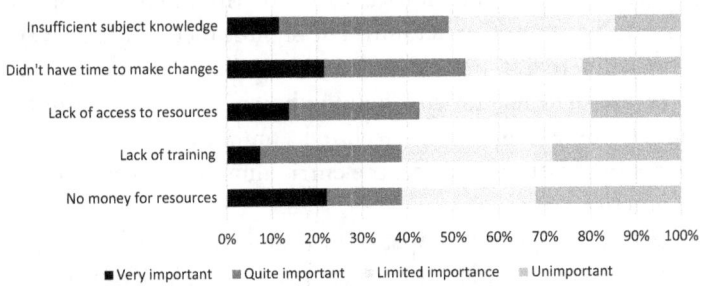

Fig. 8.1. The Most Frequently Cited Barriers to Making Change Cited by Teachers Who Had Done So.

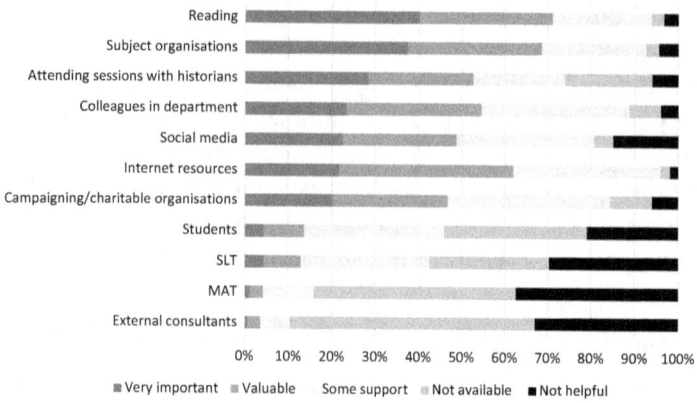

Fig. 8.2. Sources of Support Cited by Teachers Who Reported Having Made Recent Curriculum Changes.

with historical scholarship and in the work of subject associations. Hearing directly from historians (through webinars and online conferences) was also frequently cited as a very important source of support, confirming previous impressions about the impact of the pandemic in creating new digital opportunities for sharing expertise and resources.

Impact and Next Steps

Although demands for change within the history curriculum attract considerable media interest and fuel political debate, it has been difficult to make authoritative claims about what is actually being taught within KS3 (the last years of compulsory history education) because of the flexibility of the current National Curriculum. The significance of the surveys reported here lies in the detailed picture that they have begun to reveal of teachers' curriculum choices across the country and the extent to which declared commitments at least to diversity, if not decolonise, the curriculum have been realised in practice.

Despite the positive impetus for change revealed in the 2021 survey, the fact that lack of subject knowledge, lack of training, and lack of access to resources continued to be cited as obstacles to making changes (see Fig. 8.1) suggests that far more needs to be done both to alert teachers to the sources of support that are available and to enable them to access them. The following chapters in this section help to serve that purpose. Lyndon-Cohen illustrates the kinds of work that pioneering teachers are now able to share with teachers seeking to make significant changes, while Branford and Todd demonstrate how new online approaches are enabling teachers to learn more effectively from academic scholarship.

The next steps for this research are:

- To continue to map teachers' actual curricular choices and the kinds of support that they value. In addition to the Historical Association's work on this, the large-scale survey launched in 2024 by University College London and the University of Oxford as part of the 'Portrait of the teaching of the British Empire, migration and belonging' (https://portraitemb.co.uk/) will provide invaluable information as the basis for more effective professional development.

- To raise further awareness of the importance of decolonial approaches. These should not simply be adopted in response to diverse student populations in specific schools. Rather, the survey results suggest that such awareness-raising is even more urgent in all-white school contexts.

- To identify ways to share examples of leading practice more widely within the history education community.

References

Ajegbo, K., Kiwan, D., & Sharma, S. (2007). *The diversity and citizenship curriculum review*. HMSO. https://dera.ioe.ac.uk/6374/7/DfES_Diversity_%26_Citizenship_Redacted.pdf

Alexander, C., & Weekes-Bernard, D. (2017). History lessons: Inequality, diversity and the national curriculum. *Race Ethnicity and Education*, 20(4), 478–494. https://doi.org/10.1080/13613324.2017.1294571

Atkinson, H., Bardgett, S., Budd, A., Finn, M., Kissane, C., Qureshi, S., Saha, J., Siblon, J., & Sivasundaram, S. (2018). *Race, ethnicity & equality in UK History: A report and resource for change*. The Royal Historical Society. https://royalhistsoc.org/racereport/

Burn, K., & Harris, R. (2019). *Survey of history in secondary schools in England*. Historical Association. https://www.history.org.uk/secondary/categories/409/news/3826/ha-secondary-history-survey-2019

Burn, K., & Harris, R. (2021). *Historical association survey of history in secondary schools in England 2021*. Historical Association. https://www.history.org.uk/secondary/categories/409/news/4014/historical-association-secondary-survey-2021

Decolonise Keele Network. (2018). Keele manifesto for decolonizing the curriculum. *Journal of Global Faultlines*, 5(1–2), 97–99. https://www.jstor.org/stable/10.13169/jglobfaul.5.1-2.0097

Department for Education. (2013a). *Proposed programmes of study for 2014 national curriculum*. Crown Copyright.

Department for Education. (2013b). *National curriculum in England: History programmes of study*. https://www.gov.uk/government/publications/national-curriculum-in-england-history-programmes-of-study

Harris, R., & Burn, K. (2016). English history teachers' views on what substantive content young people should be taught. *Journal of Curriculum Studies*, 48(4), 518–546. https://doi.org/10.1080/00220272.2015.1122091

Harris, R., & Reynolds, R. (2018). Exploring teachers' curriculum decision making: Insights from history education. *Oxford Review of Education*, 44(2), 139–155. https://doi.org/10.1080/03054985.2017.1352498

Haydn, T. (2014). How and what should we teach about the British Empire in schools? In J. Wojdon (Ed.), *Yearbook of the international society of history didactics* (Vol. 35, pp. 23–40). Wochen Schau Verlag.

Mohamud, A., & Whitburn, R. (2016). *Doing justice to history: Transforming Black British history in schools*. IOE Press.

Moncrieffe, M. L., & Harris, R. (2020). Repositioning curriculum teaching and learning through Black-British history. In S. Gorard (Ed.), *Research intelligence* (Vol. 144, pp. 14–15). British Educational Research Association.

Petitions Committee. (2021). *MPs to debate petition relating to Black history and cultural diversity in the curriculum*. https://committees.parliament.uk/committee/326/petitions-committee/news/156079/mps-to-debate-petition-relating-to-black-history-and-cultural-diversity-in-the-curriculum/

QCA. (2007). *History: Programme of study for key stage 3 and attainment target.* HMSO. http://curriculum.qca.org.uk/uploads/QCA-07-3335-p_History3_tcm8-189.pdf

Runnymede Trust. (2016). *Our migration story: The making of Britain.* https://www.ourmigrationstory.org.uk/

CHAPTER 9

Challenging Dominant Narratives: Centring Historically Underserved Voices to Create New Enquiries for the History Classroom

Dan Lyndon-Cohen

Leeds Trinity University, UK

ABSTRACT

Although there have been many attempts over the last 30 years to diversify the history curriculum in schools, decolonisation is a relatively recent phenomenon. This article will initially explore the seminal influences that enabled teachers at Park View School to develop a curriculum that challenges the dominant narratives and provides students with alternative pathways to understand how history has been constructed and how this can be widened. It will showcase two schemes of work that re-centre voices that have been historically and colonially underserved: The Tape Letters unit draws on an oral history archive about the experiences of the British-Pakistani community and invites students to conduct their own oral history interviews; the LGBTQ+ unit enables students to navigate the subjectivity of archives and to explore, through material culture, the changing position of the LGBTQ+ communities in Britain and ultimately construct their own digital archive.

Keywords: decolonisation; oral history; archives; Tape Letters; LGBTQ+

Research Context

Since the publication of the National Curriculum for history in 1988, there have been various approaches to diversifying the content of the schools' history curriculum with varying degrees of success. These range from the integration of 'diversity' as a second-order concept in the 2008 iteration of the National Curriculum (removed under the Conservative-Liberal Democrat administration in 2010) (Harnett & Smart, 2009, p. 15) to the mandatory teaching of Black, Asian, and Minority Ethnic histories in the Welsh Curriculum in 2022 (Government of Wales, 2021). The creation of migration history courses in all the major General Certificate of Secondary Education (GCSE) history exam syllabi since the 2016 reforms has also had a trickle-down effect: in my own discussions in working with history teachers over the last 10 years, it appears that an increasing number are creating schemes of work, particularly at Key Stage 3 (KS3), that embed migration histories into their curriculum. Publishers have also responded to this shift with a range of resources being produced to support the teaching of more diverse histories in the classroom, with many written by practising teachers (Hodder Education, 2023). However, while there may be an increase in the representation of colonially and institutionally underserved communities in the history curriculum, there is a continuing need to address the substantive and substantial structural barriers that still exist which perpetuate the dominant narratives that still centre a Eurocentric curriculum and pedagogical approaches. This has been challenged by what has been called 'decolonisation', a contested term that has multiple meanings (Webb, 2020). This chapter will draw on the work of Tuhiwai-Smith (1999), Trouillot (1995), Dabiri (2019), and Cutrara (2019) to establish what a decolonised approach to the teaching of history in schools can look like.

Literature

Linda Tuhiwai-Smith's seminal work *Decolonising Methodologies* draws on multidisciplinary and indigenous approaches, to present a 'counter-story to western ideas about the benefits of the pursuit of knowledge' (Tuhiwai-Smith, 1999, p. 3).

Tuhiwai-Smith identifies specific concerns about the way in which history has been written and taught, including the conceptions that there is a 'universal history', that history 'can be told in one coherent narrative', and that 'history as a discipline is innocent' (Tuhiwai-Smith, 1999, p. 31). Her work aligns with other scholars such as Trouillot who argues that the construction of history reveals the underlying power relations that form both a dominant narrative and its accompanying 'silences' (Trouillot, 1995, p. 26), represented in the African proverb 'until the lions have their own historian, the history of the hunt will always glorify the hunter' (NPR The Two-Way, 2013).

Dabiri's (2019) book, *Don't Touch My Hair*, exposes several ways that indigenous histories and experiences have been marginalised including a fascinating insight into the Maroon community at San Basilio de Palenque, in Columbia, where female anti-slavery activists used their hair as maps to guide enslaved Africans to freedom.

Finally, Dr Samantha Cutrara, a Canadian academic, presents practical ways in which history students can be supported in navigating their way through Eurocentric and colonial narratives and pedagogies. Her article, 'The Subjectivity of Archives' (Cutrara, 2019), was a seminal influence which inspired the construction of a scheme of work about LGBTQ+ histories in Britain that was taught at Park View School in London.

Objectives and Methods

The work that was undertaken in the history department at Park View represented a pioneering approach to decolonisation in the classroom as it not only focused on the historical content that was being delivered but also addressed the pedagogy and assessment practice that underpinned the learning. In recognising that the dominant Eurocentric white heterosexual narratives are sustained by the traditional approaches to the construction of history, a concerted effort was made to challenge this. This was firstly through the acquisition of source material that broke free from the dependency on the written word. For example, the LGBTQ+ unit included a series of video interviews that were recorded specifically for the lessons in which invited speakers selected an artefact for an archive on LGBTQ+ history. In addition, the choice of assessment empowered students to participate in their own history-making process either through the construction of a digital archive or an oral history interview.

Two schemes of work were constructed, both built around a historical enquiry question. The first question being: 'How does oral history allow us to explore the experiences of Pakistanis in Britain c1960 to today?' This aimed to expose students to the *Tape Letters* (Lyndon-Cohen, 2024) archive of cassette recordings and interviews exploring themes of migration, empire, and partition through the experiences of the British-Pakistani community. Students developed a range of skills to support the output of the unit, which would consist of an oral history interview with a member of their family.

The second enquiry question was: 'Parliament, Protest or Pop Culture: Which has done more to change the position of the LGBTQ+ communities in Britain since the 1930s?' This was designed to help students to understand the subjectivity of archives and to help them to construct their own digital archive in response to the enquiry question.

The *Tape Letters* enquiry used decolonial approaches in several ways. Firstly, it centred the voices of the British-Pakistani community within the enquiry and explored their lived experiences of migration, empire, and partition. The lessons were constructed around audio extracts from the archive and deliberately limited the amount of written material that was used to support the content. This was done for several reasons, including to expose and immerse the students in the different dialects, accents, and languages that were spoken in the archive; to move away from the 'tyranny of the written word' (Green, 2020, pp. 26–27) in acknowledging the validity of oral history as a discipline; and to recognise its power as a decolonising agent. Students worked through a sequence of lessons which helped them not only to understand the historical context but also to learn the skills of effective listening, questioning, and conducting oral history research.

The LGBTQ+ enquiry was centred around the construction of a digital archive that addressed the changing position of the LGBTQ+ communities in Britain. Central to the delivery of the scheme of work was the use of material culture including songs, film, posters, badges, and other paraphernalia related to LGBTQ+ activism and experiences. It also drew on short films created specifically for the lessons from LGBTQ+ people and allies sharing their experiences and selecting an artefact for a hypothetical archive. The power dynamics related to archives were discussed, including the way in which metadata can create silences in the archive, and students were repeatedly asked to 'tag' evidential material. All of this support culminated in the final piece of work which enabled students to construct their own digital archive, selecting five sources that framed their response to the enquiry question, and justifying their choices. This decolonised approach empowered some students to identify themselves as members of the LGBTQ+ community and to reflect on the implications of these changes for their own lives.

Analysis and Findings

The *Tape Letters* enquiry was very successful in terms of student engagement and understanding of the key historical context. The use of the audio extracts enabled a much deeper understanding of the personal responses that the *Tape Letters* participants were sharing in their testimonies. For example, after listening to one extract from the interviews that were spoken in Pothwari, an oral only language from the Pakistani Punjab, the students were able to infer the emotional impact of the British Empire in India from the tone and rapid speech pattern that was used. In one lesson on the experiences of Pakistani migrants to Britain, students were also able to explore the diversity and complexity of these experiences by listening independently to (up to) 10 different audio clips.

Student feedback at the end of the unit also showed that they felt well prepared when they had to carry out their own oral history interviews, with the skills that they needed being embedded throughout the lessons (Lyndon-Cohen, 2023, p. 127). Some of the interviews that the students produced were fascinating, with questioning that facilitated interesting discussion. There were also students who interviewed a family member in their home language, which they transcribed into English, adding another dimension to the outcomes. In some of the lessons, the students were privileged to be joined by the founder of the *Tape Letters* project, Wajid Yasseen, who summed up his experience, commenting:

> *As an observer in the classroom, I sensed the children experienced a more tangible sort of history* (Lyndon-Cohen, 2023, p. 123)

The LGBTQ+ enquiry also showed how effective the decolonised approach was in supporting students to construct their own digital archive. As students had multiple opportunities to select and tag the source material used in each lesson, they were confident in using these skills in the final task. Some students used their independent research skills to select engaging and stimulating artefacts and reflected effectively on why they had chosen them to answer the enquiry question.

Strengths and Limitations

The *Tape Letters* enquiry showed the power of oral testimony being used directly in the classroom. As the creator of the source, Wajid Yasseen commented from his observations of this:

> *Applying an oral/aural approach in developing the lesson plans and drawing directly from the Tape Letters archive meant students could hear how large-scale socio-political events manifest in people's lives* (Lyndon-Cohen, 2023, p. 123)

There were also challenges, however, for some students in terms of accessing some of the audio content, particularly for those with cognitive barriers that meant processing the information was difficult.

The LGBTQ+ enquiry faced more challenges, but these largely stemmed from the response of some of the students to the content of the lessons. Although a lot of work had been done to ensure a safe and open learning environment, and there were no explicit examples of homophobic or transphobic behaviour, there was some student apathy towards the activity which resulted in a lack of engagement. Still, despite these limitations, both enquiries demonstrated that both the curriculum and the pedagogy driving it could be effectively decolonised, enabling students to engage with content that has been historically underserved, and actively engaging in the construction of historical materials.

Impact and Next Steps

Both units of study are now fully integrated into the KS3 curriculum at Park View School and will continue to be taught for the foreseeable future. They form a central part of our decolonised approach to practice which underpins the entire curriculum. Our *Tape Letters* unit of study will be hosted on the *Tape Letters* website with a teacher pack, accompanied by a film for guiding users through the lessons. The LGBTQ+ lessons formed the basis of two chapters in a new history textbook entitled: *Fights for Rights in Modern Britain*, published by Oxford University Press in September 2023. Both units of study were presented in a workshop at the 'Schools History Project' (SHP) summer conference in July 2023. Next steps for this research:

- There are plans to write an alternative *Tape Letters* unit built around the construction of sonic soundscapes for exploring migration histories.

- The LGBTQ+ history unit will be part of an SHP understanding event in 2024 which will bring together classroom practitioners with academic historians and archivists to discuss the teaching of LGBTQ+ histories.

References

Cutrara, S. (2019). The subjectivity of archives: Learning from, with, and resisting archives and archival sources in teaching and learning history. *Historical Encounters*, 6(1), 117–132. http://hej.hermeshistory.net/index.php/HEJ/article/view/122

Dabiri, E. (2019). *Don't touch my hair*. Penguin.

Government of Wales. (2021). *Learning of Black, Asian, and minority ethnic histories included in the new Welsh curriculum*. Retrieved January 12, 2021, from https://www.gov.wales/learning-black-asian-and-minority-ethnic-histories-included-new-welsh-curriculum

Green, T. (2020). *What have historians been arguing about: African history in the precolonial period? Teaching history* (Vol. 181, pp. 26–27). Historical Association.

Harnett, P., & Smart, D. (2009). The history curriculum in England: Contested Narratives. In S. Aktekin, P. Harnett, M. Ozturk, & D. Smart (Eds.), *Teaching history and social studies for multicultural Europe* (pp. 99–114). HARF.

Hodder Education. (2023). *Teaching the British empire: KS3 history: Challenges, solutions and approaches.* Retrieved January 12, 2023, from https://www.youtube.com/watch?v=0p_CWKzZJbM

Lyndon-Cohen, D. (2023). Oral history. In A. Fairlamb & R. Ball (Eds.), *What is history teaching, now?* John Catt.

Lyndon-Cohen, D. (2024). Chapter 13: Decolonising the curriculum. In M. Stanford & D. Keates (Eds.), *A practical guide to teaching history in a secondary school.* Routledge.

Lyndon-Cohen, D. (2024). *Tape letters.* Retrieved January 12, 2024, from https://tapeletters.com/

NPR The Two-Way. (2013). *Chinua Achebe and the bravery of lions.* Retrieved January 12, 2013, from https://www.npr.org/sections/thetwo-way/2013/03/22/175046327/chinua-achebe-and-the-bravery-of-lions

Trouillot, M.-R. (1995). *Silencing the past: Power and the production of history.* Beacon Press Books.

Tuhiwai-Smith, L. (1999). *Decolonizing methodologies.* University of Otago Press.

Webb, E. (2020). *What have historians been arguing about: Decolonisation and the British Empire. Teaching history* (Vol. 178, pp. 42–43). Historical Association.

CHAPTER 10

A Professional Development Model for the Teaching of British Empire, Migration, and Belonging

Abigail Branford and Jason Todd
University of Oxford, UK

ABSTRACT

The TIDE Beacon Fellowship was a professional development programme supporting a small group of history and english teachers in their teaching of the British Empire, Migration, and Belonging. The Fellowship took place over three months with three full-day workshops. This chapter seeks to assess how a sustained form of professional development could support the teaching of a complex topic like the history of the British Empire. The authors will present a single case study as a basis of hypotheses testing, arguing that teachers are best supported with professional development that draws on both academic scholarship from the relevant subject disciplines and empirical evidence from classrooms; accounts for teachers' personal beliefs; and takes place within supportive forums that facilitate dialogue.

Keywords: identity; migration; empire; belonging; professional development

Research Context

Migration and Empire

Issues of migration and empire routinely form part of political discourse in Britain. Political campaigns are 'grounded in conceptions of the past' that attempt to support political claims in the present (Bhambra, 2017). This grounding is often based on at best partial readings of these pasts – especially in relation to migration and empire. The recourse to mythical or partial historical narratives in political campaigns illustrates the urgent need for young people to have an education that enables them to accurately make sense of the ways these histories are being deployed.

Literature

Given how public discussion of migration and empire is loaded with potential controversy, the teaching of it requires sensitivity. Work such as that by Barton and McCully (2005), Kitson and McCully (2005), Traille (2007), and Kello (2016) speaks to how teachers approach teaching sensitive and controversial issues. This work suggests that teachers' own life experiences, the context of the school they are in, and the nature of the curriculum shape teachers' approaches in the classroom. However, the Historical Association expressed the need to 'improve the research and evidence base related to the teaching of emotive and controversial history' in order to offer teachers quality professional development in this area (Historical Association, 2007).

Further literature (Branford, 2023; Burn & Harris, 2021; Haydn, 2019) suggests that while the majority of schools do include teaching about the British Empire, the presence and depth of the topic is variable and inconsistent across schools. A range of issues need to be addressed to enable both a greater presence of empire and migration in teaching but also to ensure that this teaching reflects the complexity at stake.

Objectives and Methods

A Model of Professional Growth

Clarke and Hollingsworth (2002) offer an empirically grounded, interconnected model of teacher professional growth. They highlight how change is a process of reflection and enactment between four domains that constitute a teacher's world: *external domain; personal domain; domain of consequence; reflection and enaction*, p. 950.

The model demonstrates the complexity of teacher development and highlights its *ongoing* and idiosyncratic nature within a dynamic change environment like a school. It shifts attention away from the simple supply of resources (*external domain*) by instead recognising that change in the *domain of practice* (i.e. the classroom) is also related to changes in multiple other domains. As well as being influenced by external information/stimuli, classroom practice also relates to teachers' own knowledge and beliefs (*personal domain*) and teachers' ideas about the purpose of history education (*domain of consequence*). The mechanisms that trigger change in these domains (*reflection and enaction*) will be demonstrated in the analysis. In sum, Clarke and Hollingsworth help us to recognise how building knowledge, changing beliefs, and making practical changes happen in concert.

The Runnymede Trust and University of Liverpool TIDE project, led by Nandini Das, joined forces to create a fellowship programme informed by the Clark and Hollingsworth approach. The fellowship was an innovative 12-week programme of professional development for 12 participants composed of english and history secondary school teachers (and 1 museum educator). The group was atypical of the wider UK teaching population in that over 50% were from minoritised backgrounds and all highlighted their personal migration histories in their applications as part of their motivations for applying to the fellowship.

Teachers took part in three cumulative masterclasses in 2019, one in March, April, and May, respectively. Each masterclass introduced the teachers to leading experts and to current scholarship related to the themes of empire and migration. These experts included both academic specialists in these themes and experienced practitioners with an established track record in teaching empire and migration in schools (teacher facilitators). In between each masterclass, teachers took part in online forums hosted by the ERC-funded TIDE project (Travel, Transculturality, and Identity in England, 1550–1700). In each online session, fellows were presented with reading packs (e.g. historical documents, literary documents) related to a weekly keyword (e.g. 'blackamoor', 'Indian', 'native').

Below we offer a case study of a single participant to offer an in-depth and holistic examination of the impact of the fellowship for illustrative purposes (Flyvbjerg, 2006). Using pre-fellowship survey data, transcripts of fellowship sessions, online discussions, and post-fellowship interviews, we describe the impact that the fellowship had on a teacher's knowledge and her evolving practices.

Analysis and Findings

Sequence 1: Reflecting on Narratives

This illustrative case study follows a history teacher pseudonymised as Heather, whose learning over the course of the programme signals several reflections and enactments which give a sense of the utility of the fellowship and the individual journeys to which it contributed. We begin with an overview of a few of Heather's pre-fellowship characteristics and positioning before discussing her reflections and enactments over the course of the fellowship.

On entering the fellowship, Heather had been teaching for four years. In her pre-course survey, Heather self-identified as 'British and mixed race'. Heather mentioned that she studied (albeit briefly) British imperialism at university and wrote an undergraduate thesis on Black British History. Her life experiences had over time inculcated a sense of race as personally significant. She wrote:

> [As a child] I didn't really engage with my race much back then. I didn't feel like it was too much of an issue ... As I've got older it's felt like more of a bigger deal and I'm more interested in it.

Another key orientation for Heather was 'teacher as learner'. This process of learning and discovery was especially important in relation to her sense that she herself might not have been taught history with fullness and complexity, particularly in relation to empire and migration. Below, we turn to how Heather demonstrates change both in terms of her lesson content (see Sequence 1) and lesson structure (see Sequences 2 and 3).

We see that her reflections – both on the stimuli from the *external domain* and on her teaching from the *domain of practice* – had implications for her *personal domain*: building her subject knowledge and changing her beliefs about what constituted multidimensional narratives of the period.

For example, in response to a reading pack on early modern European imaginaries of Islam, Heather brought together her new learning with an assessment of her *domain of practice*, writing that:

> *The first historical document [in the reading pack] also reminded me of a conversation we were having with [a TIDE historian] about an early encounter between a British ambassador and the Mughal Empire ..., if we teach [Islamic] history at all, it's often the antagonistic interactions, wars etc, rather than the diplomatic (or romantic) ones ... I feel like Islamic history outside of the Crusades is rarely taught in schools ... So often it seems like it's linked to war (Crusades, Fall of Constantinople, terrorism etc). It seems very reductive and potentially very alienating for our Muslim students?*

Reflecting on her new learning and her previous practice revealed something about her *domain of consequence*: that her practices were not achieving inclusivity even though inclusivity was a salient goal of history education for Heather.

Engaging with a diversity of historical narratives through the fellowship enabled Heather to see heretofore hidden gaps in her lesson content. Responding to a reading pack about how the term 'Indian' was used by early modern Europeans in relation to people in Asia and North America, Heather said:

> *Currently, we only touch on India during a unit on the consequences of the British Empire for those who lived within it. The current depiction is pretty one-dimensional and negative [about India]. It would be great to build in some of what we've been discussing during this fellowship about the wealth and power that existed there. We don't really touch on the indigenous population in our America unit, except to say that many*

> indigenous people were treated badly/died because of European diseases ... it'd be great if we were able to show the students a more complex picture existed that included agency on both sides (even if those sides weren't equal).

Sequence 2: Reflecting on Enquiry

Heather described her domain of practice prior to the fellowship as containing enquiries that were essentially teacher-focused with little input from students. The purpose of enquiries was just to 'structure what I'm telling them'. However, the teacher-facilitators emphasised situating pupils as co-constructors of knowledge. This stimuli in the *external domain* prompted reflection on her beliefs about enquiry in the *personal domain*.

Heather's reflections about the role of students in enquiries started to change, exemplified by her comment that:

> [now] I want them to be more active in the enquiry whereas before I think they were very passive.

We see that this, in turn, led to reflection on her *domain of consequence* where student agency became a more salient outcome for her than it had previously been:

> We want to get the children to develop their initial hypothesis for the enquiry and then keep coming back to that as you go through the enquiry ... I think now I'm going to be like – I [still] set the parameters – but they are in a way like co-detectives a bit more.

Furthermore, Heather then sought further input from others, emailing teacher-facilitators to ask for help putting together an enquiry that would centre student agency. Seeking out further guidance via her *external domain* was an enactment of the changes in her *domain of consequence* which prioritised agency.

Sequence 3: Reflecting on Sources

Growth was also enabled by the fellowship through positioning teachers as learners. Even teachers' initially negative experiences could provide insights. Heather became frustrated engaging with the weekly reading packs (stimuli from the *external domain*), commenting that:

> *I really struggled to draw any overarching conclusions or to work out how best to use the source material.*
>
> *We do a unit on the British Empire; we just do this source dump with the kids. Like 'here are loads of sources about India' and I'm like 'we've got to not do that'*

This suggests that Heather's experiences as a learner provided her with further insights about her students' experiences when faced with a similar task. Therefore, we argue that reflecting on the stimuli from the *external domain* and her classroom practice, led to a change in Heather's beliefs about using sources, resulting in a desire to enact changes in the domain of practice.

A clear takeaway that emerges from this experience (and is underscored by Heather's case) is that professional development, especially in relation to the themes of empire, needs to consider teachers as learners and root this learning in teachers' *personal domains*, that is, their evolving knowledge and beliefs. This contributes to the literature emphasising teachers' individual learning (Hagger et al., 2008). Moreover, as the themes of empire implicate issues of race, we want to highlight the *personal domain*, how the significance of teachers' personal experiences and connections in the context of empire parallels their engagement with race, engagements emphasised by Harris (2012) and the Anti-Racism Framework for Initial Teacher Education (Lander & Smith, 2022).

Strengths and Limitations

A strength of the research was that the analytical framework from Clarke and Hollingsworth enabled an appreciation of what the data signalled about Heather's internal changes, which would have been obscured by a singular focus on changes Heather made in the classroom. This allows for a deeper understanding of the effect of the fellowship and the future potential of similar programmes. However, the impact of the fellowship on these teachers' *students* was beyond the scope of the study. Several possible issues may be revealed in such an investigation such as difficulties of enaction posed by fellows' schools or classrooms (the 'change environment' in which enaction happens).

Impact and Next Steps

We have seen that new material can provoke and revise teachers' preconceptions around pedagogies of empire and migration. However, change is not simply the by-product of this new material itself, but rather change is enabled via supported reflection between the domains of teachers' beliefs and classroom practices.

- The TIDE project inspired TRACTION, an innovative online platform providing teachers access to cutting-edge interdisciplinary research on empire and migration.
- To advance our understanding of this topic, University College London and University of Oxford are collaborating on a three-year research study called 'A portrait of the teaching of the British Empire, migration and belonging in English secondary schools'. This project will support teacher professional learning by providing empirical research to better understand classroom experiences and by mapping the academic scholarship related to these themes of empire and migration.

References

Barton, K. C., & McCully, A. W. (2005). History, identity, and the school curriculum in Northern Ireland: An empirical study of secondary students' ideas and perspectives. *Journal of Curriculum Studies*, 37(1), 85–116. https://doi.org/10.1080/0022027032000266070

Bhambra, G. K. (2017). Brexit, trump, and 'Methodological Whiteness': On the misrecognition of race and class. *The British Journal of Sociology*, 68(1), 214–232. https://doi.org/10.1111/1468-4446.12317

Branford, A. (2023). *Decoding 'balance': Learning about the British Empire in English secondary schools* [Unpublished DPhil thesis]. University of Oxford.

Burn, K., & Harris, R. (2021). *Historical association survey of history in secondary schools in England 2021*. Historical Association. https://www.history.org.uk/secondary/categories/409/news/4014/historical-association-secondary-survey-2021

Clark, D., & Hollingsworth, H. (2002). Elaborating a model of teacher professional growth. *Teaching and Teacher Education*, *18*(8), 947–967. https://www.sciencedirect.com/science/article/pii/S0742051X02000537?via%3Dihub

Flyvbjerg, B. (2006). Five misunderstandings about case-study research. *Qualitative Inquiry*, *12*(2), 219–245. https://doi.org/info:doi/

Haggar, H., Burn, K., Mutton, T., & Brindley, S. (2008). Practice makes perfect learning to learn as a teacher. *Oxford Review of Education*, *34*(2), 59–78.

Harris, R. (2012). Purpose as a way of helping white trainee history teachers engage with diversity issues. *Education Sciences*, *2*(4), 218–241.

Haydn, T. (2019). How is 'Empire' taught in English schools? An exploratory study. In K. Grindel, K. Gorbahn, & S. Popp (Eds.), *History education and (post)colonialism: International case studies* (pp. 277–296). Peter Lang.

Historical Association. (2007). *Teaching emotive and controversial history 3-19*. Historical Association.

Kello, K. (2016). Sensitive and controversial issues in the classroom: Teaching history in a divided society. *Theory and Practice*, *22*(1), 35–53. https://doi.org/10.1080/13540602.2015.1023027

Kitson, A., & McCully, A. (2005). 'You Hear About It For Real in School.' Avoiding, containing and risk-taking in the history classroom. *Teaching History*, *120*, 32–37.

Lander, V., & Smith, H. (2022). *Anti-racism framework for initial teacher education*. Newcastle University, Leeds Beckett University, National Education Union.

Traille, K. (2007). 'You Should Be Proud about Your History. They Made Me Feel Ashamed:' Teaching history hurts. *Teaching History*, *127*, 31–37.

CHAPTER 11

Decolonisation in Further Education: Engaging Diverse Students in the Delivery of a Decolonised Curriculum for A Level Biology in the Heart of the Former Empire

Samantha Hughes and Neil Hart

City and Islington College, UK

ABSTRACT

Biology is broadly speaking a colonised subject and as such exemplification of the material to a non-white non-western centric narrative can elicit deep thought, debate, and analysis of the subject. Recent curriculum changes in England (post 2015) present little time for non-curricular content and staff can struggle to engage students in meaningful debate, analysis, and social-scientific thinking. Staff at City and Islington College took radical and long-term change to exemplify biology within a decolonisation narrative, using various methods to ensure that critical topics were covered while looking at the colonisation and colonialism of the subject. The staff ensured that decolonisation was a key agenda item in curriculum development to maintain an interwoven approach to the subject. Structured student interviews provided student feedback and student voice. Early discussion with students suggests the use of context has allowed students to be more confident in expressing their views and analysing unfamiliar contexts.

Keywords: biology; post 16; metacognition; student voice; context-led approach

Research Context

We teach in the sixth form centre of a large Further Education college in central London, part of the largest post-16 education provider in the city. Our centre delivers only A levels, a programme with a persistent and significant attainment gap for disadvantaged students (Tuckett et al., 2021), within which people of colour are disproportionately represented (UK Government, 2020). We are as inclusive and comprehensive as we can be for an institution delivering only A levels. White British students in our classrooms are fewer than the greater number of students we teach coming from South Asian, Middle Eastern, and African diasporic backgrounds.

Dominating the view from our south-facing windows, and a little over half a mile down the road from our college, is the City of London – the economic centre of the British empire; the major location for the arrival of resources and wealth generated from centuries of occupation; military violence; enforced trade monopolies; slavery and indentured labour; and other violences of British colonisation and imperialism across a large part of the globe. The students we teach represent the contemporary face of London, a city that continues to pull people in from across its former empire and beyond, lured by the wealth that still sits here, visible in the ever-changing skyline of the financial centre as seen from our classrooms.

With such an ethnically diverse student body, the biology department set about updating all schemes of work to frame the curriculum within the socio-science narrative to ensure there were a variety of activities that allowed students to analyse and evaluate scientific theory, as well as state their views, and engage with the subject in a context led approach. These activities involved all staff collaboration to ensure that all students have a similar experience across the department and used metacognitive skills to develop subject understanding as well as broader engagement with decolonisation in line with self-regulated learning.

Literature

Biology is broadly speaking a colonised subject, and as such, sharing exemplifications of the subject's material to a non-white non-Euro-American-centric narrative can elicit deep thought, debate, and analysis of the subject. Chamany et al. (2008) argue that biology can and should be exemplified within a social construct, while Gilbert and Fausto-Sterling (2003) state that societal contexts enliven the course as well as encourage a wide variety of students to engage in further scientific study. Many science teachers still do not engage in socio-scientific discussion, and student views often do not feature prominently (Day & Bryce, 2011).

Euro-American knowledge production for teaching and learning biology is so hegemonic that this can lead to the understanding of biology as a universal truth by many (Trinos & Mudaly, 2020; Walsh, 2021). A richer teaching and learning of biology has been identified by exploring possibilities for including indigenous knowledge (Trinos & Mudaly, 2020) and as required to decolonise the narrow Euro-American subject content. The specification content for A level biology is largely a list of facts to be remembered and applied, which reflects the way that Euro-American society views scientific knowledge (Trinos & Mudaly, 2020; Walsh, 2021). This uncritical delivery of scientific-knowledge-as-fact is beginning to be unpicked at the university level, where there is an increasing awareness of the influence of the historically white, male, researcher in influencing experimental design and interpretation of data (see Liboiron, 2021; Wall Kimmerer, 2020).

Objective and Methods

The 2020 Black Lives Matter anti-racism movement across the globe was a catalyst for our biology department to formalise decolonial practices within both planning and delivery of lessons. Developing this work was also on the agenda for all subject meetings so that it could be discussed where the topic provided opportunities to problematise mainstream knowledge, incorporate diverse examples, and make space for untold stories. Discussion during meetings allowed us to build a cohesive approach that allowed teachers to develop resources based on their own interests and expertise and share these with colleagues so that all students were exposed to similar activities and encouraged to develop similar critical thinking.

Given the makeup of the student body, and our sixth form centre location within the heart of the former British empire, as teachers we felt compelled to do justice to the students we teach by integrating an anti-racist and decolonised approach to biology within the constraints and structure of the A level biology curriculum. Our primary goal was to make the subject more relevant to students from minority ethnic diverse backgrounds, the majority of whom come from families who have been the victims of British colonial practices. Our goal was in seeking to reverse the erasure of the stories of people of colour in traditional telling of the story of biology. As the largest post-16 institution in London, the centre of colonial Britain, and the centre of the UK's diversity, we recognised our uniquely important position to lead on challenging colonial narratives that still inform much of current biology curricula.

We worked to create space in the A level biology curriculum, and in the ingrained beliefs of students, to challenge the dominant stories of biology and to share stories that recognise valuable knowledge production marginalised by Euro-American science, and to hear the voices of the global majority currently engaged in science (or fighting against those engaging in science). We saw this to acknowledge the untold (or undertold) stories of marginalised people who have contributed to scientific knowledge production through history, either willingly or unwillingly.

We were informed by Chamany et al. (2008) in their writing about the importance of biology teachers to include information on the wider social and historical context into biology teaching, to improve retention of information, and to model the learning behaviour that allows students to understand the subject through an expanded concept framework. Day and Bryce's (2011) writing on socio-scientific discussion in science lessons helped to shape the way discussions with students were conducted, aiming for open-ended enquiry during classroom dialogue, rather than other types of approaches that might limit open discussion.

Using action research, introducing new approaches to the classroom, and then reflecting and evaluating these was a natural fit of methods when undertaking this work. Action research involves very practical methods and aims since the key objective is to enhance practice as part of everyday encounters (Koshy, 2010). But, this approach also aimed to create a community of practice, where all stakeholders are involved in knowledge making as well as evaluation of interventions in the classroom (Reason & Bradbury, 2006). In this instance, this involved planning, delivery, and reflection by staff, as well as metacognitive and student voice activities by students.

Our efforts to decolonise our teaching of biology were enacted through four strands:

1. Acknowledging worldviews beyond dominant science.

This strand focuses on broader, animist, views of the material and biological world around us – to consider ideas themes on living and non-living. For example, an exploration of life supporting resources such as sources of water, sun, moon, and rocks. We also aim to acknowledge complex and diverse gender identities beyond the XX and XY chromosomes. In learning about microorganisms and disease, we would aim to decentre Euro-American knowledge focusing on the need to control spread of diseases, that were limiting empirical expansion, and instead build in space for consideration of cultures with extensive knowledge on using microorganisms and preventing disease. Links could then be made to well-developed understandings of the wider ecological interactions of microorganisms that have preserved these practices for centuries or millennia.

2. Examples of people from the global majority engaged in science or the fight against dominant science.

For example, this included our emphasis on showcasing working Biologists in the UK with ethnic diasporic origins stemming from Africa, Asia, and the Middle East. We shared how their engaging pioneering work can be linked to the curriculum content of A level biology. We also used the story of the indigenous and marginalised communities at risk of biopiracy through the human diversity genome project who have been able to get their genomes legally protected. We also taught of the cotton farmers in India pushing back against multinational corporations selling access to genetically modified cotton with links to worse outcomes for local farmers.

3. Telling the untold or under-told stories of marginalised people and their contributions to science throughout history.

For strand three, we incorporated the stories of researchers such as Marie Maynard Daley at the many points where her work links to the A level specification and Janaki Amal who links Kew Gardens to conservation of land exploited by farming practices in India and resistance to British rule in India. We also include those people who contributed against their will, such as Henrietta Lacks and her infinite cell line.

4. Acknowledging the problematic history that sits within biology.

For strand four, we introduced the erasure of the stories of the local experts who were foundational to the knowledge gained of beneficial species by European colonisers making 'discoveries' throughout their empires, the origins of modern farming practices in the plantation model of agriculture made possible by enslaved workers and so destructive to global ecosystems. We include ideas about dominance and control that were foundational to the origins of Biological classification.

Analysis and Findings

Having undertaken this action research project, trialling, and reflecting on practices and outcomes, there has been a realisation that there are more opportunities for developing this work than we had originally envisaged. This has also highlighted the importance of developing this work further. However, student voice activities have also raised an awareness of the resistance among students to digress too far from the obvious content of the examination specification and, consequently, to spend time on learning which will not be formally examined at the end of the course.

Early discussion with students suggests the use of context has allowed some students to be more confident in expressing their views and analysing unfamiliar contexts. However, our personal experiences in delivering the content at times leave us feeling that there is resistance from the students to deep critical engagement with the ideas.

The fact that our students do not always value the time spent on decolonising the subject can also be tied to complex relationships with power structures and the ongoing effects of European colonisation. Our students consider studying A levels at our college a mark of success and a step on a journey towards improved opportunities and professional and economic outcomes. These students feel worthy of an experience that they feel will improve their chances of moving onto university and understandably that requires a focus on the knowledge and skills required for A level assessment. Our attempts to empower these students through deviating from A level content creates a tension that we are always aware of.

Strengths and Limitations

Within the department, we all identify as white, British, or of the white British diaspora. We saw problems in the power dynamic related to white teachers and students of colour in the delivery of anti-racist content by white teachers in this context. We are careful to avoid falling into white-saviourism but, while the content and its delivery are coming from us, it is arguably a practice we are engaged in. Students are not necessarily comfortable to engage in critical conversations around race and racism with teachers who represent the most empowered group and occupy a position as teacher that traditionally holds power in the classroom.

While some students remain passive, there are some who can be depended on to engage in discussion with these ideas. But there are issues around who dominates classroom discussion and how this shapes the sharing of ideas by the whole class. In a diverse group of students, the discussion does not always represent the ideas of all class members and potentially further marginalises the experiences of those who do not feel represented.

Impact and Next Steps

The work can be advanced in a series of ways that engage community, the wider scientific community, the community of A level providers, and the students themselves within their community.

- Further work with students might provide opportunities to evaluate their perceptions in relation to questions that have arisen from this action research. For example: What is the impact of learning about the negatives of colonialism on the development of a subject that you have chosen to study, as led by a white teacher, in the centre of that empire? How does this impact on your ability/interest/desire to engage with this material? Would you feel differently if you were taught by teachers of colour?

- Further research could also explore how decolonial praxis may affect students' perceptions about careers in science and perhaps inform their future career choices.

- Finally, the key questions coming out of this research include: How can we instigate sharing practice between different institutions to ensure that anti-racist and decolonial practices continue to be explored and developed? How can this lead to changes in the narrative of the A level syllabus?

References

Chamany, K., Allen, D., & Tanner K. (2008). Making biology learning relevant to [Database] students: Integrating people, history, and context into college biology teaching. *CBE Life Sciences Education*, 7(3), 267–278.

Day, S. P., & Bryce, T. G. K. (2011). Does the discussion of socio-scientific issues require a paradigm shift in science teachers' thinking? *International Journal of Science Education*, 33(12), 1675–1702.

Gilbert, S. F., & Fausto-Sterling, A. (2003). Educating for social responsibility: Changing the syllabus of developmental biology. *International Journal of Development Biology*, 47(2–3), 237–244. PMID: 12705676.

Koshy, V. (2010). *Action research for improving educational practice. A Step-by-step guide* (2nd ed.). SAGE Publications.

Liboiron, M. (2021). *Pollution is colonialism*. Duke University Press.

Reason, P., & Bradbury, H. (Eds.). (2006). *Action research participative inquiry & practice* (2nd ed.). SAGE Publications.

Trinos, K., & Mudaly, R. (2020). Exploring possibilities for including indigenous knowledge into the biology teacher education curriculum: Leveraging insights from Karanga knowledge holders. *Alternation*, 27, 76–116.

Tuckett, S., Robinson, D., & Bunting, F. (2021). *Measuring the disadvantage gap in 16-19 education*. Education Policy Institute. https://epi.org.uk/wp-content/uploads/2021/02/Measuring-the-16-19-disadvantage-attainment-gap_EPI-2021.pdf

UK Government. 2020. *Ethnicity facts and figures: People living in deprived neighbourhoods*. https://www.ethnicity-facts-figures.service.gov.uk/uk-population-by-ethnicity/demographics/people-living-in-deprived-neighbourhoods/latest/

Wall Kimmerer, R. (2020). *Braiding Sweetgrass*. Penguin Books.

Walsh, L. L. (2021). *Developing decolonial consciousness in biology students through critical reflection assignments*. CourseSource. https://pdfs.semanticscholar.org/6fb1/7ae753362f25f0dc0080aa1849ad59e3ed59.pdf

CHAPTER 12

Decolonising Language Teaching: More Than a Box-ticking Exercise

Christina Richardson, Jane Jones and Tanya Linaker

King's College London, UK

ABSTRACT

Language teaching has traditionally offered a space for the development of cultural knowledge and intercultural understanding as well as language learning. Furthermore, language teachers have recently become more critically race aware in their roles. In this research, we found a shift towards the decolonisation of the language curriculum within a more general trend towards increasing diversity and inclusion in school and university curricula. This research was aimed at exploring those developments in a collaborative team project that included both lecturers and post-graduate certificate in education (PGCE) students who, following training, undertook classroom research. Data analysis delivered insights regarding personal understanding of decolonisation and teachers' implementations. Despite constructive work evident in Modern Foreign Language (MFL) teaching and resources, there was considerable insecurity about the process and student voice was lacking. However, the arts-based approach enabled creative and positive representation of perspectives and the student researchers expressed a transformation of their mindset into one of activism.

Keywords: language teaching; student research; reflexivity; arts-based methods; emotionality

Research Context

Issues around coloniality and decolonisation for equity and inclusion in education have been the focus of reflection and debate (see Moncrieffe 2019a, 2019b, 2020, 2021, 2022; Moncrieffe et al., 2020). We were inspired to explore decolonisation issues in our subject area of language teaching that promotes a diverse pedagogy and intercultural learning, and for a critical approach to the study of language and culture.

In 2022, the School of Education, Communication and Society (ECS) and King's Language Centre (KLC) at King's College London secured a grant for a collaborative project aimed at Decolonising Language Teaching Curricula. The project involved volunteer facilitators – lecturers from both departments, five PGCE students, and three KLC students as co-researchers. Throughout the academic year, the project facilitators organised staff development events with external speakers, reading groups, and discussions on curriculum decolonising with a specific focus on French, Spanish, Italian, and German language teaching. The students carried out action research in modern foreign language teaching in secondary school and higher education contexts. They interviewed language teachers, observed lessons, and analysed reading lists, resources, teaching methodologies, and pedagogies. This was followed by further discussions on data analysis, self-reflections, and practical recommendations from the students for a decolonising agenda. Working within the training partnership between ECS and the training partnership schools, students and staff were able to develop deeper understanding of issues related to decentring and decolonising Eurocentrism through guided self-reflection and practical workshops. The results of the project and practical recommendations for teachers were disseminated at two conferences, internal workshops and via our King's College London internal publications.

Literature

The literature informing this research project was addressed directly in the reading group set up by the team, also in seminar sessions with guest speakers. It drew on a broad discussion of issues relating to decolonising curriculum knowledge from national, transnational, international, and interdisciplinary perspectives (Moncrieffe, 2022; Moncrieffe et al., 2020). This literature was explored alongside research addressing wider issues of racism in secondary MFL teaching, and guiding principles for decolonising the curriculum that were more specific to MFL in secondary school teaching contexts (Panford & Irvine, 2021), as well as literature relating to decolonising language teaching within the academy (Arday et al., 2021). The work of Said (1978) on orientalism informed the discussion of exoticisation and 'othering'. The specific focus of the KLC team on decolonising the teaching of Arabic and Russian drew on the work of Columbu (2022) and Nasibullov and Kopylova (2020). Underpinning the research project was a shared commitment to arts-based methodology, drawing on key texts such as Leavy's (2017) handbook of arts-based research and the work of Murris (2016) on post-humanism.

Objectives and Methods

A primary objective was to deepen our own understanding and awareness of coloniality and decolonisation to pursue our agentive agenda. The aims of the project involved progressing curriculum decolonising of modern foreign language teaching in secondary schools and universities by transforming the way we teach and learn as an inclusive community. We were also concerned with facilitating the engagement of students from KLC and ECS as curriculum co-creators and co-researchers by providing students with research experience and developing their analytical skills. The question underpinning the research was how to foster student and staff collaboration through involvement in action research that would lead to policy change and transformative action.

Taking a collaborative, arts-based approach, the research team explored teachers' perspectives and reviewed curriculum provision within their programme or partnership teaching spaces. Following Leavy (2017), an arts-based methodology is defined as a cross-disciplinary approach employed across all stages of research from data collection through analysis to representation that employs 'the tenets of the creative arts' (pp. 2–3) and intertwines theory and practice in a holistic way.

Embodying a participatory and reflective approach, this research project put the student researchers at the heart of the study. This involved systematic reflection throughout, to develop a critical awareness and promote rich potential for the sharing of critical insights. Innovative reflective activity by the research team was enacted in arts-based sessions involving participants describing an object, artefact, or visual which had meaning for them in relation to decolonising the curriculum. Thus, arts-based research enabled student participation through reflection on identity and meaning.

Within ECS, student-led research by trainee teachers was conducted in their PGCE teaching placement schools. This involved carrying out semi-structured interviews with their school mentors, a curriculum review, and arts-based reflections. Students studying a language at the King's Language Centre were asked to observe a series of lessons in Italian, Arabic, Russian, and Punjabi and to conduct interviews with teachers of those languages. In addition, the co-researchers conducted reviews of the teaching curricula in these languages. Research project co-leads trained students in research in workshops and training sessions including interview conduct and qualitative data analysis.

Analysis and Findings

The project team worked individually and collaboratively to code and analyse the data on a thematic basis from which emerged clear findings.

The overarching finding from our research was that, although there is a consensus about the concerns of decolonisation, it is often generationally framed and has different meanings for everyone. These meanings made visible through the arts-based approach were linked to individual/family histories and personal lived experiences evidenced in artefacts such as dolls, posters, photos, pieces of embroidery, and ancestral trinkets.

We concur with Braun and Clarke (2019) that qualitative research is about meaning-making and is… 'context-bound, positioned and situated' and that data analysis is about: '... telling stories, about interpreting and creating... the product of deep ... data immersion, thoughtfulness and reflection' (p. 591).

The schoolteachers were greatly inspired by the project, and decolonisation of the curriculum was considered by MFL teachers as an opportunity to pioneer in this field. The teachers participating in this research were shown to be proactive in the decolonisation process in their teaching. One remarked on developing an:

> [...] understanding of how we can incorporate opportunities within the curriculum to create a perspective beyond Eurocentric ideas while teaching L2.

A shift was advocated from the focus from European (or Eurocentric) to a broader experience of, for example, people in the world who speak Spanish in Latin America and French in the Caribbean, as well as advocacy for the inclusion of other languages in mainstream language learning.

Nonetheless, teachers felt insecure about how to implement the process of decolonising the curriculum. For example, one interviewee asked:

> Where does one start? And what does it entail?

Many questions were posed in this respect. These included the time frame, the data highlighting consensus that this is a long-term process with no 'quick fixes'. Although, in the short term, some speedy action planning was declared possible on policy decisions regarding schemes of work, resourcing, and display items. Decolonisation, it was asserted, needed a whole school focus, with school leadership and support of the core vision to ensure a holistic approach.

Teachers had, without exception, scrutinized and created resources to ensure diverse and culturally sensitive representation of their school communities and the globality of languages they were teaching. Furthermore, the teachers dug deep in actioning a duty of care to students involving getting to know students, their interests, and backgrounds, to teach content that is relevant to their lives. Decolonisation, the teachers stressed, was not just curriculum but concerned the identity construction of each student and included intersectional issues pertaining to, for example, their family units, gender, race, and class. These are issues that lend themselves to an arts-based approach, the use of photographs, for example, to show pride in back generations, dolls and trinkets that sparked memories of family connections and visits, sewing crafts that chimed with family traditions, all of which reinforced pride in identity.

Language teaching, we have concluded, has moved away from political rhetoric towards a practical implementation of curriculum decolonisation. It is happening in a way that makes sense to the teachers and students, drawing on their linguistic expertise and cultural knowledge, and shared purpose in teaching as a valuable collaboration. The arts-based approach enabled a reconciliation of the general aims and themes of the research with the highly personalised interpretations of the research findings, an approach that the student researchers vowed to implement in their schools with their pupils.

Strengths and Limitations

The project was considered by the research team and by relevant authorities and interest groups at King's College, as well as communities outside as highly successful, and impactful on our community in generating action and enlarging the network. Schoolteachers and university colleagues found useful practical experience from presentations. A better understanding and more secure personal positioning of the project staff engendered action regarding curriculum content and teaching approach to align much more with university decolonisation and globalisation aims. The greatest success was perhaps the enthusiastic initiation of a new generation of teachers into critical research, in which an arts-based approach was central to thinking.

As with all small-scale research, however valuable, we identify limitations as to the generalisability of the findings. Only a small number of schools, students, and teachers were involved, and furthermore, they were restricted to the KCL partnership schools and to students and staff in the King's Language Centre. At the same time, we became aware that our findings resonated with other research activities in other contexts and believe strongly that we have disseminated important knowledge to inspire and concur with others.

All was not completely harmonious, and we had instances of pushback from some teachers. One teacher said decolonisation was a 'fad', another said it was a 'tick box exercise', and a third participant claimed she had 'no idea what was being talked about'. By contrast, their work evidenced inclusivity and representativeness. We respect conflicting even negative views; however, due to time restrictions, we did not have a chance to explore these differences of opinion in full. Students also commented on not always being able to '*see themselves represented in the curriculum*' and generally lacking a voice although student voice was strongly advocated by teachers to include and involve students.

Impact and Next Steps

This successful project was celebrated with a series of expressions of galvanizing and positive learning. We have applauded this positivity since the topic of decolonisation can evoke feelings of insecurity and anxiety, even fear. Decolonising work is sensitive, personalised, and contested. Therefore, awareness of the sensitive nuances of this project is crucial to progressing our overall understanding and implementation of it. The project has fuelled a constructive and enabling mindset and led to changes that bear the hallmark of transformed practice such as student voice inclusion, new pedagogies, and resources. The participants felt strongly that the process is ongoing and continuous. This continuity provides spaces for hope, encouragement, and agency for sustaining the project ethos and for the next steps that for us include:

- Follow up projects that focus on lesser taught languages and have an international dimension working with schools and universities in the Global South as well as elsewhere in Europe.
- The exploration of teachers' progress and concerns in a safe space for discussion of these such as in ECS school mentor meetings.

- Embedding successful project strategies such as enabling student teachers as researchers into our programmes.
- The inclusion of other schools in the network.
- Providing ongoing support for a new generation of activists and potential leaders in curriculum decolonisation.

Even though the number of activists participating in the project is limited, change often starts in small ways and is only ever implemented with teacher-led action in their classrooms.

References

Arday, J., Belluigi, D. Z., & Thomas, D. (2021). Attempting to break the chain: Reimaging inclusive pedagogy and decolonising the curriculum within the academy. *Educational Philosophy and Theory*, 53(3), 298–313. https://doi.org/10.1080/00131857.2020.1773257

Braun, V., & Clarke, V. (2019). Reflecting on reflexive thematic analysis. *Qualitative Research in Sport, Exercise and Health*, 11(4), 589–597. https://doi.org/10.1080/2159676X.2019.1628806

Columbu, A. (2022). Decolonising Arabic language teaching: A case study. *Language Cultures Mediation*, 8(2), 101–118.

Leavy, P. (2017). *Handbook of art-based research*. Guilford Press.

Moncrieffe, M. (2022). Why decolonising curriculum knowledge? In M. L. Moncrieffe (Ed.), *Decolonising curriculum knowledge: International perspectives and interdisciplinary approaches* (pp. 1–14). Palgrave Macmillan. https://doi.org/10.1007/978-3-031-13623-8_1

Moncrieffe, M. L. (Ed.). (2019a, July). *Decolonising the curriculum: Teaching and learning about race equality* (Issue 1). University of Brighton.

Moncrieffe, M. L. (Ed.). (2019b, December). *Decolonising the curriculum: Teaching and learning about race equality* (Issue 2). University of Brighton.

Moncrieffe, M. L. (Ed.). (2020, July). *Decolonising the curriculum: Teaching and learning about race equality* (Issue 3). University of Brighton.

Moncrieffe, M. L. (Ed.). (2021, May). *Decolonising the curriculum: Teaching and learning about race equality* (Issue 4). University of Brighton.

Moncrieffe, M. L., Harris, R., & Race, R. (Eds.). (2020, Spring). *Decolonising the curriculum – Transnational perspectives. Research intelligence* (Issue 142). British Educational Research Association.

Murris, K. (2016). *The posthuman child*. Routledge.

Nasibullov, K., & Kopylova, N. (2020, Spring). Decolonising the curriculum in hybrid spaces: Muslim schooling in Russia. In M. L. Moncrieffe, R. Harris, & R. Race (Eds.), *Decolonising the curriculum – Transnational perspectives. Research intelligence* (Issue 142, pp. 24–26). British Educational Research Association.

Panford, L., & Irvine, M. (2021). *What does a decolonised MFL curriculum look like?* Association of Language Learning. https://www.alllanguages.org.uk/about/community/special-interest-groups/de-colonising-the-curriculum

Said, E. W. (1978). *Orientalism*. Penguin Classics.

CHAPTER 13

HEADSUP: Using Deliberate Reflexive Practice to Strengthen Decolonial Thinking and Action

Balqis Mohammed, Anna Olsson Rost and Karen Pashby

Manchester Metropolitan University, UK

ABSTRACT

This chapter examines the role that guided collaborative reflection can play in teachers' development of decolonial thinking. Following research undertaken with teachers in England, Finland, and Sweden, this chapter uses data collected from preservice history teachers in England to investigate how HEADSUP resources can be applied in aid of encouraging preservice teachers to start to undertake the task of developing and interrogating their ways of knowing, to begin the process of decolonising their practices. Our research shows how HEADSUP can be applied to stimulate collaborative reflection among practitioners as a key starting point for the work of decolonising curricula and practices, in a bid to try and avoid issues of performative decolonisation.

Keywords: decolonising; reflective practice; preservice teachers; professional development; HEADSUP

Research Context

This chapter draws on findings from a small-scale research project undertaken with 15 preservice teachers (secondary, history), involving a workshop and focus group. The main aim of this project was to engage preservice teachers with the revised ethical global issues pedagogy (EGIP) resource based on research carried by Pashby et al. (2019, 2020) undertaken with 26 teachers from across England, Finland, and Sweden.

The EGIP teacher resource was informed by Andreotti's (2012) HEADSUP checklist: Hegemony, Ethnocentrism, Ahistoricism, Depoliticisation, Salvationism, Uncomplicated Solutions, and Paternalism. This challenges perpetuated patterns of oppression in the educational context (Pashby et al., 2020). The EGIP resource is a collection of activities based on HEADSUP that teachers can adapt and use to teach about global issues or to reflect on their current teaching practices (Pashby et al., 2020). Participants in this study were specifically tasked with reviewing the EGIP resource to explore the potential for adapting HEADSUP for use in the history classroom. As we are engaging with the HEADSUP framework through the EGIP resource, we will refer to the EGIP activities as HEADSUP in this chapter for simplification and consistency.

The original research findings by Pashby et al. (2019, 2020) indicate that HEADSUP can support critical reflection. In view of this, this chapter focuses on the potential of utilising the HEADSUP resources (Andreotti, 2012; Pashby et al., 2020) to specifically support deliberate reflexive practice in individual practitioners at different phases of their careers and in their decolonial thinking. Indeed, Dominguez (2019) writes that the process of developing decolonial thinking requires re-thinking about what we know and how we came to know it. In this process, novice teachers are engaged in uncomfortable conversations about how coloniality shapes our epistemologies and ontologies and, ultimately, how we define progress (Dominguez, 2019). This chapter will examine what role the HEADSUP resources can play in facilitating this 're-thinking'.

Literature

Existing literature has emphasised the importance of the process of re-learning, or un-learning, as an integral aspect of the process of decolonising one's practices (Pinar in Le Grange, 2023). Le Grange (2023) suggests that although structures and systems need to be decolonised, 'without the transformation of the self, decolonisation will not occur' (p. 16). However, the process of this transformation is complex, and for time-poor teachers (Olsson Rost, 2022), this can be very challenging.

Pinar (in Le Grange, 2023) has stressed the importance of providing spaces where individuals can find their voices, providing opportunities to 'construct their understanding of what it means to teach, to study, to become [decolonised]' (p. 16). Pinar refers to this work as 'complicated conversations', which are not solely about exchanging information, but rather about providing opportunities for continual self-criticism that can mitigate against power relations that otherwise hinder productive conversations (Le Grange, 2023).

There have also been critiques of what has sometimes been described as gestural, superficial or performative decolonisation (Moosavi, 2020), or what Sinha (2003) has described as 'mention and inclusion' where 'lip service is paid to critical voices … [and then] issues are deemed to have been raised, highlighted, addressed and resolved' (p. 12).

Objectives and Methods

The research undertaken by Pashby et al. (2020) indicated that practitioners were able to use the resources to direct their critically reflexive practice. Our study sought to add to these findings by addressing the question:

- What role can reflexive practice play in teachers' development of decolonial thinking and action in the classroom?

Considering some of the issues raised in the literature, our study proposed that the type of guided reflection undertaken by the participants aided by the HEADSUP resources (Andreotti, 2012; Pashby et al., 2020) can provide a valuable starting point for practitioners on their decolonial journey.

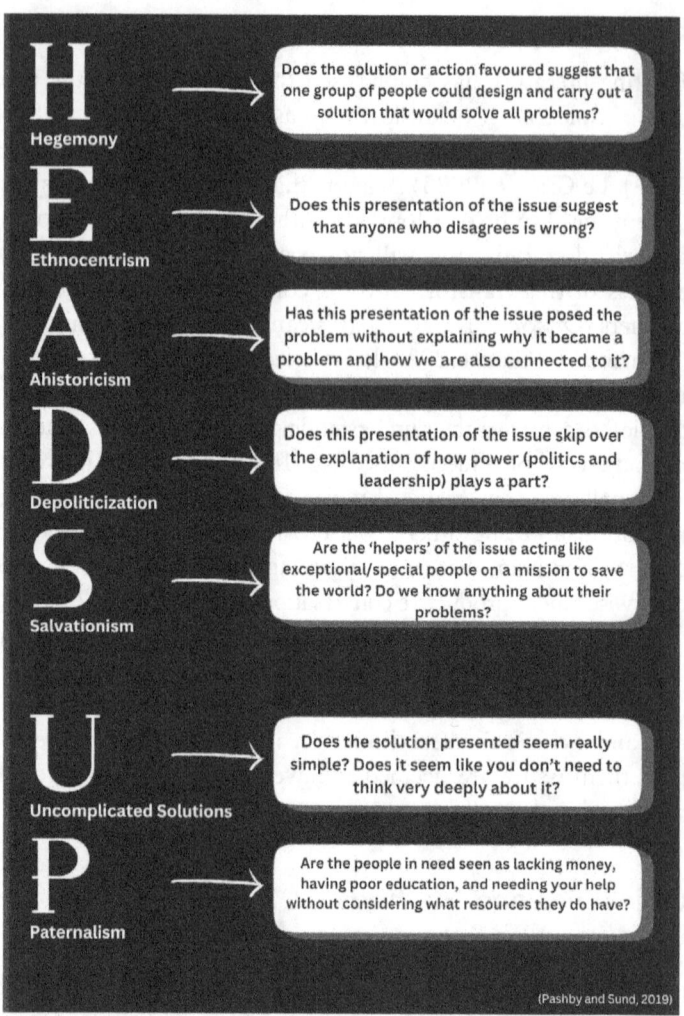

Fig. 13.1. HEADSUP factors explored through evaluative questions. Adapted from Pashby and Sund (2019, p. 7).

Source: From Pashby, K., & Sund, L. (2019). *Teaching for sustainable development through ethical global issues pedagogy: A resource for secondary teachers.* https://www2.mmu.ac.uk/esri/teacher-resource/

A group of preservice teachers, a majority of whom identified as white females, were invited to participate in a three-hour research workshop and a follow-up focus group (one hour). Fifteen preservice teachers participated in the workshop, and three of them attended the focus group. In the workshop, participants were tasked with reviewing the HEADSUP resources through reflections on their experiences, exploring potentials for adapting the analytical tool for use in the history classroom. During the focus group, participants were asked to elaborate on their workshop experiences.

We used page 7 of the EGIP teacher resource (see Fig. 13.1) as an introduction to HEADSUP in the workshop. Additionally, we used pages 5 'Reflections for Teachers' and 9 'Breaking Down an Issue 2' in the focus group to guide the discussion.

Data produced included recordings from the workshop and focus group and scans of workshop materials (handouts for the participants). The data was analysed using reflective thematic analysis (RTA) (Braun & Clarke, 2021) to identify key emergent themes. Following Braun and Clarke's (2021) RTA, themes were not predetermined but generated through a process of reflection, interrogation, and thorough immersion in the data. This study was awarded ethical approval by the Research Ethics and Governance Committee at Manchester Metropolitan University.

Analysis and Findings

Focusing specifically on the role that HEADSUP played in guiding reflections among participants, and developing their thinking, some of the findings reveal opportunities for the kind of re-education (Le Grange, 2023) that may be needed *before* practitioners begin to decolonise practices and curricula. One participant emphasised this by saying:

> *It's good to have something like a framework [HEADSUP] in mind to think of whenever you're about [to] talk about an issue, or how it's being taught, it helps you to be critical of it, which is good.*

Another participant concurred:

> [...] *even your frame of reference is a product of that [colonial structures] and having been taught in quite a not decolonialised [decolonised] way yourself, so having to do that teaching of yourself beforehand before you can teach them successfully. So, yeah, I thought it was really good.*

We see that these quotes exemplify how participants experienced working with the HEADSUP resources. Despite the intended focus of the workshop being on how to adapt the resources for teaching history, the reflections returned to how HEADSUP had guided participants' own thinking, and how this presented opportunities for re-educating oneself before adapting teaching practices or curricula.

The sense that HEADSUP could have a positive role to play in developing criticality among practitioners was also a recurring theme that participants referred to. As an example, another comment provided in the focus group referred to this:

> *Yeah, I think it's useful for, even if we're not showing them that full acronym of HEADSUP, it's useful, I suppose, for us to have a, almost, checklist, because we can critically think about how we want to use that checklist, rather than students: 'Done, tick'.*

Here, the participant purposefully moves the discussion away from using HEADSUP in the classroom. This was a recurring theme in the workshop and focus group, where participants identified potential limitations to introducing HEADSUP to their pupils and were hesitant in their ability to confidently engage in this equity work. As an example, a participant expressed their worry that:

> *Some teachers would probably roll their eyes at all this because kind of like, [they would think] 'More academic research, more people telling me what to do. I know how to teach'.*

Another participant made a similar comment regarding the wider school structure:

> *When a history department in a school finds something that works for them, and that gets them good results, it's*

going to be very hard to get them to change what they're doing [due to] the limited time, Ofsted, results tables.

Participants further critiqued what they saw as the routinised ways of teaching and explained that real change may require individual teachers to understand the value of encouraging critical thinking:

They [teachers] would need to realise the value of getting kids to think really critically about sources and about history, ... how it's remembered now, as well ... it would be great if we all had to teach a module about, like, the politics of remembering history, because that's so interesting.

Even when participants did not consciously reflect on how HEADSUP might enhance criticality, the development of critical thinking could be discerned through the discussions taking place:

Yeah. I remember reflecting quite a lot on the hegemony, like the first point of the HEADSUP tool, and how, I don't know, how fraught that can be, and how you can very unintentionally start promoting something that's very [much] part of the problem, as a way of trying to get to a solution.

An analysis of the data reveals that the 'hegemony' and 'salvationism' categories of the HEADSUP resource were able to act as triggers for critical thinking. Firstly, in relation to practitioners' roles in 'promoting something that is very [much] part of the problem' and secondly, as the quote below illustrates, requiring participants to interrogate these concepts themselves in the process of considering how to use them in the classroom:

Then, if you bring in the salvation as an aspect late, like after that, and say, 'God, isn't it also a little bit patronising? Does it play on, like, a power dynamic?' and try and tease that out of them so they see that, I don't know, they see what ... they understand why that's superficial, rather than me just telling them.

The findings exemplify the discussions that were generated among participants as they contemplated the practical use of the

HEADSUP teacher resources. Participants clearly appreciated the resources for enabling re-education and promoting criticality. However, they were concerned with the potential limitations of presenting the resources to students in the classroom.

Strengths and Limitations

The limited teaching experience of the participants in this project seemed to have an impact on their ability to envisage how to take a different approach to their teaching. Beyond the potential resistance of individual teachers, participants referred to constraints imposed by the curriculum, Ofsted, and school departments, and how this would make using the resources challenging. However, these limitations pushed them to collectively investigate alternative methods of using the resource in the classroom, without this being too disruptive to the norm. For example, they argued that HEADSUP could be used to scaffold students' learning and encourage critical thinking, instead of presenting them with the resource, by asking questions such as: 'Whose responsibility is it, then, to try and fix all these problems?'.

Impact and Next Steps

These findings illustrate how the research project engaged student-teachers in thinking reflexively about the effectiveness and limitations of using HEADSUP in their teaching and their decolonial thinking. The resources showed great possibilities for promoting criticality and for encouraging preservice teachers to push their subject-language repertoire as they became comfortable with using and adapting the HEADSUP terminology.

Through collaborative reflective discussions, participants moved from talking about the potential barriers of using HEADSUP in the classroom, to imagining how else the resource could be used and, particularly, how it can be used to develop their own thinking. This highlights an awareness among preservice teachers of the need to develop their decolonial thinking and undergo a process of re-education. As shown above, one participant commented that our 'frame of reference' is intrinsically a product of coloniality, acknowledging that coloniality is deeply entrenched in our ways of thinking and being.

The next steps proposed for this work are to:

- Raise awareness of the HEADSUP resources among preservice and in-service teachers in England.
- Develop HEADSUP resources further to emphasise aspects of re-education of practitioners.
- Develop a programme of continued professional development with a focus on re-education prior to changes to classroom practice.
- Incorporate activities which enable practitioners to identify superficial or performative decolonisation practices and to go beyond them.

References

Andreotti, V. (2012). Editor's preface: HEADS UP. *Critical Literacy: Theories and Practices*, 6(1), 1–3. andreotti_-_preface_-_critical_literacy_org_-_headsup__1_.pdf (oregoncampuscompact.org)

Braun, V., & Clarke, V. (2021). One size fits all? What counts as quality practice in (reflexive) thematic analysis? *Qualitative Research in Psychology*, 18(3), 328–352.

Domínguez, M. (2019). Decolonial innovation in teacher development: Praxis beyond the colonial zero-point. *Journal of Education for Teaching*, 45(1), 47–62.

Le Grange, L. (2023). Decolonisation and anti-racism: Challenges and opportunities for (teacher) education. *The Curriculum Journal*, 34, 8–21.

Moosavi, L. (2020). The decolonial bandwagon and the dangers of intellectual decolonisation. *International Review of Sociology*, 30(2), 332–354.

Olsson Rost, A. (2022). *Strengthening teacher networks: Decolonising secondary school history curricula*. British Educational Research Association. https://www.bera.ac.uk/publication/strengthening-teacher-networks-decolonising-secondary-school-history-curricula

Pashby, K., da Costa, M., & Sund, L. (2020). Pluriversal possibilities for global education in northern Europe. *Journal of Social Science Education*, 12(4), 45–62.

Pashby, K., & Sund, L. (2019). *Teaching for sustainable development through ethical global issues pedagogy: A resource for secondary teachers*. https://www2.mmu.ac.uk/esri/teacher-resource/

Pashby, K., Sund, L., & Corcoran, S. (2019). *Teaching for sustainable development through ethical global issues pedagogy: Participatory research with teachers*. Manchester Metropolitan University. https://www2.mmu.ac.uk/media/mmuacuk/content/documents/education/final-mmu-report-ba-project-teaching-for-sustainable-development-through-ethical-global-issues-pedagogy.pdf

Sinha, V. (2003). Decentring social sciences in practice through individual acts and choices. *Current Sociology*, *51*(1), 7–26.

SECONDARY AND TERTIARY EDUCATION – SUMMARY

The confidence and expertise afforded to subject specialists because of their knowledge and understanding of the traditional discipline itself offers insights into the limitations of traditional ways of knowing within the boundaries of the discipline. This also involves an engagement with choices in relation to language use within disciplines and considerations as to how underserved narratives can be brought to the fore. In seeking to illustrate decolonial thinking and praxis, the chapters in this section have advocated for conscious critical disruption of given subject knowledge for transforming and advancing equity and inclusion in teaching and learning. The findings across the chapters have given emphasis to the importance of critical reflection on teaching and learning to foster decolonial thinking and praxis.

The teaching and learning themes that have emerged from this section interrelate with each other in various ways. Action research and reflexive practice have been connected and related to enacting decolonial teaching and learning as subversive (to curriculum and pedagogical norms) individual initiatives. Key insights from the contributions in this section guide and encourage practitioners who seek to follow in undertaking decolonial praxis.

Reflective Questions

1. To what extent is the implementation of decolonial praxis inherently reliant on individual initiative? What are the benefits and challenges of this peculiarity? To what extent can continued advanced professional development be designed with this particularity in mind?

2. To what extent can subject- and discipline-specific perspectives be utilised to encourage further engagement with/confidence in decolonial practice in secondary/tertiary education?

3. How can we move this work – which relies on plurality and diversity – forward within English secondary and tertiary contexts where, currently, curriculum homogeneity is the mark of success?

Recommended Reading

Donaldson, L., Jefferson, J., Panford, L., Saleh, A., Smee, K., Wells-Dion, B., & Hemmings, E. (2022). Making spaces for collaborative action and learning: Reflections on teacher-led decolonising initiatives from a professional learning network in England. *The Curriculum Journal, 34*(1), 100–117. https://doi.org/10.1002/curj.186

Gandolfi, H. E. (2021). Decolonising the science curriculum in England: Bringing decolonial science and technology studies to secondary education. *The Curriculum Journal, 32*(3), 510–532.

Glowach, T., Hicks-Beresford, T., & Mitchell, R. (2023). Decolonising the curriculum in English secondary schools: Lessons from teacher-led initiatives in Bristol. In Y. Hutchinson, A. A. C. Ochoa, J. Paulson, & L. Tikly (Eds.), *Decolonising Education for Sustainable Futures* (pp. 136–150). University of Bristol Press. https://doi.org/10.51952/9781529226119.ch007

Joseph-Salisbury, R. (2020). *Race and racism in English secondary schools*. Runnymede Trust. https://assetsglobal.websitefiles.com/61488f992b58e687f1108c7c/61bcc0cc2a023368396c03d4_Runnymede%20Secondary%20Schools%20report%20FINAL.pdf

Moncrieffe, M. L., Harris, R., & Race, R. (Eds.). (2020). *Decolonising the curriculum – Transnational perspectives* (Research Intelligence; Vol. 2020, Issue 142). British Educational Research Association.

Nayeri, C., & Rushton, E. A. (2022). Methodologies for decolonising geography curricula in the secondary school and in initial teacher education. *London Review of Education, 20*(1), n1.

Olsson Rost, A. (2022). Strengthening teacher networks, decolonising secondary school history curricula: Challenges & opportunities in a (post-) pandemic context. In M. L. Moncrieffe (Ed.), *Pandemic, protests, recovery opportunities: Repositioning of educational research, teaching & learning* (Research Intelligence; Issue 151, pp. 26–28). BERA.

Pashby, K., & Sund, L. (2019). *Teaching for sustainable development through ethical global issues pedagogy: A resource for secondary teachers*. Manchester Metropolitan University. Ethical-Global-Issues-English.pdf (mmu.ac.uk)

Philpott, C. (2022). What does it mean to decolonise the school music curriculum?. *London Review of Education, 20*(1), 7. https://doi.org/10.14324/LRE.20.1.07

Smith, L., Magaji, A., Wragg, J., Coombes, S., & Hornsby, R. (2023). Decolonising the secondary initial teacher education curriculum in a university in England: A journey. *International Journal of Multidisciplinary Comparative Studies, 9*(1), 48–56.

Vauzour, S., & London, L. (2024). Decolonising initial teacher education and anti-racist education in 'white spaces': Feelings of uncertainty and optimism: Listening to student teachers' and university tutors' voices to critically evaluate a project to decolonise their PGCE. *Teacher Education Advancement Network Journal, 15*(1), 136–148.

HIGHER EDUCATION – INTRODUCTION

This section on higher education highlights different approaches towards decolonisation at individual, national, and institutional levels. Differences in the policy landscape at the national level are apparent in the dichotomous picture portrayed in *Smith and Lander* (Chapter 14) (with a focus on England) and *Davis and Olusola* (Chapter 15) (focus on Wales). Smith and Lander note the deracialisation of the initial teacher education (ITE) curriculum in England, pointing to the lack of reference to race or racism in the initial teacher training core content framework and its precedent teacher standards. By contrast, Davis and Olusola describe the 'diversity wind' across educational (and non-educational) settings triggered by the murder of George Floyd in 2020. This they described has spawned the Welsh government's 'Anti-racist Wales Action Plan' published in 2022. This policy drives initiatives such as diversity anti-racist practice and professional learning which brings together partners across Wales to develop their decolonial praxis. The importance of policy at the national level and the impact on institutional policy is reiterated by *Engman* (Chapter 17) and *Sattarzadeh* (Chapter 18), adding perspectives from Northern Ireland and the USA, respectively. The authors, including *Akbar & Fakunle* (Chapter 16) and *Taylor et al.* (Chapter 19) describe different individual initiatives and approaches to decolonise the curriculum involving reflexivity, positionality, and decentring of hegemonic constructions of knowledge. Key themes captured in these diverse chapters of decolonial research are discussed briefly:

1. *Connecting policy and practice through ITE*. The role of ITE in the decolonisation process cannot be over-emphasised. *Smith and Lander* (Chapter 14) point to the issues concerning

a lack of explicit national policy to guide and support practice, while *Davis and Olusola* (Chapter 15) uncover possibilities through their research and decolonial praxis. They share on how the research conducted by Welsh Initial Teacher Educators to decolonise ITE provision focuses on staff skill development in racial literacy, decolonial pedagogy, and recruitment and retention of diverse students. National policy and the implications for language teaching featured in *Engman's* (Chapter 17) paper, with a focus on internationalised classrooms which is a theme across other chapters.

2. *Fostering reflective and reflexive positionalities.* The authors across these chapters remind us of the importance of individual awareness of their own positionality, and an acknowledgement of inherent hegemonic constructions of knowledge as they seek to enact change in their practice. *Akbar and Fakunle's* (Chapter 16) reflection on their cultural and experiential knowledge affords critical engagement with the course content and broadens the class experience beyond a single frame of knowing. The authors provide examples of how this approach is enacted in their classroom practice.

3. *Co-constructing knowledge through indigenous values and language.* Equity and inclusion via decolonial praxis is emphasised by *Engman* (Chapter 17), *Sattarzadeh* (Chapter 18), and *Taylor et al.* (Chapter 19). *Engman* (Chapter 17) uses her relational language reclamation approach to the curriculum to facilitate engagement with multiple voices from both local and international students, ensuing a rich exchange of ideas, cultures, and languages. *Sattarzadeh* (Chapter 18) reveals how a practical course offers a transformational learning experience for students, including an awareness of the depiction of Black stories or lack of in institutional narratives and subversion. This serves as a critical learning opportunity for students to understand anti-Blackness and to re-imagine what a university archive with representation of different voices could and should be. Underpinned by non-western values,

Taylor et al. (Chapter 19) describe a buddying programme to foster a sense of community and togetherness across cultural differences and national boundaries. These approaches adopted within and across cultural boundaries share a sense of the rich possibilities inherent through decolonial praxis.

CHAPTER 14

Creating the Anti-racism Framework to Transform the Curriculum for Student Teachers in England

Heather Jane Smith[a] and Vini Lander[b]

[a]Newcastle University, UK
[b]Leeds Beckett University, UK

ABSTRACT

This chapter presents findings from a global literature review (LR) into anti-racism in initial teacher education/training and a national survey for England which was constructed following the review to gain a contemporaneous picture of anti-racism work in initial teacher education/training (ITE/T) in England. Both the LR and survey revealed a pressing need for student teachers to become racially literate and for guidance for ITE/T providers in teaching student teachers about race, racism, and anti-racism. The findings from the LR and survey were then utilised to construct the anti-racism framework (ARF) for ITE/T for England, which was written to provide such guidance within a policy landscape which is argued as de-racialised. The chapter concludes with an imagined case study demonstrating how the framework could be used to support critical and informed reflections on the content of the current ITE/T curriculum to avoid damaging deficit assumptions about Black and global majority (BGM) pupils and their schooling.

Keywords: anti-racism; anti-racism framework; initial teacher education/training; anti-racist pedagogy; decoloniality

Research Context

In 2019, the then Conservative UK government published the first de facto curriculum for Initial Teacher Education/Training for England – ITT Core Content Framework (2019) (henceforth referred to as CCF). This followed publication of the extant Teacher Standards (Department for Education, 2011). Both documents are deracialised in an absence of (and in terms of the Teacher Standards, a removal of) reference to race or racism, mirroring a more general policy trend in education (Gillborn et al., 2016; Smith, 2023). There is no mandatory requirement for ITE/T to teach about racism specifically in training future teachers in England today.

Juxtaposed to this policy and regulatory frame, however, there is:

- continued inequities in education outcomes for BGM pupils as evinced by the government's own statistics, including in permanent and fixed term exclusions, see House of Commons Library (2023), whereas permanent exclusion for racial abuse is extremely rare (Ibid),
- evidence of continued escalation of racist incidents in schools (Batty & Parveen, 2021; YMCA, 2020),
- an estimated 46% of all ethnic minority children living in poverty in England (Runnymede Trust, 2024),
- continued under-representation of BGM teachers and especially school leaders,
- a curriculum in which fewer than 1% of students at GCSE level study a book by a BGM writer (Runnymede Trust, 2024).

Contrary to current policy therefore, the need for teacher training to address racism is clear. The following sections will explain the research which underpinned the production of the ARF for ITE/T (Smith & Lander, 2022).

Literature

The research underpinning the ARF began with a global LR for anti-racism in ITE/T (Smith & Lander, 2022). The review highlighted that literature focussing on directives from the state avoiding reference to racism were all from England, whereas the majority of examples of anti-racist pedagogy and practices in ITE/T came from the United States. The literature revealed a clear need to embed anti-racist pedagogies in ITE/T with substantial evidence that 'one-off' or stand-alone anti-racist workshops were ineffective in developing student teachers' critical thinking and proactive responses to racism in education. The LR indicated where anti-racism work existed, responsibility tended to rest with one or two ITE/T tutors who had the skills and confidence to deliver anti-racist pedagogies. Overall, there was a lack of knowledge and confidence in teacher educators, and this was perceived as a barrier to anti-racist teaching in ITE/T, along with a lack of time. Training on anti-racist teaching for ITE/T tutors was cited as a need in several studies, along with greater encouragement from the institution/provider to embed anti-racist teaching. The impact of not teaching anti-racism in ITE/T was identified in several studies in the review as resulting in for example: lower admission and higher non-completion rates for BGM student teachers; BGM student teachers experiencing racism on the ITE/T course and on school placement; and student teachers' lack of confidence and knowledge to challenge racism and/or embed anti-racist teaching in their practice.

Objectives and Methods

Given the findings of the LR, we wanted a contemporaneous picture of anti-racism work in ITE/T in England. The purpose of the LR and national survey was to provide a foundation to the creation of a research-informed ARF for ITE/T. The aim of the framework was to enable ITE/T providers to transform their curriculum and practices to improve student teachers' racial literacy and enable them to become anti-racist pedagogues.

The research leading to the ARF was essentially exploratory to reveal ITE/T practices in England understood in light of the global literature on anti-racism and teacher education. The LR utilised keywords associated with ITE/T and race, racism, and anti-racism, cognisant of the lexical variations across the English-speaking world for teacher preparation. We employed snowballing until 'data saturation' was reached and final themes emerged. Although not exhaustive, it was an extensive global review, revealing 123 relevant research/scholarly publications from 1986 up to 2021 (most publications were in the 2000s).

The survey was designed with the research partners [UCET (Universities' Council for the Education of Teachers), NASBTT (National Association of School-Based Teacher Trainers), NALDIC (National Association for Language Development in the Curriculum: The EAL National Subject Association), Centre of Race Education and Decoloniality, Show Racism the Red Card, National Education Union, Universities of Sanctuary, BAME Ed Network] and constructed via JISC (Joint Information Systems Committee) online surveys. It opened in May 2021 for approximately six weeks and was shared via the weekly newsletter issued by UCET to all HEI (Higher Education Institution) ITE/T providers in England. Strict confidentiality was maintained, and results were handled in accordance with general data protection regulations. The survey responses were initially analysed quantitatively using JISC. Together with the free text responses in the survey, a qualitative analysis was then undertaken to look for consistencies and contradictions between the survey and the LR.

Analysis and Findings

The online survey was opened 80 times, but there were only 26 usable survey returns. Nevertheless, the respondents represented a wide range of ITE/T provision, subject areas, and educational stages (early years, primary and secondary).

The first headline finding was an unequivocal support for anti-racism appearing as an aspect of ITE/T provision. As one respondent put it, 'we can't expect teachers to be anti-racist if we haven't taught them how to do this'. Free text responses mirrored the global LR findings in highlighting the role of education in developing a racially equitable society; the importance of anti-racist pedagogies, racial literacy, and understanding white privilege; a recognition of the need for a more racially diverse teaching population; and an overt acknowledgement of institutional racism as prevalent in society including in education systems.

The survey asked respondents to rate 13 characteristics of anti-racism in ITE/T (as revealed in the LR) in terms of their importance (Table 14.1), and 65% of respondents rated each of the areas listed as very important (the highest rating).

68% of respondents agreed that they taught student teachers to become anti-racist pedagogues in their classrooms, and this was primarily undertaken through an embedded approach across the course and formed part of a series of work addressing a range of equality issues. For respondents who did not do this teaching, the main reasons for this centred around a lack of knowledge or confidence, suggesting the need for training. The survey revealed the existence of a mix of formal and informal training, where less formal training in working with colleagues was perceived

Table 14.1. Characteristics of Effective Anti-racist Pedagogy in ITE/T.

1. Knowledge of the equality act and their responsibilities as a teacher as reflected in the National Curriculum and the Teachers' Standards
2. Being able to deal with incidents of racism or racial harassment in school
3. Understanding the ways racism is manifested in interpersonal interactions including, for example, racial microaggressions
4. Understanding the ways in which school systems can act to discriminate against pupils from BAME communities
5. Developing knowledge of critical theories, pedagogies, and anti-racism approaches in education
6. Drawing on knowledge of these theories, pedagogies, and approaches to ensure better outcomes for all pupils, especially those from BAME heritage
7. Developing knowledge of ways to provide BAME representation in the curriculum to include achievements and experiences – decolonising the curriculum
8. Knowledge of acronym 'EAL' – identifying pupils and their languages
9. Developing inclusive teaching practices for pupils with English as an additional language (EAL) to promote better outcomes
10. Developing inclusive teaching practices in understanding the needs of pupils who have refugee/asylum seeker experiences
11. Developing inclusive teaching practices for pupils who are Roma
12. Developing inclusive teaching practices for Traveller pupils
13. Raising awareness of 'unconscious' teacher bias; for example, in understanding societal stereotyping of pupils from BAME communities and how this affects deficit assumptions and the lowering of teacher expectations and disparities in exclusion rates

as more useful than official online training. Respondents agreed with all barriers to teaching anti-racism in ITE/T found in the LR, with the following being the most prevalent:

- lack of school-based mentors' expertise;
- lack of importance in teachers' standards;
- lack of importance in CCF;
- lack of time;
- lack of colleagues' confidence in teaching anti-racism.

Strengths and Limitations

Although the survey captured a picture of ITE/T provision in England, which mirrored the global LR findings and indicated a clear need for anti-racism teaching in ITE/T, there were acknowledged limitations. Firstly, in terms of the LR, there is an acknowledgement that most studies were small scale, and social anxieties in talking about race and racism may have limited the number and efficacy of studies published. Also, importantly, the studies referred to in the LR were limited to those written in English, resulting in literature from only seven countries (the UK and Ireland, Australia and New Zealand, the USA and Canada, and South Africa). In terms of the survey, the most obvious limitation was the small number of returns, which perhaps is not surprising given the policy context presented at the outset of this chapter.

Impact and Next Steps

Analysis of the LR and national survey were used to devise the ARF. This section will explain the construction of the ARF and suggest a way it can be meaningfully used for future impact.

The ARF is divided into three sections:

(a) Overarching values and understandings

(b) Executive summary of the global literature review

(c) *Themes*: pedagogy and curriculum; student teacher and placements; leadership in teacher education; staff training – teacher educators and school-based mentors; course evaluation processes.

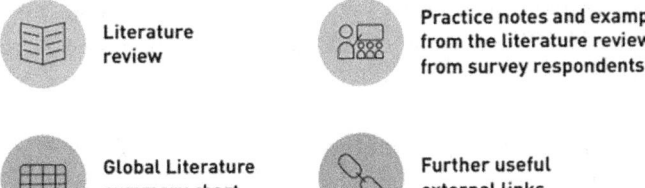

Fig. 14.1. Sources of Evidence in the ARF.

Source: Taken from Smith and Lander (2022, p. 4).

The themes are presented as a series of questions to support critical reflection and course development and are linked directly to the sources of evidence and practice as in Fig. 14.1.

The ARF launched in September 2022 to a large online audience. Since then, we have worked with agencies across England (e.g. the NASBTT) and in Scotland (e.g. the Building Racial Literacy programme) and Wales, liaising with Cardiff Metropolitan University to understand the changes underway in preservice and in-service teacher education to realise the Welsh government's ambitious aim for Wales to become an anti-racist country.

We held a national conference in March 2023 to hear from providers about their engagement with the ARF and have continued to provide online support to organisations and individual courses.

1. We are currently in the process of making an animated video to accompany the ARF for training purposes to support further impact.
2. We are also working with Show Racism the Red Card in their use of the ARF to develop modules for student teachers on anti-racism.

An Imagined Case Study

Let us consider one case of how the ARF could support a transformed ITE/T curriculum. 'In every year covered by this data [from 2006 to 2019], the rate [of permanent exclusion] for pupils from Black and Mixed backgrounds was higher than the national average' (Ethnicity, Facts and Figures, 2023). So, what does the ITE/T curriculum teach student teachers about pupil behaviour?

1. There are 35 references to behaviour(s) in the CCF, relating to both pupils' and teachers' professional behaviour, but no reference to the lived experiences of contextual circumstances such as racism (interpersonal and structural). Furthermore, explanation for (mis)behaviour and the 'ability to self-regulate one's emotions' (p. 26) are narrowed considerably to deficits (presumably the wrong sort of identity or values) internal to pupils and families, echoing the assertion made in the report by Commission on Race and Ethnic Disparities (2021, p. 77) that 'socioeconomic status, family strain, community culture, climate and context [but not institutional or systemic racism] along with peer pressure are all significant influences of behaviour'.

2. Without critical and informed reflections upon assumptions of colour-blindness, meritocracy, and familial/cultural deficit as advocated in the ARF (Fig. 14.2), a focus on individualised *identity and values* could easily lead to damaging assumptions that: (i) a pupil's identity and values are pupil-specific and somehow innate rather than socially constructed; (ii) that particular cultures, families, and pupils are, therefore, more prone to be less motivated to behave well; and hence (iii) this exclusively explains (mis)behaviour rather than factors arising from lived experiences of racism within a society and within the structural elements of schooling (policies, practices, and curriculum).

3. Consideration of such extrinsic factors is absent in any of the wider and ITE policy documents or the recommended readings in the CCF. If we have any hope of a sustainable transformation of inequities in our schooling system, we would argue that the ARF is a crucial tool in addressing the de-racialisation of ITE/T policy in England, and the consequential damaging impact on teachers of the future.

> Anti-racism pedagogy refers to how and what you teach; it is therefore relevant to all subject areas.
>
> Based on your understanding of racism, what are the central tenets and tensions you explore with your student teachers relevant to your subject areas to support their developing critical racial literacy?
>
> **For example:**
>
> - colour-blindness or race cognisance (LR, pp. 44; 47-48);
> - race/racism as a-historical versus historical creation of whiteness; (LR, p. 43; 50-51)
> - debt versus the discourse of closing the gap? (LR, p.43)
> - meritocracy (myth or reality)
> - assumptions/discourses of deficit, lack of expectations, hard to reach families, lack of cultural integration, or structural or institutional racism as explanatory factors for education disparities (LR p. 50; 52-53; 54)
> - questions around whose knowledge is legitimised, how this is shared and who has/had access (LR p. 42-43; 50).

Fig. 14.2. Excerpt from the ARF.

Source: Taken from Smith and Lander (2022, p. 10).

References

Batty, D., & Parveen, N. (2021, March 28). UK schools record more than 60,000 racist incidents in five years. *The Guardian*. https://www.theguardian.com/education/2021/mar/28/uk-schools-record-more-than-60000-racist-incidents-five-years

Commission on Race and Ethnic Disparities. (2021). *Commission on race and ethnic disparities the report*. https://assets.publishing.service.gov.uk/media/6062ddb1d3bf7f5ce1060aa4/20210331_-_CRED_Report_-_FINAL_-_Web_Accessible.pdf

Department for Education. (2011). *The teachers' standards*. https://www.gov.uk/government/publications/teachers-standards

Ethnicity, Facts and Figures. (2023, February). *Permanent exclusions by ethnicity*. Gov.UK https://www.ethnicity-facts-figures.service.gov.uk/education-skills-and-training/absence-and-exclusions/permanent-exclusions/latest/#permanent-exclusions-by-ethnicity

Gillborn, D., Rollock, N., Warmington, P., & Demack, S. (2016). *Race, racism and education: Inequality, resilience, and reform in policy & practice. A two-year research project funded by the Society for Educational Studies (SES) National Award 2013.* https://soc-for-ed-studies.org.uk/wp-content/uploads/2019/02/GillbornD-et-al_Race-Racism-and-Education.pdf

House of Commons Library. (2023). *Racial discrimination in schools (Number CDP-0049).* House of Commons Library Debate Pack. https://researchbriefings.files.parliament.uk/documents/CDP-2023-0049/CDP-2023-0049.pdf

Runnymede Trust. (2024). *The UK's leading race equality think tank.* https://www.runnymedetrust.org

Smith, H. J. (2023). The doublespeak discourse of the race disparity audit: An example of the White racial frame in institutional operation. *Discourse: Studies in the Cultural Politics of Education,* 44(1), 1–15. https://doi.org/10.1080/01596306.2021.1931035

Smith, H. J., & Lander, V. (2022). *The anti-racism framework for initial teacher education/training.* https://www.ncl.ac.uk/mediav8/humanities-research-institute/files/LBU_Anti_Racism_11-compressed.pdf

YMCA. (2020). *Young, discriminated, and Black: the true colour of institutional racism in the UK.* YMCA England & Wales. https://www.ymca.org.uk/press-statements/young-discriminated-and-black

CHAPTER 15

Decolonial Praxis in Wales: Reflections on Research, Policy, and Anti-racist Action

Susan Davis and Jeremiah Adebolajo Olusola
Cardiff Metropolitan University, UK

ABSTRACT

This chapter reflects upon a distinct decolonisation journey taking place in Wales, and how a Welsh government organisation called diversity anti-racist practice and professional learning (DARPL) is contributing to changing the Welsh educational landscape through decolonial praxis. We describe how a research collective of Welsh Initial Teacher Educators worked on decolonising their professional practice, curricula, and their own minds. This research runs parallel to curriculum changes in Wales that are part of a broad suite of Welsh government policies and commitments based on anti-racist thinking and professional learning in education. DARPL, which is funded by the Welsh government and housed within Cardiff Metropolitan University (CMU), is a community of practice working with a wide range of partners and networks across Wales. DARPL operates via a 'virtual campus', delivering in-person and online training, delivered by staff with lived and professional experience of racism. It provides a national model of professional learning for those working across all tiers of education to develop an understanding of anti-racist practice and leadership.

Keywords: decolonial praxis; reflection; anti-racism; racial literacy; self-reflexivity

Research Context

Despite ongoing attempts within the academy to correct higher education's past complicity in colonial projects, it is widely acknowledged that coloniality endures within the UK's educational systems (Arday et al., 2021). As well as being visible within student culture and in the aspirations imparted to young learners, it is deeply embedded within the literature taught to our children, in established measurements of academic aptitude and in the positioning of Western epistemologies as the universal way of knowing (Bhambra et al., 2018). As Imadojemun (2023) notes 'the fundamental imperialistic philosophies of colonialism have been internalised throughout universities' (p. 91). In recent years and following the murder by white police in the USA of the Black man George Floyd in 2020 leading to anti-racism protests across the world, we noticed that there has been something of a diversity wind blowing across public institutions, including in education. In Wales, this has taken the shape of the Government's 'Anti-racist Wales Action Plan' published in 2022 (Welsh Government, 2022a). This ambitious plan was co-produced with organisations and individuals who possess both scholarly insight and lived experiences of racism. Prior to this, the Welsh government funded a working group, helmed by Professor Charlotte Williams, to explore diversity in the curriculum. The resultant report, *Black, Asian and Minority Ethnic Communities, Contributions and Cynefin in the New Curriculum Working Group* was published in 2021 (Williams, 2021). The report included 51 recommendations which were accepted by the Welsh government and resulted in the country becoming the first in the UK to make the teaching of Black, Asian, and minority ethnic history mandatory within the school curriculum. The implications of these ground-breaking initiatives are profound and resonate closely with wider efforts to decolonise education. While a theoretical distinction is to be acknowledged between efforts to expand diversity, which tend to operate within existing structures of inequality, and efforts to expand decolonisation, which seek to transform existing structures, and tend to operate outside of the enfranchised epistemological framework (Bhambra et al., 2018; Ramgotra, 2019), these developments in Wales represent a significant step in the journey to decolonise the academy. The Welsh government's commitment to tackling racism has manifested also in the development of the new curriculum for Wales, which came into force in 2023 (Welsh Government, 2022b). A key component of the sweeping changes taking place in Wales has been the government's commissioning of professional learning for educators on racism and anti-racism through the DARPL.

Objectives and Methods

As part of wider decolonial praxis, a research collective of Welsh Initial Teacher Educators within CMU set out to decolonise Initial Teacher Education (ITE) provision (Davis et al., 2024). We recognised that ITE programmes in Wales undoubtedly touch upon issues of equality, diversity, and inclusion (EDI). However, there is more focus on disability, poverty, or gender. Matters pertaining to race equity, which are complex and emergent, are often side-lined or sanitised in EDI offerings (Conn & Davis, 2023). Moncrieffe et al. (2019) suggest the drive towards embedding anti-racist education into ITE programmes is diluted. Our research took place across the academic year 2022/23 and saw the collective working in tandem with wider ITE colleagues who were at different stages in their journeys of discovery. Our explicit aims in this research were:

- Upskilling staff knowledge on racial literacy/decolonial practice.
- Recruitment and retention of diverse students.
- Decolonising module delivery/teaching and learning provision.

The research is significant in a national and international context as it is situated within a policy window (Kingdon, 1984), notably a specific period of opportunity, running parallel to cutting edge Welsh government anti-racist policy and initiatives.

Given the contextual backdrop of the Welsh education system, we realised that embarking on this decolonisation process would be challenging and would likely involve synergies of discomfort, a term we coined to describe the inevitable unpredictability of the process. Our work was situated within a Welsh context, as it mirrored changes which were ongoing within Wales. For example, the new Welsh curriculum envisaged learners as 'global citizens of Wales and the World' (Welsh Government, 2022b).

Inspired by Bell's (2018) warning, not to reinforce coloniality by overlooking the unconscious dynamics of oppression, we were careful to utilise an intentional and reflexive approach in our work. This thinking animated our deployment of methodological tools such as reflective practice, notably the experience, reflection, and action model (Jasper, 2013). Our research was underpinned by a theoretical framework of Critical Race Theory. This furnished us with a supporting knowledge base and a heightened sensitivity to colonial structures of power, which are present in society and curricula (Rollock & Gillborn, 2011). The adoption of a patchwork methodology (Higgins et al., 2016) offered us the flexibility of an iterative approach, well suited to decolonial reflections. It gave us space to ponder and be creative. Allowing us the luxury of taking a deep dive into this area, provoking reflection, not only around new questions, but thoughts, feelings, and our own positionality.

Thus, we were acutely aware of the synergy between our personal and professional thinking (Gökçe et al., 2020).

As a research collective of six ITE colleagues (three academics of colour and three white), we had a common focus in exploring pedagogy, expanding the use of global knowledges in curricula, and probing issues of systemic inequality. As previously intimated, a key feature of this project was finding other ITE colleagues committed to shifting personal allyship into a course of action. To this end, we rolled out a series of staff meetings; without a prescriptive agenda, this provided a safe space in which to elicit ideas and reflections. During meetings, we tasked colleagues with examining their lesson plans for colonial content, recording thoughts on their decolonisation journey, and completing questionnaires which detailed their current thinking. Data were collated and thematically analysed to form a vision map of the current shape and existing limitations in our institution's ITE provision, related to decoloniality. Evaluation of these insights formed the stimulus for initiating change.

Analysis and Findings

Through valuable time spent in deep self-reflexivity, we began to uncover the inherent discomfort of the decolonisation process. The initial 'forming, storming, norming and performing' (Tuckman, 1965) within the research collective acted as a form of peer debriefing, which lent our project credibility (Spall, 1998).

Among the range of findings uncovered by this research are:

- ITE colleagues across the institution were at varying stages in their understanding of decolonisation.
- Staff expressed a shared sense that hegemonic tools of cultural exclusion existed within their curricula; this newfound insight threw up many more questions than answers.
- Acts of learning and generating questions were an integral element of the overall research project.
- Staff wanted to include the narratives of racialised communities within modules. A demand for more honest portrayals of the UK's colonial histories and the lasting effects of colonialism upon the world was apparent. This related to the underlying realisation that Wales itself is a colonised nation (Davies, 1974).
- ITE colleagues were keen to embed diversity and decolonisation more widely across the university.

Strengths and Limitations

Working towards a decolonised curriculum was an emotional endeavour for members of our ITE research collective and, to an extent, wider ITE colleagues. This demanded the establishment of a supportive work family, centred upon trust and collegiality. Providing a safe space within which colleagues could learn, discuss, and make mistakes was vital. We realised that colleagues of colour within the research collective did not know all the answers to the questions raised, and nor should they be expected to.

Impact and Next Steps

It is anticipated that the work undertaken by CMU/DARPL in this decolonisation process will impact the ITE provision in our own institution and add momentum to broader decolonisation efforts taking place in Wales. There is a clear impetus for change in the Welsh context given the comments of Jeremy Miles, the previous Minister for Education and Welsh Language, who stated, 'I'm pleased that we are building on the important work DARPL is delivering to achieve our vision for an anti-racist Wales by 2030' (Welsh Government, 2023). It is conceivable that meaningful change is on the way in our small country. The methods of research in our approach could be used by teacher educators across the UK who may be in the embryonic stages of their own decolonisation processes, and who may be inspired to replicate the model of collegiality and reciprocity outlined in this chapter. We assert the intrinsic value of global knowledges and posit that decolonising curricula should be approached as a journey of discovery. That journey will involve taking time, listening to a diverse range of voices, and reflecting critically on positionality in new ways to decolonise not only professional practice but our minds.

Some possible next steps with this research are:

- To drive the momentum of this research in seeking to bridge the gap between research, policy, and practice implementation.

- To see if change developed in Wales by this research can be replicated more widely across other nations (England, Scotland, Northern Ireland).

References

Arday, R. J., Belluigi, D. Z., & Thomas, D. (2021). Attempting to break the chain: Re-imaging inclusive pedagogy and decolonising the curriculum within the academy. *Educational Philosophy and Theory*, 53(3), 298–313. https://doi.org/10.1080/00131857.2020.1773257

Bell, D. (2018). A pedagogical response to decoloniality: Decolonial atmospheres and rising subjectivity. *American Journal of Community Psychology*, 62(3–4), 250–60.

Bhambra, G. K., Gebrial, D., & Nişancıoğlu, K. (Eds.). (2018). *Decolonising the university*. Pluto Press.

Conn, C., & Davis, S. (2023). Policy implications of collective agency for inclusion: Evidence in the Welsh context. *Journal of Education Policy*, 39, 127–148. https://doi.org/10.1080/02680939.2023.2222372

Davies, R. R. (1974). Colonial wales. *Past & Present*, 65, 3–23. http://www.jstor.org/stable/650335

Davis, S., Watkins, S., Haughton, C., Oliver, E., Farag, J., Webber, P., Goold, S. (2024) Re-imagining a decolonised, anti-racist curriculum within initial teacher education in a Welsh university. *British Educational Research Journal*. https://doi.org/10.1002/berj.4007

Gökçe, G., Varma, S., & Watanabe, C. (2020, June 9). *A manifesto for patchwork ethnography*. Member Voices, Fieldsights. https://culanth.org/fieldsights/a-manifesto-for-patchwork-ethnography

Higgins, M., Madden, B., Berard, M., Lenz Kothe, E., & Nordstrom, S. (2016). De/signing research in education: Patchwork(ing) methodologies with theory. *Educational Studies*, 43(1), 16–39. https://doi.org/10.1080/03055698.2016.1237867

Imadojemun, M. (2023). 'It's the colonisation of the mind': How the legacy of the British Empire has impacted the University of Greenwich. *Compass: Journal of Learning and Teaching*, 16(2), 91–120. https://doi.org/10.21100/compass.v16i2.1386

Jasper, M. (2013). *Beginning reflective practice*. Cengage Learning.

Kingdon, J. W. (1984). *Agendas, alternatives and public policies*. Harper Collins.

Moncrieffe, M. L., Asare, Y., Dunford, R., & Yousef, H. (2019). *Decolonising the Curriculum: Teaching and learning about race equality* (Issue 1). https://cris.brighton.ac.uk/ws/portalfiles/portal/6443632/Decolonising_the_curriculum_MONCRIEFFE

Ramgotra, M. (2019). Political voice in a changing world. *Critical South (blog)*. https://criticalsouth.blog/tag/manjeet-ramgotra/.

Rollock, N., & Gillborn, D. (2011). *Critical race theory (CRT)*. British Educational Research Association. https://www.bera.ac.uk/publication/critical-race-theory-crt

Spall, S. (1998). Peer debriefing in qualitative research: Emerging operational models. *Qualitative Inquiry*, 4(2), 280–292.

Tuckman, B. W. (1965). Developmental sequence in small groups. *Psychological Bulletin, 63*(6), 384–399. https://doi.org/10.1037/h0022100. PMID 14314073.

Welsh Government. (2022a). *Anti-racist wales action plan*. https://www.gov.wales/sites/default/files/publications/2022-06/anti-racist-wales-action-plan_0.pdf

Welsh Government. (2022b). *Curriculum for wales*. https://hwb.gov.wales/curriculum-for-wales

Welsh Government. (2023). *Press release: Anti-racist training launched for childcare and playwork professionals*. https://www.google.com/url?sa=t&rct=j&q=&esrc=s&source=web&cd=&cad=rja&uact=8&ved=2ahUKEwiLs_nlyrKDAxXq_7sIHcU2D5sQFnoECA8QAQ&url=https%3A%2F%2Fwww.gov.wales%2Fanti-racist-training-launched-childcare-and-playwork-professionals&usg=AOvVaw1ufmSC2w2NKCGrb5-p4rfW&opi=89978449

Williams, C. (2021). *Black, Asian and minority ethnic communities, contributions and Cynefin in the new curriculum working group*. gov.wales/sites/default/files/publications/2021-03/black-asian-minority-ethnic-communities-contributions-cynefin-new-curriculum-working-group-final-report.pdf

CHAPTER 16

Decolonising the Curriculum in Higher Education: Introducing a Practice-informed Framework from Two Non-white Academics in a UK University

Farah Akbar and Omolabake Fakunle

University of Edinburgh, UK

ABSTRACT

There is no shortage of discussion on decolonising in higher education, but a lack of insight regarding the practical implications for staff who aim to embed decoloniality in their teaching practice. This chapter contributes towards addressing this gap. Informed by a decolonial lens, two scholars articulate three stages in their pedagogical approach, and the impact, in an internationalised classroom in a UK university. This systematic approach centres on 'deconstruction' of dominant knowledge constructs, 'empowerment' to enable knowledge co-construction, and 'reflection' on pedagogical experience as part of students' educational journey. Hence, through observation, reflection, action, and refinements in our practice, we provide practical suggestions that legitimise diverse knowledge, create a sense of responsibility for own learning within a safe space for critical conversations, and reject the deficit-based approach for asset-based approach. The chapter, thus, contributes to discourses around decolonising curriculum with implications for pedagogy, practice, and policy development in higher education.

Keywords: decolonising curriculum; higher education; critical conversations; co-creating teaching; international staff

Research Context

This study examines the practical application of decolonisation in higher education. The aim is to demystify theory by providing practical insights based on the experiences of two UK-based scholars with 20 years of teaching experience on a Postgraduate Taught programme. The study takes place at a Russell Group University in Scotland, a highly internationalised institution with non-EU international students constituting 44% of the total student body. This context provides an environment to understand possibilities and constraints towards the adoption of a decolonised pedagogy in higher education.

Literature

Decolonisation in higher education, as suggested by Moosavi (2023), is a transformative process aimed at challenging the dominance of Western-centric content by introducing the often-excluded perspectives due to coloniality. However, despite the renewed call to 'decolonise' the university curriculum, integrating a transformative decolonial approach in practice is not without difficulties (Moncrieffe et al., 2019). While the cultural diversity within an internationalised classroom can afford a space for decolonialisation discourses (Fakunle et al., 2022), it is less discussed, how teachers and students jointly confront and address the continuing impact of colonialism in the production of knowledge and the unequal power dynamics between the so-called Global North and Global South.

Representation of diverse people and perspectives matters within an internationalised classroom. But efforts to increase inclusion and representation, such as diversifying the curriculum or hiring more academics from ethnic minority groups, are not sufficient for decolonising higher education (Abdelnour, 2022).

In other words, while important, targeted diversity initiatives by themselves do not address the structural and institutionalised state of coloniality characterised by hegemonic construction of knowledge and ways of knowing.

It is crucial to emphasise that diversity is about increasing the variety of voices and experiences present in academia, while decolonisation is about fundamentally rethinking and restructuring how knowledge is produced and disseminated (Icaza Garza & Vázquez, 2018). As such, to meaningfully decolonise teaching, academics must radically transform how knowledge is produced and shared, disrupting Western-centric frameworks and questioning their inherent biases. This process includes giving marginalised perspectives a central role in knowledge creation and representation.

This chapter articulates the practical manifestation of a transformative way of thinking about knowledge production in the internationalised classroom. The principle of equality underpins the aims to push the boundaries of educational practice towards a more meaningful action on decolonisation. This extends beyond a tokenistic nod towards divergent knowledge systems.

Objectives and Methods

This chapter provides a reflective account that articulates a systematic and practical application of decolonisation in higher education. The goal is to make theoretical concepts more understandable by offering practical insights drawn from the experiences of two UK-based scholars. The paper addresses two overarching questions:

1. What strategies can be employed in higher education to decolonise the curriculum?
2. What are the impacts of these strategies on both students and teachers?

The method adopted to frame this paper aligns with the principles of action research, relying primarily on reflective practice. The two scholars engaged in systematic, cyclic processes of observation, reflection, action, and refinements in their practice. They maintained learning journals throughout the semesters to document their teaching practices, observations, insights, challenges, adjustments, successes, and student responses (Schon & DeSanctis, 1986). In line with Abu Moghli and Kadiwal (2021) in these journals, the scholars reflected on their strategies and efforts to de-centre Western knowledge, legitimise diverse forms of knowledge, and their attempts to create a learner-centred, inclusive, and equitable learning environment. This method mirrors the iterative, reflective approach of action research and provides rich, contextual data for analysing the practical implementation of decolonisation in higher education.

Analysis and Findings

Our reflection on our teaching practice informs our analysis and findings that capture how we rethink our pedagogical approaches, engage with our learners, and create an inclusive environment as a process of decolonisation. This process is discussed below framed as a three-stage process: deconstruction, empowerment, and reflection.

Deconstruction

We first deconstructed the learning process to dismantle innate assumptions of students as passive receivers of knowledge rather than active contributors to knowledge creation. A crucial aspect of this transformation is the application of 'translanguaging' in our teaching. 'Translanguaging' offers students the flexibility to use their entire linguistic repertoire, including their first language (L1), which can be typically undervalued in conventional academic settings (Wang, 2022). We made efforts to encourage students to express themselves and communicate with others in the classroom using their L1. This led to an increased exchange of ideas and a deeper connection among learners while disrupting the monolingual mindset and power imbalance between the dominant and minority students. For example, students were encouraged to incorporate words and phrases from their L1 if it helped express their ideas better. We encouraged open and honest conversations around potential unintended consequence of alienation within mixed groups during group discussion. Liberty of expression was, thus, moderated with underlying ethos of respect and reciprocity.

In our teaching, we also experimented with aspects of co-creation in the curriculum in two ways. Firstly, student agency in course content selection was encouraged by presenting a list of potential topics from which students could select a few to be the focus for the following weeks. This list was shared early in the semester to give students ample time to contemplate and communicate their preferences. The most popular topics were then incorporated into the schedule for subsequent weeks. Secondly, questions were interposed into weekly lectures to facilitate discussions during follow-on interactive workshop sessions. Students were encouraged to work in groups to discuss their viewpoints on the prompting questions and related thoughts on the weekly topics, with positive feedback, for example, a student quote from the course enhancement questionnaire (CEQ):

> *[names lecturer] provides the perfect lectures and workshops for us. Lectures are very interesting [with] many questions which are worth considering ... so we can give our opinions during the workshops.* (anonymous student feedback, CEQ 2021)

These intentional processes afford students' autonomy to direct their learning journey in a meaningful way. The transition from a traditional, institutionalised curriculum development approach facilitated shared authority, inclusion, and student agency.

This deconstruction, however, required further actions. We realised that students needed to be confident to use their voice, ask challenging questions, share unique insights, and present diverse perspectives. This empowerment would foster academic courage, a sense of belonging in the academic community, and a space for meaningful knowledge exchange. We tried to achieve this by focusing on alternative epistemologies and non-Western perspectives within the reading lists (Grosfoguel, 2015). For example, in one workshop, we discussed the Common European Framework of Reference (CEFR) for languages from the perspective of Confucianism (Leung & Lewkowicz, 2013; Xiao & Chen, 2009). The CEFR, a widely used framework, evaluates language proficiency based on Western standards, potentially marginalising many learners who cannot meet these criteria, thus perpetuating a colonial 'dominant language versus less dominant language' (Moosavi, 2020) paradigm in knowledge acquisition. This reading prompted students to consider context and culture in language learning, effectively highlighting the marginalising nature of dominant systems.

Beyond the classroom, we encouraged our PhD students to explore their own cultural knowledge and scholarly works written and published in their own languages. This practice challenges the usual academia approach that draws heavily from existing concepts and frameworks from the Global North. By drawing on diverse knowledge systems, our students can counter Western-centric views and create contextually relevant taxonomies in their research. This approach not only enriches their research but also emphasises cultural relevance.

Empowerment

The deconstruction activities outlined above sparked a reconsideration of Western paradigms and advanced our efforts to decolonise academic practice. Students were encouraged see the legitimacy of 'other' knowledges that were more relevant to their personal and cultural experiences. This made them feel validated and empowered to share their unique perspectives. We also noticed students taking 'risks' as they began to interrogate previously unquestioned norms. Their probing questions enriched academic discussion and demonstrated critical thinking. As they began to feel a sense of belonging in the academic community, their academic courage flourished.

In our courses, we emphasised empowerment through extracurricular activities exposing students to real-world scenarios. Activities like school visits and classroom observation help empower students by exposing them to varying settings and teaching methods, expanding their view beyond the dominant Western model. These activities prompt critical reflection on established norms, encouraging students to consider context-relevant alternatives. 'Meet the experts' sessions further enhance empowerment.

These sessions, featuring practitioners from diverse backgrounds, challenge traditional single-narrative frameworks. Hearing from practitioners who represent non-Western epistemologies broadens students' perspectives, fostering understanding of diverse knowledge systems, subsequently empowering them to challenge and enrich traditional dialogues.

Reflection

Previous research attests to international students' reflexive capabilities to assess the best course of actions to achieve their academic and non-academic objectives (Fakunle & Pirrie, 2020). We encourage reflection in the design of assessment options. Instead of predetermining what students should say or think, we give them the space to delve into and verbalise their own comprehension and application of the course content. For instance, on one of our courses, an assignment might involve designing a lesson plan. In another course, the assignment allows students to critically appraise any topic of interest in the syllabus. We find that many students use a decolonial approach in their essay to interrogate normative constructions in the field of international higher education. This affirms the interest of the students and the relevance of a decolonial framework discussed as part of the course context. The task, therefore, allows students to apply theoretical knowledge in a practical way, and to use approaches within various cultural contexts, consider potential challenges, and envision strategies to encourage inclusive and diverse learning environments. This introduces a reflective practice that actively engages students in the process of decolonisation.

Strengths and Limitations

The strengths of our decolonising practices include an enhanced appreciation for non-Western perspectives and a more inclusive, engaging learning environment. Classroom debates and critical reflective exercises foster independent thinking, while real-world experiences enrich theoretical understanding. However, there are limitations. Challenging ingrained normative assumptions may necessitate difficult conversations. We, therefore, do not underestimate the time and effort required for educators to plan, facilitate, and embed an ethos of decoloniality in their pedagogy. Crucially, notwithstanding individual efforts, institutional structures can constrain or enable decolonisation in the curriculum.

Impact and Next Steps

Our decolonising practices have had significant impact on staff and student interactions in our internationalised classroom. We facilitate safe learning spaces for students to enact their agency to challenge dominant knowledge constructs. Students feel empowered to share diverse epistemologies and knowledges that enrich our learning. This instils greater confidence in their personal and cultural identities. As teachers, we continue to evolve in our pedagogical approach towards a more inclusive and dynamic classroom environment.

To further decolonise our teaching, our goals include:

- Continuous improvement of teaching practices through peer learning opportunities and students' feedback.

- Expanding course content to encompass non-Western resources, enhancing global inclusivity.

- Advocating for the inclusion of decolonisation as a central aspect in the transformation of the curriculum, aligning it with the university's strategic objectives.

References

Abdelnour, S. (2022). What decolonizing is not. *M@n@gement*, 25(4), 81–82. https://doi.org/10.37725/mgmt.v25.9029

Abu Moghli, M., & Kadiwal, L. (2021). Decolonising the curriculum beyond the surge: Conceptualisation, positionality, and conduct. *London Review of Education*, 19(1), 1–16. https://doi.org/10.14324/LRE.19.1.23

Fakunle, O., Kalinga, C., & Lewis, V. (2022). Internationalization and decolonization in UK higher education: Are we there yet? *International Higher Education*, 110, 1–3.

Fakunle, O., & Pirrie, A. (2020). International students' reflections on employability development opportunities during a one-year Masters-level program in the UK. *Journal of International Students*, 10(S2), 86–100. https://doi.org/10.32674/jis.v10iS2.2719

Icaza Garza, R. A., & Vázquez, R. (2018). Diversity or decolonization? Researching diversity at the University of Amsterdam. In G. K. Bhambra, D. Gebrial, & K. Nişancıoğlu (Eds.), *Decolonizing the University* (pp. 108–128). Pluto Press. http://hdl.handle.net/1765/113362

Leung, C., & Lewkowicz, J. (2013). Language communication and communicative competence: A view from contemporary classrooms. *Language and Education*, 27(5), 398–414.

Moncrieffe, M., Dunford, R., & Asare, Y. (2019). Decolonising the curriculum: Challenges and opportunities for teaching and learning. In G. Wisker, L. Marshall, J. Canning, & S. Greener (Eds.), *Navigating with practical wisdom* (p. 20). University of Brighton Press.

Moosavi, L. (2023). Turning the decolonial gaze towards ourselves: Decolonising the curriculum and 'decolonial reflexivity' in sociology and social theory. *Sociology (Oxford)*, 57(1), 137–156. https://doi.org/10.1177/00380385221096037

Moosavi, L. (2020). The decolonial bandwagon and the dangers of intellectual decolonisation. *International Review of Sociology*, 30(2), 332–354. https://doi.org/10.1080/03906701.2020.1776919

Grosfoguel, R. (2015). Epistemic racism/sexism, westernized universities and the four genocides/epistemicides of the long sixteenth century. In M. Araújo & S. R. Maeso (Eds.), *Eurocentrism, racism, and knowledge: Debates on history and power in Europe and the Americas* (pp. 23–46). Palgrave Macmillan UK. https://doi.org/10.1057/9781137292896_2

Schon, D. A., & DeSanctis, V. (1986). The reflective practitioner: How professionals think in action. *The Journal of Continuing Higher Education*, 34(3), 29–30. https://doi.org/10.1080/07377366.1986.10401080

Wang, D. (2022). Translanguaging as a decolonising approach: Students' perspectives towards integrating Indigenous epistemology in language teaching. *Applied Linguistics Review*, 2022, 1–22. https://doi.org/10.1515/applirev-2022-0127

Xiao, X., & Chen, G. (2009). Communication competence and moral competence: A Confucian perspective. *Journal of Multicultural Discourses*, 4(1), 61–74.

CHAPTER 17

Relationality, Plurilingualism, and Place: Language Education in Higher Education in Northern Ireland

Mel M. Engman
Queen's University Belfast, UK

ABSTRACT

Efforts towards decolonising the higher education curriculum in Northern Ireland reflect the complex and often contradictory character of the structures, relations, and identities in place. The author draws on his experiences as a settler researcher and learner of Ojibwemowin (an Indigenous language in North America) to explore how these complexities intersect with language in one English language teaching (ELT) programme at a university in Northern Ireland. The author describes the tensions inherent in teaching ELT-related curriculum from a place where language policy has been uneven for many years. The author then explains how language reclamation research has informed teaching practices that de-centre English and draw on relationality. These practices are examined through decolonising and anticolonial lenses to highlight the value of relationships and place as an underexplored pathway in English language and language education curricula in higher education in Northern Ireland and elsewhere.

Keywords: English language teaching; anticolonial curriculum; language reclamation; relationality; Northern Ireland

Research Context

Efforts towards decolonising the higher education curriculum in Northern Ireland reflect the complex and often contradictory (Nic Dháibhéid et al., 2021) character of the structures, relations, and identities in place. Longstanding community relationships with the land and language sit in tension with structures instantiated through projects of Church and empire (Jenkins, 2021), as well as with settler colonial technologies old and new. I draw on my experiences as a settler researcher and learner of indigenous language to explore how these complexities intersect with language in one ELT programme at a university in Northern Ireland.

The English language has been an instrument of empire for centuries, facilitating the invasions, extractions, settlements, and alliances that fuelled the growth of the British Empire (e.g. Lin & Motha, 2021). On the island of Ireland, English was central to the control, management, and erasure of indigenous lifeways. This was evident in the desire expressed by Sir John Davies, an architect of the Ulster plantation, that future generations of Irish speakers would not only *learn* English but would 'in tongue and heart and every way else *become* English' (Donlan, 2003, p. 11; *emphasis* author's). And while it shares official language status with Irish (*Gaeilge*) in the Republic of Ireland, there is no question as to the political supremacy of English in the North. It promises cultural capital and is unironically presented as a 'neutral' means of communicating amidst linguistically diverse populations, particularly in higher education (MacKenzie et al., 2022). Yet, contemporary scholarship on ELT around the world notes that rather than a binary of powerful-powerless, English learning is a 'site of struggle' (Motha, 2006, p. 76) where negotiations of power are constantly underway.

I teach in a post-graduate programme that aims to help students further their careers as teachers or academics through a research-oriented degree that focuses on ELT and language education. A few of the students in this programme come from the islands of Ireland and Britain, though cohorts are majority international students, with diverse geographic, linguistic, and economic backgrounds. Some of the students are not yet practising teachers, having just finished undergraduate programmes before their arrival, while others have been in the workforce for years. Managing these diverse experiences and expectations is a challenge. How do we prepare plurilingual language teachers to think critically about the power relations that are embedded in their subject matter?

Literature

It is important to conceptualise language learning as 'situated amid historical and structural circumstances, and a multiplicity of desires' (Liyanage & Canagarajah, 2019, p. 431). Though I am not teaching English per se, my students are learning how to use English for academic purposes in our university, and intersections of language and desire are integral to the curriculum. As I work to prepare a global workforce of English teachers at an institution in Northern Ireland, I perceive the tensions in these desires through a lens of coloniality. This lens has been shaped in large part by my research with Ojibwe[1] language educators in the United States. Despite a few linguistic similarities between Ojibwemowin and Irish grammar, there are many points of resonance in the movements by communities in North America and in Northern Ireland to resist the supremacy of English and to sustain and reclaim their languages.

Indeed, it is through *language reclamation* (Engman & Hermes, 2021; Leonard, 2018, 2019; McCarty et al., 2018) that these cross-community resonances become apparent, along with their relevance to the curriculum informing the development of all language teachers. Language reclamation is an intentionally decolonising approach to language education. By viewing language as a relational phenomenon (Henne-Ochoa et al., 2020; Leonard, 2019), rather than as an object to be transmitted, language reclamation projects intervene in the disrupted and severed relations that result from colonial structures. A language reclamation approach to curriculum centres relationships between humans and non-humans and land (Hermes et al., 2023). It is not necessarily anti-English use, but it deliberately disrupts the status quo, disallowing English the 'elbow room' it is accustomed to (Engman et al., 2023).

Objectives and Methods

A curriculum that promotes the global teaching and learning of English is unlikely to remove colonising structures, as the field itself 'stems from long histories of global empire and capitalist conquest' (Hsu, 2017, p. 112). As such, the word 'decolonising' seems inappropriate to describe work in an ELT programme in Northern Ireland of all places. Returning to Liyanage and Canagarajah's (2019) sentiment about the 'situated'-ness of language learning, we cannot ignore the importance of *place* in shaping people's relationships to language. Much of the language ecology in Northern Ireland is intensely place-based, influenced by local histories and practices (MacKenzie et al., 2022; Mitchell & Miller, 2019). As I necessarily think with land and place in the reclamation research I do, I have begun to embed thinking with place in my teaching; asking: *what are some affordances for anticolonial transformation in the education curriculum that are unique to Northern Ireland?*

Sterzuk (2015) writes about the linguistic conformity of higher education and how the pursuit of English standards can be seen as an 'institutional investment in whiteness' (p. 56). I counter this in teaching by introducing non-prestige varieties of English into the classrooms, holding space for languages other than English, and elevating ways of knowing and being that are Indigenous, queer, and/or from the Global South. While literature provides a starting point (leveraging the legitimacy of the academy), it is the plurilingual international students, the indigenous knowledges they bring with them, and the students from Northern Ireland with their specific local knowledge that provide the richest sources of anticolonial transformation (Zembylas, 2022). We share sociolinguistic observations (and questions!) about life in Northern Ireland. We bring objects, songs, and stories into the classroom that have roots in distant homelands or strong tethers to the island of Ireland. There is also space in the curriculum for students to teach each other the languages we know or are learning. Micro-teaching sessions invite future English teachers to practise by teaching languages of home – for instance, Bangla, Catalán, Ojibwemowin, and Irish. Students are also invited to lead English-based skill sharing sessions with young people from refugee and asylum-seeking (RAS) backgrounds. For some, this is a critical opportunity for encountering the *'multiplicity* of desires' that neoliberalism attaches to English (Liyanage & Canagarajah, 2019, p. 431, *emphasis* mine), and for developing relationships with bilingual learners whose own relationships to Northern Ireland may differ greatly from those of international and local students.

Analysis and Findings

This language reclamation approach to the curriculum decentres English and prioritises building and strengthening relationships with humans, more-than-humans, and land. Students find that there are many ways to learn and know. Learning can be done quietly, noisily, plurilingually, and in interaction with non-human beings. Asking students to draw on their own knowledges and relationships to place in Northern Ireland and elsewhere allows for an emergence of anticolonial curiosity. Deliberately bringing minoritised languages into ELT spaces, facilitating work with RAS English learners to campus, and holding space for international students' own local and indigenous ways of knowing demands more of these future English teachers than a standardized curriculum would. But it also allows for curiosity and practice to bloom against linguistic and epistemological conformity – something that is evident in critical student work and professional trajectories.

Strengths and Limitations

One significant challenge to this project of transforming the curriculum for language teachers comes from the academy's mechanisms of 'disciplining' our thinking (Cushing-Leubner et al., 2021). This is not unique to Northern Ireland. As with any other subject area the ELT and language education curriculum is bounded or tracked into a 'discipline' that is not always amenable to the application of ideas, concepts, and methods from other disciplines. Additionally, students are not immune to the colonial ideologies that pervade much of the modern world.

A language education curriculum that de-centres English tends to disrupt some students' expectations and assumptions about what a language teacher 'needs to know'. Initial resistance to learning through relationships and indigenous and local knowledges can be a part of the learning process, and ultimately, it is the relationality across humans, language, and place that is a core strength of the curriculum.

Impact and Next Steps

More than 20 years after the Good Friday Agreement, Northern Ireland is widely presented as a 'post-conflict' place, though segregation in the education sector remains – including both higher education and further education (Irwin, 2019).

Incorporating the relational perspectives that underpin language reclamation work appears to offer anticolonial pathways for English and language education curricula, regardless of a student's socio-political orientation. The impact of this on even a relatively small scale results in a classroom space that is noisier – filled with the sounds of a diverse range of sense-making mechanisms. Student projects once concerned with prestige varieties of English are now more likely to address questions of plurilingualism that are relevant to home contexts. And along with the development of relationships among students, I see evidence of investment in relations with place, as students bring questions, problems, and triumphs into the classroom that come from deeper engagement with the complexity of coloniality in Northern Ireland.

A curriculum that moves towards heterogeneity (Sterzuk, 2015) and towards human- and land-based relationships can open up anticolonial possibilities for students as future practitioners. The next steps for this convergence of place-based practitioner research are to:

- Investigate curricular moves that might balance the 'inequalities of English' (Park, 2015) with the multitude of desires related to it through practice-based assignments for students. How do students recognise inequality in language curriculum and use? Where do these inequalities converge with and upend complex student desires?

- Explore the learning potential of introducing indigenous language learning (e.g. Ojibwemowin, Irish) as an aspect of the ELT curriculum to further develop student plurilingualism and to offer alternative instructional models and conditions. How might the learning of a minoritised indigenous language shift student perceptions of 'mainstream' instructional practices and expectations?

- Examine the possibilities of embedding engagement with local language education and activism efforts in the curriculum. What can international students learn from visits with local language activists? Where might there be points of resonance between language policies in Northern Ireland and elsewhere? How might hands-on engagement with local language concerns empower students to 'see' inequalities elsewhere and to better visualise possible routes of intervention as future practitioners?

Note

1. Ojibwe, also called *Ojibwa*, *Anishinaabe*, or *Chippewa*, are diverse and widespread peoples indigenous to North America. Ojibwe peoples' name for their language is Ojibwemowin or Anishinaabemowin.

References

Cushing-Leubner, J., Engman, M. M., Ennser-Kananen, J., & Pettitt, N. (2021). Imperial straightening devices in disciplinary choices of academic knowledge production. *Language, Culture and Society*, 3(2), 201–230. https://doi.org/10.1075/lcs.21001.cus

Donlan, S. P. (2003). 'Little better than cannibals': Sir John Davies and Edmund Burke on property and progress. *Northern Ireland Legal Quarterly*, 54, 1–24.

Engman, M. M., & Hermes, M. (2021). Land as interlocutor: A study of Ojibwe learner language in interaction on and with naturally occurring 'materials'. *The Modern Language Journal, 105*(S1), 86–105.

Engman, M. M., McGurk, Ó., & MacKenzie, A. (2023). Teanga sa chistin: A qualitative study of bilingual families, baking bread, and reclaiming Irish in the home. *Teanga, 30,* 169–200.

Henne-Ochoa, R., Elliott-Groves, E., Meek, B. A., & Rogoff, B. (2020). Pathways forward for Indigenous language reclamation: Engaging Indigenous epistemology and learning by observing and pitching in to family and community endeavors. *The Modern Language Journal, 104*(2), 481–493.

Hermes, M., Engman, M. M., Meixi, M. M., & MacKenzie, J. (2023). Relationality and Ojibwemowin in forest walks: Learning from multimodal interaction about land and language. *Cognition and Instruction, 4*(1), 1–31.

Howe, S. (2008). Questioning the (bad) question: 'Was Ireland a colony?' *Irish Historical Studies, 36*(142), 138–152.

Hsu, F. (2017). Resisting the coloniality of English: A research review of strategies. *The CATESOL Journal, 29*(1), 111–132.

Irwin, T. (2019). Further education and skills in Northern Ireland: Policy and practice in a post-conflict society. *Journal of Education and Work, 32*(3), 266–276.

Jenkins, S. (2021). Ireland, first colony of the British Empire: A Celtic story of Indigenous resistance, resilience, and cultural renewal. In H. N. Weaver (Ed.), *The Routledge international handbook of indigenous resilience* (pp. 21–34). Routledge.

la paperson (2017). *A third university is possible.* University of Minnesota Press.

Leonard, W. Y. (2018). Reflections on (de)colonialism in language documentation. In B. McDonnell, A. L. Berez-Kroeker, & G. Holton (Eds.), *Reflections on Language Documentation 20 Years after Himmelmann 1998. Language Documentation and Conservation Special Publication 15* (pp. 55–65). University of Hawai'i Press.

Leonard, W. Y. (2019, September 19). Indigenous languages through a reclamation lens. *Blog Post.* https://www.anthropology-news.org/index.php/2019/09/19/indigenous-languages-through-a-reclamation-lens/.

Lin, A. M. Y., & Motha, S. (2021). 'Curses in TESOL': Postcolonial desires for colonial English. In R. Arber, M. Weinmann, & J. Blackmore (Eds.), *Rethinking languages education: Directions, challenges, and innovations* (pp. 15–35). Routledge.

Liyanage, I., & Canagarajah, S. (2019). Shame in English language teaching: Desirable pedagogical possibilities for Kiribati in neoliberal times. *TESOL Quarterly, 53*(2), 430–455.

MacKenzie, A., Engman, M. M., & McGurk, Ó. (2022). Overt and symbolic linguistic violence: Plantation ideology and language reclamation in Northern Ireland. *Teaching in Higher Education, 27*(4), 489–501.

McCarty, T. L., Nicholas, S. E., Chew, K. A. B., Diaz, N. G., Leonard, W. Y., & White, L. (2018). Hear our languages, hear our voices: Storywork as theory and praxis in Indigenous-language reclamation. *Daedalus, 147*(2), 160–172.

Mitchell, D., & Miller, M. (2019). Reconciliation through language learning? A case study of the Turas Irish language project in East Belfast. *Ethnic and Racial Studies, 42*(2), 235–253.

Motha, S. (2006). Deecolonizing ESOL: Negotiating linguistic power in US public school classrooms. *Critical Inquiry in Language Studies, 3*(2–3), 75–100.

Nic Dháibhéid, C., Akhtar, S., Hassett, D., Kenny, K., McAtackney, L., McBride, I., McMahon, T. G., & Ohlmeyer, J. (2021). Round table: Decolonising Irish history? Possibilities, challenges, practices. *Irish Historical Studies, 45*(168), 303–332.

Park, J. S.-Y. (2015). Structures of feeling in unequal Englishes. In R. Tupas (Ed.), *Unequal Englishes: The politics of English today* (pp. 59–73). Palgrave Macmillan.

Sterzuk, A. (2015). 'The standard remains the same': Language standardization, race, and othering in higher education. *Journal of Multilingual and Multicultural Development, 36*(1), 53–66.

Tuck, E., & Yang, K. W. (2012). Decolonization is not a metaphor. *Decolonization: Indigeneity, Education & Society, 1*(1), 1–40.

Wrangel, C. T. (2017). Recognizing hope: US global development discourse and the promise of despair. *Environment and Planning D: Society and Space, 35*(5), 875–892.

Zembylas, M. (2022). Affective and biopolitical dimensions of hope: From critical hope to anti-colonial hope in pedagogy. *Journal of Curriculum and Pedagogy, 19*(1), 28–24.

CHAPTER 18

'Hunting' for a Black Feminist Decolonial 'Archive' at a Predominantly White University

Sahar D. Sattarzadeh
The University of Texas at Arlington, USA

ABSTRACT

Based on classroom learnings from a course lesson on de/coloniality of African and Black diasporas in higher education at a small private historically, predominantly white university in the rural United States, this chapter is an invitation to critically and meaningfully engage with our own higher education institutions (HEIs) as ideal laboratories for individual, community, and institutional transformation. Engaging in a university scavenger hunt, co-designed by faculty and students, various meanings, and implications of 'decoloniality' and 'decolonisation' within contexts of higher education are interrogated and reimagined through individual and collective counternarratives in the shape of a Black feminist decolonial 'archive'. This archive challenges and reimagines narratives in/visibilised in the university's current archival records, which are characterised by anti-Blackness, anti-Indigeneity, colonial innocence, and white supremacy. This chapter focuses on un/learning varying (de)colonial and decolonising worldviews of HEIs and academia through participatory narrative and archival reproduction.

Keywords: Black feminism; decolonial archive; counternarratives; higher education; scavenger hunt

The classroom remains the most radical space of possibility in the academy ... Urging all of us to open our minds and hearts so that we can know beyond the boundaries of what is acceptable, so that we can think and rethink, so that we can create new visions ....
(hooks, 1994, p. 207)

Research Context

When first arriving at college or university, students are rarely invited – or even aware of the possibilities – to study the history and purpose of their own HEIs, particularly those that are inherently Euro-American and colonial in design. Consequently, students may often be deprived of the opportunity to identify in/direct oppressive forces within their own HEIs and how to address and dis/engage with them. This chapter attempts to capture how an undergraduate course lesson was collaboratively designed with and for students to create a 'Black feminist decolonial archive' that celebrates Black life, countering anti-Blackness within their historically and predominantly white university.

Upon arriving at the 'About' section of the history of Noble Raile University's (NRU)[1] website, a prideful archive of historical narratives and photographs greet you. As a small, private, predominantly white liberal arts university, located in a small, predominantly white rural town in the United States, one might imagine what the archives comprise. Although NRU currently has its first woman *and* Black president in its nearly 200-year history, like most historically and/or predominantly white institutions (PWIs) in the United States, NRU continues to pivot upon an institutional foundation that prioritises whiteness, Euro-Americanness, heterocispatriarchy, Christianity, and neoliberalism – all of which are reinforced in its digital and physical university archives. Besides, as Shirley Anne Tate (University College London, 2014) reminds us, in higher education, Black women are considered dispensable and invisible. The recent deaths of US university Presidents JoAnne A. Epps and Orinthia T. Montague and the suicide of Vice President of

Student Affairs Antoinette 'Bonnie' Candia-Bailey, as well as the forced resignation of Harvard University President Claudine Gay, underscore that even in leadership positions, Black women become the 'collateral damage' (Hudson-Ward, 2023; Weismann, 2024).

NRU self-reports that 19% of its student population are people of colour, 21% are international students, and 29% of the faculty are 'multicultural'.[2] Thanks to a $40 billion donation for a business school from a few wealthy white donors, the university recently opened a business school and closed a number of programmes in the arts, humanities, and social sciences, including an interdisciplinary programme track option. Halfway through the year, university administrators also formally severed ties with a community partnership programme that has significantly contributed to NRU's diverse US ethnic/racial student population over the past two decades. These students were openly told they were recruited to the university to increase 'diversity numbers' (Anonymous Email Communication, 2023). Aside from a few faculty members of colour, most of the initiative to serve historically and systematically marginalised US and international students of colour on campus falls upon the students themselves, particularly through their student organisations and their involvement with the 'diversity and inclusion' centre on campus.

A rupture surfaced in 2018 when the Black Student Association on NRU's campus led protests demanding action in response to racist incidents on campus and the pervasive whiteness of the curriculum. In response, NRU administration eventually issued a policy requirement that all enrolled students must enrol in a university-approved 'diversity' and 'global'-designated courses before graduation. To date, there is no evidence that such courses have resulted in a social transformation of the university's current racially polarised climate. Most of the staff, faculty, students – and curriculum – at NRU are of white Euro-American heritage. Thus, NRU has a history with Blackness that needs to be critically interrogated.

Literature

The Archive

Mbembe (2002) describes the archive as both the physical edifice and the documents it contains or holds, and that '[t]he status and the power of the archive derive from this entanglement' between them (p. 19). 'Documents' include digitised texts, as well as the cached and current websites of HEIs. People working within such institutions and the 'buildings' containing such documents also comprise archives – not solely physical buildings that hold physical archival records.

Countering the notions of individual archivists and their edifices, *community archives* include a collaborative collecting and gathering of oral histories, curated projects, and 'reassessments of existing collections and relationships to see what they might produce' (Crummé, 2024, p. xvi). Community archives have the potential to challenge the dominant individualist, whitewashing of institutional archivists and archives. Community archiving, thus, creates space for historically and systematically marginalised communities to 'disrupt this flow of privilege' through archival creating and collecting by sharing new stories and visibilising narratives that are consistently erased and omitted; such efforts simultaneously challenge stereotypical images and tropes of these communities (Caswell, 2014). In like manner, there is a shift in 'power', whereby Black narrators and archivists, for example, create and share the missing truths of incomplete stories they wish to tell (Funderburk, 2024). Decolonial archival work is inherently community-based (McCracken & Hogan-Stacey, 2023).

On Decolonisation and Decoloniality

Discourses on anti-Blackness, anti-Indigeneity, and PWIs usually include conversations about decoloniality and/or decolonisation, but rarely are they studied deeply. They are often used synonymously with one another. Furthermore, they are often conflated, fetishised, and overused without regard for unique historical, geographical, political, and sociocultural contexts (Tuck & Yang, 2012) and examples of what decoloniality and decolonisation may look like. Echoing Ngũgĩ wa Thiong'o in *Decolonisation of the Mind*, Sabelo Ndlovu-Gatsheni differentiates between his approach to decolonisation and decoloniality, explaining that within the context of colonisation, *decolonisation* demands an unlearning deeply embedded in one's consciousness since colonialism becomes deeply internalised (Omanga, 2020). Decoloniality, on the other hand, is an intentional countering of Eurocentric/settler colonial violences of modernity that erase, racialize, and objectify those from the so-called 'Global South'. Popularly adjudicated and reinforced by white and patriarchal proponents, decolonial discourses often disregard, erase, and invisibilise Black and Afro Indigenous feminist decolonial contributions that must be encountered, visibilised, and celebrated (Faniyi, 2024; McKittrick, 2006; McKittrick, 2021; Tamale, 2020; Wynter, 1994). In this chapter (and in the course), instead of introducing singular definitions for decoloniality and decolonisation, respectively, the intent is to problematise, as well as contextualise their various meanings across diverse African and Black Indigenous diasporas as an attempt to avoid generalisations and conflations of the two terms (Zeleza, 2010).

Black Feminisms

Black feminisms are locally and globally diverse, intersectional, and relational to other feminisms. Black feminisms do not belong to or emerge from the United States and the so-called 'Global North' but are birthed in global liminalities of struggle (Steady, 1996) and liberation (Combahee River Collective, 1977). Although differing in perspective and approach, critiques of patriarchy are a shared motivation. Black feminisms are counter-narratives to white/dominant feminisms and colonial-imperialist patriarchies that erase Blackness (hooks, 1981; Lorde, 1979; Tamale, 2020; Wynter, 1990). Sylvia Tamale defines Afro-feminism as a creation of 'theories and discourses that are linked to the diversity of African realities ... reclaim the rich histories of Black women in challenging all forms of domination, in particular as they relate to patriarchy, race, class, sexuality and global imperialism' (p. xiii).

Objectives and Methods

Although in the United States there is growing scholarship that addresses the excavation of complicit HEI histories and presents in slavery, genocide, and displacement in the name of capitalism at the horrific costs of Black and/or Indigenous peoples' lives (Lee et al., 2020; University of Virginia, 2024; Wilder, 2013), there is not much scholarship that addresses actions at the course or classroom level – one which includes students working alongside faculty. Also, US-centric approaches to such investigations deprive us of opportunities to learn and apply relevant epistemologies and ontologies from diverse global Black diaspora.

The purpose of this chapter, therefore, is to highlight a collective, course-based interrogation of a small, private predominantly white university's physical 'archive' through a campus scavenger hunt in search of the university's Black and Indigenous[3] histories and knowledges. By co-designing and engaging in the scavenger hunt, students identify all the blind/white spots of the university campus and craft interactive counternarratives of Black humanity and visibility that challenged concurrent dominant representations of whiteness, Black tokenisation, damage, marginalisation, and erasure (Tuck, 2009) present in NRU's current physical and digital archive. What Caswell (2014) refers to as 'archival absences' are equally *archival invisibilities*.

Thus, the motivating questions underlying this work are: What are the archival representations of Blackness at NRU? What are the stories we need that celebrate Blackness, feminism, and decoloniality on campus?; and how do we share such stories through a reimagined 'Black feminist decolonial archive'?

In a hybrid elective course highlighting the de/coloniality of African and Black diasporas in higher education, 12 undergraduate students – two Afro Caribbean American women, two international Black African women, two African American women, two Latina women, one international Asian woman, two white women, and one white man – collaboratively designed and exercised a scavenger hunt based on an integrated global Black decolonial feminist framework studied at the beginning of the course. The course was designed and taught by the author, a Southwest Asian junior scholar, who relies on her engagement and learnings on higher education transformation with and from artists, activists, community members, and scholars of African, Black, and Indigenous diasporas.[4]

At the beginning of the course, the meaning(s) and nuances of decoloniality and decolonisation defined by various scholars from Black, Afro-Indigenous, and Indigenous were discussed and carried throughout the academic term. As the course progressed, one of the primary learnings was that students were challenged in understanding what 'decolonisation' actually meant; and how I taught it left it ambiguous for students because it was difficult for them to comprehend without putting them into practice. Decolonisation and decoloniality do not begin and end with words. They must be enacted. Many activists, artists, and scholars whose work we engaged with used 'decolonial' and/or 'decolonisation' interchangeably without ever defining or explaining it. We discussed the genealogy of decoloniality, the consequences of its fetishisation and overuse (McCracken & Hogan-Stacey, 2023; Tuck & Yang, 2012), as well as the many meanings of decolonisation within various contexts of higher education (Stein & de Andreotti, 2016). Its dis/association from Indigenous relations with the Land is rarely discussed within the context of African and Black diasporas outside of Turtle Island/ North America. African and Black decolonial and decolonisation scholars often address African relations to Land – but not Indigenous relations. One of the main objectives of the course was to introduce students to concepts and frameworks such as decoloniality and decolonisation, but also to problematise them.

As a class, we first discussed how to define what 'Black feminist decoloniality' characterised in order to have a unified – yet diversified – understanding of how to engage with the physical and digital artefacts during an NRU scavenger hunt. Based on the texts we initially engaged with, it was collectively understood that we were defining Black decoloniality as: feminist; globally comparative across intersectional Black diasporas; an excavation of and counter-response to settler colonial entanglements and relations; a (re)humanising of Black, Indigenous life; and a responsibility to teach and learn with others.

As an ever-evolving scholar-learner of 'critical university studies' or 'higher education transformation', it became routine to conduct digital and physical archival research about NRU, as well as 'settler colonial walking tours' of the university campus. Such preliminary research invites collaborative opportunities with students in our courses together. Minthorn and Nelson's (2018) 'rearticulating' of a racist university campus tour at a minority-serving institution (MSI) through critical Indigenous theoretical and conceptual frameworks, centring concepts of Power and Place from Deloria and Wildcat's (2001) scholarship, was an affirmation that a scavenger hunt motivated by creating a Black decolonial feminist archive would be a unique, relevant contribution and exercise to engage with at this small, private white liberal arts university.

It is believed that scavenger hunts evolved from 'ancient folk games' (Schaller, 2020), whereby a specific 'treasure' is secretly hidden for all those participating in the activity to search and find, as they rely on a list or series of clues. At HEIs, scavenger hunts have been adopted for 'experiential learning' (Schaller, 2020) and studying 'organisational culture' (Barclay & York, 1996). Along these lines, in this particular course lesson, titled 'Decoloniality at NRU University Scavenger Hunt', the scavenger hunt positions Black history and knowledge at the university as a 'hidden treasure' for students to identify. It is *hidden*, because like most predominantly white universities, Blackness and Indigeneity are erased, invisibilised, pathologised, displaced, undervalued, and devalued. Breaking into four small groups, students split up across campus for a total of 1.25 hours during class time navigating the campus, seeking out answers to the clues and questions in the scavenger hunt. A few selected scavenger hunt clues and questions are provided in Table 18.1 for context. After completing the scavenger hunt, students collaboratively curated a digital exhibit (via photos, videos, graphic design, animation, and infographics) of personal and collective counternarratives to share with their peers.

Creating a counter story is not possible without knowing the stories that precede them. By understanding and learning the physical, living, and digital stories of Black life on campus, students invested in narratives that subverted them.

Analysis and Findings

Although what students learned about their university during the scavenger hunt was not surprising or unique to NRU, it was

Table 18.1. Selected Sample NRU Scavenger Hunt Clues and Questions.

Clue/Question	Objectives
Photograph/screenshot memorials, monuments, murals, street names, buildings, offices, centres, rooms, etc., across campus that honour any individual/collective Indigenous ethnic, racial, national individual(s)[a]	To navigate NRU's physical and digital campus 'archive' in order to determine which histories and presents are in/visibilised
Who was/are the first local and international student(s) from the Black diaspora to study at NRU? What did they study, and where did they come from?	To assess whether and how NRU's historical archive centres US white narratives and if their international recruitment efforts include Black diasporas
This campus building occupies the site of a former church for a Black congregation established in the 1870s	To understand if and how universities are complicit in the historical erasure of Black communities

[a] Since photographs and screenshots are identifiable, none were included here in order to maintain anonymity of the identity of students and the university.

still eye-opening for students, motivating them to share their own stories. In conversations with students regarding their post-scavenger hunt reflections, it was evident that Blackness was not celebrated institutionally, but any publicly accessible, visible narratives of students of African descent are written through 'NRU's voice' rather than the voices of the students themselves, almost romanticising their experiences at NRU as a form of diversity tokenisation guised as institutional branding/marketing. The few Black students who are celebrated are all men. Settler colonial whiteness – especially men, on the other hand, is celebrated all across campus through university statues, memorials, artwork, monuments, and building names, for example. There is a deep sense of oppressional omission when whiteness, particularly centring white men's complicities in genocide and displacement are erased in the name of innocence-making. A frustrated student remarked, 'Andrew Carnegie's foundation helped fund a study on poor whites in South Africa to justify racial apartheid. This is who built this library! And we have a monument honouring Columbus?!?'

Global representations of Blackness in NRU's archive are non-existent. Although prideful of its internationalised student body, NRU's archive is US-centric. The concept of 'global' is also depicted and enforced through a white saviour-voyeuristic gaze, where images of smiling white students and curricula 'exploring the exotic other' are plastered across NRU's archives. Lack of archival knowledge among academic faculty and staff across campus reinforced this belief. Students' inquiries from NRU employees during the scavenger hunt revealed that the university lacks a commitment to creating an inclusive, justice-oriented archive that does not solely centre whiteness and the US staff and faculty ethnic, racial, and Indigenous critical literacies of the university are nearly non-existent (but it must be noted that students did not engage with *all* faculty and staff, including those who may have personal/intellectual knowledge about the scavenger hunt clues and questions). Regardless, those who *were* encountered by students did not even suggest and/or were unaware of alternative re/sources (individuals, websites, centres, programmes, departments, etc.) across campus.

Students' counternarratives celebrating Blackness on campus highlighted NRU's complicities and contradictions of anti-Blackness. Students' digital gallery of counter stories not only visibilised anti-Blackness, but they also centred and celebrated the diversity of Blackness at NRU. One student adapted a feminist Kenyan 'queering' of NRU's visual arts spaces. Another student addressed the plantation metaphor to address the prevailing white masculinisation of sports that Black students experience on campus, complemented by a fellow student's interrogation of power and space as the only Black athlete on her softball team as compared to the men's baseball team. 'Black digital archivists' at NRU – how a student identified her university peers – were honoured through evidence of Black joy represented in their social media posts. Although students declined to have their counter stories shared here, it reinforces the reality that we are all archivists, and some stories are sacred and should not be archived for public display, institutional gain, or personal academic advancement.

Strengths and Limitations

Having the time and space to create an archive of their own, it became clear that students were empowered to reimagine, visibilise, and celebrate Black and Afro Indigenous diasporas on campus in various ways, including celebration of some of the students' respective Caribbean, African, and/or African American identities. They refused damage-centred narratives (Birnbaum, 2004; Tuck, 2009) through counternarratives that centre Black life, particularly joy, love, and kinship (Chilisa, 2019); they identified anti-Black culture and practices on campus; and they reimagined what they individually and collectively believed a Black archive *should* look like on and beyond campus.

As far as limitations are concerned, this study is clearly based on a one-time, brief course activity in one classroom session co-created with a small number of undergraduate students at a small, private predominantly white university in a rural US municipality. Our findings, therefore, should be generalisable.

Impact and Next Steps

This scavenger hunt was the first invitation these students ever received to independently and collectively investigate the truth of their university campus and to reimagine transformative counternarratives through a Black decolonial feminist lens. It can also be replicated university-wide and at other HEIs globally. Although those enrolled in the course have graduated from NRU since the writing of this chapter, the remaining time they spent at the university was characterised by critical engagement with the university space. 11/12 students decided to choose research projects that intersected Black identities/Blackness and their university. Upon learning of the scavenger hunt, NRU's diversity officer also personally reached out to me to help inform her own work across campus.

Learnings from the scavenger hunt have inspired:

- Co-designing other course, departmental, programmatic, and institutional scavenger hunts across various departments and programmes as a means of addressing intersectional oppressions within higher education.

- Utilising the scavenger hunt as a methodology for research inquiry at the institutional level, particularly to excavate and redress the university's historic and contemporary injustices and inequities in its 'archives'.
- Identifying and soliciting additional creative, collaborative opportunities within and beyond campus that foster counter storytelling.

Notes

1. This is a fictitious name used to conceal the identity of the higher education institution. All names of students included in this paper are also pseudonyms.
2. It is uncertain why and how the university defines 'multicultural'.
3. In order to avoid both their conflation *and* separation, in this chapter, 'Black and Indigenous' knowledges and histories also include Afro Indigenous histories and knowledges.
4. There were many internal and external meditations in the conceiving and designing of this course. Questions such as 'Who am I to be teaching such a course?'; 'Should I teach this course?'; 'If I don't teach it, will someone else?' On the other hand, as the only comparative global studies scholar in the education department who critically studies higher education, it seemed I *had* to teach it in order to fill a gap, especially since there were no previous African/Black diaspora courses offered in the education department and almost every other department. Offered as an elective course rather than a required core education course, it was not surprising, therefore, that course comprised mostly students of colour (75%) from various fields and disciplines across campus, including peace and conflict studies, global health, and gender studies. Indebted to insightful questions and reflections shared with sister scholars/mentors at NRU, I eventually decided to design and teach the course …. Questions regarding students also surfaced. For example, can students who do not self-identify as Black utilise a Black feminist decolonial interpretation of a counternarrated archive? Can a SWANA feminist professor curate and teach Black decolonial feminisms (even if Black SWANA feminisms exist)?

References

Anonymous Email Communication. (2023, April 13).
Barclay, L., & York, K. (1996). The scavenger hunt exercise: Symbols of organizational culture. *Journal of Management Education*, 20(1), 125–128. https://doi.org/10.1177/105256299602000113
Birnbaum, R. (2004, April 20). Edwidge Danticat. *The Morning News*. https://themorningnews.org/article/birnbaum-v.-edwidge-danticat
Caswell, M. (2014). Seeing yourself in history: Community archives and the fight against symbolic annihilation. *Public Historian*, 36(4), 26–37. https://doi.org/10.1525/tph.2014.36.4.26
Chilisa, B. (2019). *Indigenous research methodologies* (2nd ed.). Sage.
Combahee River Collective. (1977). *The Combahee River collective statement*. https://www.loc.gov/item/lcwaN0028151
Crummé, H. L. (Ed.). (2024). *Community archives: Inclusive strategies in practice*. ALA.
Deloria, V., & Wildcat, D. (2001). *Power and place: Indian education in America*. Fulcrum Resources.
Faniyi, O. (2024, February 27). An African feminist manifesto. *The Republic*, https://republic.com.ng/february-march-2024/an-african-feminist-manifesto/
Funderburk, A. R. (2024). 'Talking White': An anti-oppression view toward transcribing and archiving Black narrators. In H. L. Crumm (Ed.), *Community archives: Inclusive strategies in practice* (pp. 1–22). ALA hooks, b. (1981). *Ain't I a woman: Black women and feminism*. South End Press.
hooks, b. (1994). *Teaching to transgress*. Routledge.
Hudson-Ward, A. (2023, September 27). *Two Black women university presidents have died, spurring heartrending accounts of workplace discrimination*. Choice. https://www.choice360.org/tie-post/two-black-women-university-presidents-have-died-spurring-heartrending-accounts-of-workplace-discrimination/
Lee, R., Ahtone, T., & Pearce, M. (2020). Land-grab universities. *High Country News*. https://www.landgrabu.org/
Lorde, A. (1979). *Your silence will not protect you*. Silver Press. Mbembe, A. (2002). The power of the archive and its limits. In C. Hamilton, V. Harris, J. Taylor, M. Pickover, G. Reid, & R. Saleh (Eds.), *Refiguring the archive* (pp. 19–26). Springer. https://doi.org/10.1007/978-94-010-0570-8_2
McCracken, K., & Hogan-Stacey, S.-S. (2023). *Decolonial archival futures*. ALA-Neal Schuman.
McKittrick, K. (2006). *Demonic undergrounds: Black women and the cartographies of struggle*. University of Minnesota Press.

McKittrick, K. (2021). Footnotes (Books and papers scattered about the floor). In *Dear Science and Other Stories* (pp. 14–34). Duke University Press.

Minthorn, R. S., & Nelson, C. A. (2018). Colonized and racist Indigenous campus tour. *Journal of Critical Scholarship on Higher Education and Student Affairs*, 4(1), 73–88.

Omanga, D. (2020, January 14). *Decolonisation, decoloniality, and the future of African studies: A conversation with Dr. Sabelo Gatsheni-Ndlovu items*. Social Science Research Council. https://items.ssrc.org/from-our-programs/decolonization-decoloniality-and-the-future-of-african-studies-a-conversation-with-dr-sabelo-ndlovu-gatsheni/

Schaller, T. K. (2020). Exploring the marketplace: Scavenger hunts as field-based experiential learning. *Marketing Education Review*, 30(2), 118–124. https://doi.org/10.1080/10528008.2020.1755602

Steady, F. C. (1996). African feminism: A worldwide perspective. In R. Terborg-Penn & A. Benton-Rushing (Eds.), *Women in Africa and the African diaspora* (pp. 3–21). Howard University Press.

Stein, S., & de Andreotti, V. O. (2016). Decolonisation and higher education. In M. Peters (Ed.), *Encyclopaedia of educational philosophy and theory* (pp. 1–6). Springer. https://doi.org/10.1007/978-981-287-532-7_479-1

Tamale, S. (2020). *Decolonisation and Afro-feminism*. Daraja Press.

Tuck, E. (2009). Suspending damage: A letter to communities. *Harvard Educational Review*, 79(3), 409–427. https://doi.org/10.17763/haer.79.3.n0016675661t3n15

Tuck, E., & Yang, K. W. (2012). Decolonisation is not a metaphor. *Decolonization: Indigeneity, Education, & Society*, 1(1), 1–40.

University College London. (2014, September 9). *Why isn't my professor Black?: Shirley Anne Tate* [Video]. http://www.dtmh.ucl.ac.uk/videos/isnt-professor-black-shirley-ann-tate/

University of Virginia. (2024). *Universities studying slavery*. https://slavery.virginia.edu/universities-studying-slavery/

Weismann, S. (2024, January 12). *Inside Higher Ed*. https://www.insidehighered.com/news/governance/executive-leadership/2024/01/12/lincoln-university-administrators-suicide-roils

Wilder, C. S. (2013). *Ebony and ivy*. Bloomsbury Publishing.

Wynter, S. (1990). Afterword: Beyond Miranda's meanings: Un/silencing the 'demonic ground' of Caliban's Woman. In C. B. Davies & E. S. Fido (Eds.), *Out of the Kumbla: Caribbean women and literature* (pp. 355–370). Africa World Press.

Zeleza, P. T. (2010). African diasporas: Toward a global history. *African Studies Review*, 53(1), 1–19. http://www.jstor.org/stable/40863100

CHAPTER 19

Decolonising Teaching and Research: A Student Buddying Programme Between Burundi and the UK

Louise Taylor[a], Jill Childs[a], Susan Muchiri[b], Naomi King[a], Diana Wanjagi[a] and Frankii Charles[a]

[a]Oxford Brookes University, UK
[b]Hope Africa University, Burundi

ABSTRACT

Social work departments at Hope Africa University (HAU) (Burundi) and Oxford Brookes University (OBU) (UK) created an innovative buddying programme for their students. The project design and evaluation were based on the Burundian principle 'Ikibiri' (working together) and the African principle 'Ubuntu' (I am because we are). Although this project stemmed from the need to decolonise curricula in the UK, it was mutually beneficial: students from both institutions learned about social work from another culture and strengthened their communication skills. Evaluation of the project took a decolonial lens, attempting to examine the extent to which students experienced a sense of *Ubuntu*. This chapter will share lessons learned in attempting to decolonise teaching and research, and inspire others to do the same.

Keywords: buddying; Ubuntu; social work; decolonising; student partnerships

Research Context

The social work team at OBU, UK, has worked on developing a decolonised curriculum since 2017. We are building on global strategic priorities for social work, informed by principles inherent in the Sustainable Development Goals (Childs, 2023). Social work education typically attracts a high proportion of students from the global ethnic majority, especially Black African/Afro-Caribbean students (c. 33%), compared to OBU and UK higher education (HE) averages (c. 6%). Our initial work attempted to understand poorer overall experiences and degree outcomes of global ethnic majority students (Bunce et al., 2021). This evolved into a broader project to embrace decolonial theory from the Global South (Childs & Clarke, 2022) and go beyond the 'decolonial bandwagon' and its multiple limitations (Moosavi, 2020).

Our move towards a more truly decolonialised approach was greatly supported by Susan Muchiri from HAU, Burundi. Our cross-cultural collaboration began at a social work conference in Rwanda, where we sought to create an African partnership to expand and enrich our work (Childs et al., 2024). This has inspired and enabled us to promote indigenous values of the Global South, such as interconnectedness, sharing, and mutual respect. We now draw on the African paradigms of *'Ubuntu'*, 'A person is a person through others', and *'Ikibiri'*, the 'spirit of coming together for the good of the individual and the community' (Muchiri et al., 2019). These paradigms speak to collectivistic values based on the concept of coming together to succeed, which have a strong resonance with social work values. Our goal is to cultivate an environment that enables all students and staff members to inhabit a space, to the extent that one can say, 'This is my home. I am not a foreigner. I belong here' (Mbembe, 2016).

Literature

We have drawn on a large body of literature, including Global South research on *Ubuntu* and *Ikibiri*, and their relevance to social work (e.g. Muchiri et al., 2019; Mupedziswa et al., 2019) and education (e.g. Biraimah, 2016; Mugumbate et al., 2023; Waghid, 2020). Muchiri et al. (2019) argued that *Ikibiri* can play an important role in social work practice, as both focus on the social nature of societies and how to resolve social issues. By promoting solidity, cohesion, and collaboration, social workers can use *Ikibiri* to draw communities together, encourage and empower people, and help to find ways of overcoming societal conflicts and challenges. Although focused on East Africa, their findings could also be valuable for social work in the Global North. Similarly, Mupedziswa et al. (2019) proposed that *Ubuntu* has great potential as a guiding framework for social work in Africa, describing how the profession and the paradigm share a great deal of their visions, missions, values, and principles.

Mugumbate et al. (2023) described the roles of *Ubuntu* in social work education in Africa, arguing that it provides a useful and appropriate philosophical foundation for training social workers. They outlined how it facilitates optimal forms of reciprocal teaching and learning, indigenises and decolonises the curriculum, and provides students with useful skills for practice. They also detailed how it could benefit social work globally. Waghid (2020) and Biraimah (2016) discussed the potential benefits of applying *Ubuntu* to the development of African HE and school education, respectively, with the latter focusing specifically on Namibia.

Our literature search did not, however, find any studies that offered empirical evidence of the effects of drawing on *Ubuntu* and *Ikibiri* in social work education in the Global North, or of facilitating opportunities for social work students from the Global North and Global South to collaborate and learn from each other. Our project was, therefore, designed to address this gap and to advance understanding and development of novel and innovative ways to decolonise social work curriculums.

Objectives and Methods

We created an online buddying programme for OBU and HAU social work students. The specific objective was to enhance students' sense of *Ubuntu* by working together (*Ikibiri*) to understand cultural similarities and differences between social work in each country. The aims of the programme were to promote intercultural awareness, open-mindedness, and collaboration, and to support the development of culturally sensitive social work practice.

The use of an international buddying programme grounded in indigenous models from the Global South is a unique way to develop an anti-racist environment that furthers the decolonisation of social work curriculums on a national and international scale. Our research question was: 'Could participation in the buddying programme support students' sense of *Ubuntu*?'.

The buddying scheme is in its third year. In total, 24 students each year (12 from each institution) meet up to 6 times online in small groups to discuss a range of predetermined topics. The sessions enable participants to get to know each other, discuss their educational experiences, and discover what social work involves in their countries. The sessions have been mostly conducted in English because HAU students are taught in English, although their primary language is French. One buddying group held parts of some sessions in French because an OBU student could speak French, and translated for both groups.

To evaluate the scheme, all students on both courses were invited to complete a short online questionnaire that measured their sense of *Ubuntu* (see Mutsonziwa, 2020). We invited students to complete the questionnaire before and after the scheme, but received low numbers of responses from the latter, so combined the pre- and post-participation data. The questionnaire was translated into French for HAU participants. Students responded to 17 items on a 5-point scale whereby 1 = strongly disagree and 5 = strongly agree. Example items included, 'You treat other people with dignity', and 'Your life is richer because you share it with other people'. Students also provided qualitative feedback on the scheme. Ethical approval was obtained from OBU for all students because ethical approval processes were not in place at HAU.

Analysis and Findings

In line with our aims, we established that the buddying groups facilitated intercultural exchange between students studying social work in two different countries. Student comments on the scheme supported this, for example:

> *Our session this morning, where we talked about humanity, was really inspiring. It is indeed the essence of life. Looking forward to our next session. (HAU student)*

Another student said:

I totally enjoyed this meeting as I was able to learn from the others and received answers to my questions about what social workers do in Burundi. (OBU student)

One student described the value of learning about *Ubuntu*:

I do think I increased my understanding of Ubuntu, and I applied it to my first social work placement. [...] It is a nice concept, and should be applied more in social work settings, so I found it extremely useful to learn about. (OBU student)

Although she noted that *Ubuntu* was not mentioned explicitly by the HAU students, she observed:

I think there is a sense of community and social mobilisation in African societies that forms a social bond and well-being, and that interventions [...] in these contexts are very much around the community to improve individual well-being. I don't think that happens to the same extent in social work in the UK – we very much focus on the individual, and the family as an extension – so I do inherently think that the Burundi students may 'live it' without labelling it. (OBU student)

In terms of the *Ubuntu* questionnaire, 38 students from OBU and 69 students from HAU completed it. Unfortunately, response errors meant that it was not possible to separate responses from students who participated in the buddying scheme from those who were studying social work on the two courses but who did not participate in the scheme; therefore, we looked at data from all students combined. The mean *Ubuntu* score of OBU and HAU students was almost identical (OBU $M = 4.36$, $SD = 0.55$; HAU $M = 4.36$, $SD = 0.47$), suggesting that all students from both courses experienced high levels of *Ubuntu*, irrespective of whether they participated in the buddying scheme.

However, there were two notable differences between HAU and OBU students for two questions (see Table 19.1). OBU students scored higher than HAU students when rating their belief in the humanity of other people, whereas HAU students scored

Table 19.1. Means (and Standard Deviations) of Student Responses from OBU and HAU to Two Questions from the *Ubuntu* Questionnaire.

Question	OBU	HAU
You believe in the humanity of other people	4.68 (0.57)	3.96 (1.21)
You like living together with other people	3.63 (1.22)	4.62 (0.73)

higher than OBU students when rating whether they like living together with others.

Further work is needed to explore the validity of attempting to measure *Ubuntu* using this online questionnaire and to explore whether the mere presence of the buddying scheme in each department had a positive benefit for all students, including those who did not take part.

Strengths and Limitations

In terms of strengths, we created an innovative scheme that valued and prioritised theoretical perspectives from the Global South. Students were very willing to participate and brought with them a rich knowledge base of their country and cultural practices which they shared openly and honestly. They appreciated the opportunity to find out how learning is structured in a different cultural context, gave regular feedback to the leader about their learning, and raised key information to bring to the attention of their wider teaching team and peer group.

The groups were conducted in English, which gave HAU students the opportunity to practise and develop their English skills. Although English has a problematic hegemonic position, fluent English is considered essential for Burundian academics (Nduwimana, 2020), and HAU's vision is to encourage bilingualism in its students, putting them at an advantage for moving within different African countries. For the group that conducted parts of some sessions in French, this was a good opportunity for OBU students to experience communication challenges first-hand and to collaboratively develop ways of overcoming them.

Limitations included power dynamics, stemming from historical colonial injustices, including the comparative wealth of UK students and disparities in technology access. A major challenge for HAU students was internet connectivity and obtaining suitable devices to access the internet. Holding the groups in English created communication challenges for some students. The group timing was challenging due to different academic year schedules, for example, the academic year at HAU begins in February then restarts in August, whereas at OBU, it begins in September and restarts in January. This meant that students had limited times to meet when not in assessment periods or away from university, and some dropped out owing to frustrations at finding appropriate times.

Impact and Next Steps

This project set out to further decolonise social work curriculums in the UK and Burundi, and create an anti-racist environment through an international buddying programme that promoted the indigenous Global South models of *Ubuntu* and *Ikibiri*. Specifically, it aimed to enhance students' sense of *Ubuntu* and increase their understanding of social work in each country through collaborative work (*Ikibiri*). Students from both OBU and HAU appeared to benefit from the programme, gaining increased intercultural awareness and collaborative skills, and the *Ubuntu* questionnaire indicated that all students experienced high levels of *Ubuntu,* although further research is needed to determine whether participation or the mere presence of the scheme had this effect. As well as the individual benefits gained by students, the scheme benefitted both departments and universities in various ways, such as helping them to move away from the dominating perspectives of the Global North towards the indigenous values of the Global South. Any work that supports local solutions to capturing indigenous approaches in social work education, informed by the principle of *Ubuntu* along with the implementation of other indigenous ideas, is of high future value. Therefore, the answer may lie in work that transforms curriculums and prioritises the importance of locally based solutions that apply ideas from non-western contexts in an international context. Applying these in social work education may have the potential to shape future decision-making of regulators, HE leaders, policymakers, teachers, and practitioners of social work in both the UK and Africa (Childs, 2023).

The next steps of advancing our work will involve:

- Engaging in further research on the concept of *Ubuntu*, including investigation of the validity of Mutsonziwa's (2020) questionnaire and other potential ways to assess *Ubuntu*. This will be highly beneficial for future projects at national and international levels.

- Overcoming more fundamental challenges in the overall development of social work curriculums. There exists a heavy reliance on Anglo-American theory, literature, and practice in the UK and East African contexts, and although changes are being made to teaching materials, more fundamental transformations need to take place. At OBU, for example, we intend to draw on our learning from the buddying scheme to embed *Ubuntu* philosophy more deeply into our curriculum and ways of teaching, instead of engaging in more superficial decolonising actions such as simply trying to diversify reading materials.

- Promoting in both countries the value of supporting indigenous approaches in social work education. At OBU, for example, we intend to enable students to draw on and apply *Ubuntu* in their placements and careers, and be able to share the merits of this with colleagues and clients on a much wider scale.

References

Biraimah, K. (2016). Moving beyond a destructive past to a decolonised and inclusive future: The role of ubuntu-style education in providing culturally relevant pedagogy for Namibia. *International Review of Education*, 62, 45–62. https://doi.org/10.1007/s11159-016-9541-1

Bunce, L., King, N., Saran, S., & Talib, N. (2021). Experiences of black and minority ethnic (BME) students in higher education: Applying self-determination theory to understand the BME attainment gap. *Studies in Higher Education*, 46(3), 534–546. https://doi.org/10.1080/03075079.2019.1643305

Childs, J. (2023, July 20). Collaborating on an anti-racist curriculum. *Wonkhe Blog*. https://wonkhe.com/blogs/collaborating-on-an-anti-racist-curriculum/?utm_content=buffer2f713&utm_medium=social&utm_source=twitter.com&utm_campaign=buffer

Childs, J., & Clarke, L. (2022, March 8). Viewpoint: Decolonising the social work curriculum – A university's journey. *Professional Social Work*. https://www.basw.co.uk/resources/professional-social-work-psw

Childs, J., Mohamed, O., Pike, N., Muchiri, S., Bell, J., Dibo, A., & Ndabarushimana, A. (2024). Learning from Ikibiri and Ubuntu to decolonise social work research in higher education. *Practice*, 36(2), 159–171. https://doi.org/10.1080/09503153.2023.2223362

Mbembe, A. (2016). Decolonizing the university: New directions. *Arts and Humanities in Higher Education*, 15(1), 29–45. https://doi.org/10.1177/1474022215618513

Moosavi, L. (2020). The decolonial bandwagon and the dangers of intellectual decolonisation. *International Review of Sociology*, 30(2), 332–354. https://doi.org/10.1080/03906701.2020.1776919

Muchiri, S., Murekasenge, J., & Nzisabira, S. (2019). *Ikibiri in Burundian society: An indigenous model of solidarity and collaboration*. Fountain Publishers.

Mugumbate, J., Mupedziswa, R., Twikirize, J, Mthethwa, E., Desta, A., & Oyinlola, O. (2023). Understanding Ubuntu and its contribution to social work education in Africa and other regions of the world. *Social Work Education*, 43(4), 1123–1139. https://doi.org/10.1080/02615479.2023.2168638

Mupedziswa, R., Rankopo, M., & Mwansa, L. (2019). Ubuntu as a pan-African philosophical framework for social work in Africa. In J. Twikirize & H. Spitzer (Eds.), *Social work practice in Africa: Indigenous and innovative approaches* (pp. 21–38). Fountain Publishers.

Mutsonziwa, I. (2020). *Ubuntu: Development and validation of a scale to measure African humanism* [Doctoral dissertation]. University of Pretoria. https://repository.up.ac.za/handle/2263/79761

Nduwimana, A. (2020, August 7). Should Burundians care about English as a global language? https://blogs.lse.ac.uk/africaatlse/2020/08/07/should-burundians-care-about-english-global-language-politics/

Waghid, Y. (2020). Towards an Ubuntu philosophy of higher education in Africa. *Studies in Philosophy and Education*, 39(3), 299–308. https://doi.org/10.1007/s11217-02

HIGHER EDUCATION – SUMMARY

The chapters in this section have illustrated the challenges involved in deconstructing the colonial project through a decolonial agenda, such as, discomfort with the decolonial process, from all actors involved. However, change is imperative, and the authors have described different ways of tackling the decolonial project at the individual, national, and institutional levels. The decolonial process occurs within and beyond nationally created state borders. The authors have given recognition to the possibilities afforded through internationalised classrooms in advancing decolonial praxis. It is recognised that the hegemonic position of the English language remains an area of contestation across different global regions, from the South to the North. This suggests that initiatives to decentre English language can serve as a veritable and equitable approach, driven by decolonial praxis. The point here is to highlight the importance of other languages which the English language colonial tool sought to erase. Hence, decentring the English language through a decolonial lens may help with addressing re-imagined conceptions of 21st century literacy. However, there remains a need to consider the valuing of different knowledges and ways of being beyond the Western gaze, and this includes and extends beyond language learning.

Reflective Questions

1. To what extent has national policy impacted the approaches to embedding decolonisation in initial teacher training/education?
2. How can there be a better integration of decolonisation in learning and teaching to address the continuing legacy of colonialisation that emerges in the form of systemic inequalities in the classroom and beyond?

3. How can higher education scholars and practitioners address the discomfort encountered by actors involved in the process of decolonisation?

Recommended Reading

Andreotti, V. O., Stein, S., Ahenakew, C., & Hunt, D. (2015). Mapping interpretations of decolonization in the context of higher education. *Decolonization: Indigeneity, Education & Society*, 4(1), 21–40.

Bhambra, G. K., & Holmwood, J. (2021). *Colonialism and modern social theory*. Polity Press.

Fakunle, O., Kalinga, C., & Lewis, V. (2022). Internationalization and decolonization in UK higher education: Are we there yet? *International Higher Education*, 110(2022), 1–3.

Gopal, P. (2021). On decolonisation and the university. *Textual Practice*, 35(6), 873–899. https://doi.org/10.1080/0950236X.2021.1929561

Lander, V. (2014). Special issue race ethnicity and education: Initial teacher education: Developments, dilemmas, and challenges. *Race, Ethnicity, and Education*, 17(3), 299–303. https://doi.org/10.1080/13613324.2013.832917

Martin, F., & Pirbhai-Illich, F. (2016). Towards decolonising teacher education: Criticality, relationality and intercultural understanding. *Journal of Intercultural Studies*, 37(4), 355–372.

Mignolo, W. D. (2017). Coloniality is far from over, and so must be decoloniality. *Afterall*, 43(1), 38–45. https://doi.org/10.1086/692552

Moncrieffe, M. L. (Ed.). (2020). *Decolonising the curriculum: Teaching and learning about race equality* (Issue 3). University of Brighton. https://www.researchgate.net/publication/343211837_Decolonising_the_Curriculum_Teaching_and_Learning_about_Race_Equality_Issue_3_July_2020

Ndlovu-Gatsheni, S. J. (2020). *Decolonization, development and knowledge in Africa: Turning over a new leaf* (1st ed.). Routledge. https://doi.org/10.4324/9781003030423

Pirbhai-Illich, F., Martin, F., & Pete, S. (2023). *Decolonizing educational relationships: Practical approaches for higher and teacher education*. Emerald Publishing Limited.

Tuck, E., & Yang, K. W. (2012). Decolonization is not a metaphor. *Decolonization: Indigeneity, Education & Society*, 1(1), 1–40.

Winter, J., Webb, O., & Turner, R. (2024). Decolonising the curriculum: A survey of current practice in a modern UK university. *Innovations in Education and Teaching International*, 61(1), 181–192. https://doi.org/10.1080/14703297.2022.2121305

CONCLUSION

CHAPTER 20

What Are the Next Steps to Advancing Equity and Inclusion in Teaching and Learning Through Decolonial Educational Research and Practice?

Marlon Lee Moncrieffe[a], Omolabake Fakunle[b], Marlies Kustatscher[b] and Anna Olsson Rost[c]

[a]*British Educational Research Association, UK*
[b]*University of Edinburgh, UK*
[c]*Manchester Metropolitan University, UK*

The purpose of this guide has been to share examples of impactful decolonial evidence-informed research in teaching and learning in early childhood and primary education, secondary and tertiary education, and higher education so that this praxis can be fostered more widely. A wide range of methodological approaches grounded by decolonial theory have been shared, leading to the question: What are the next steps to advancing equity and inclusion in teaching and learning through decolonial educational research and practice?

Opposition and Challenges

This guide opened by pointing to examples of the social and educational contexts across the world from which the public provocation and demand for a decolonised curriculum have emerged such as: through the Black Lives Matter anti-racism protests of 2020; and the student-led 'Rhodes Must Fall' and

'Why is my curriculum white?' movements across UK and South African universities in 2015. Following the Black Lives Matter anti-racism protests of 2020 in the UK, government (Conservative) policymakers were called to parliament to answer a list of the public's concerns. They had petitioned for educational reform to see the teaching and learning of Black history in schools, to counter the epistemic violence of whiteness they saw imposed on children and young people through early childhood, primary education, and secondary education curriculum content (UK Parliament Committees, 2020). Despite the expert evidence of this epistemic violence shared by leading practitioners, academics, and educationalists, and their remedies for diversification of curriculum knowledge, the government (Conservative) policymakers did not uphold the public's concerns. Instead, they argued that national curriculum contents were broad and balanced enough in their current form (see Moncrieffe, 2023).

In higher education, Stokes (2021) appeared to provide a double view that the new wave of interest in decolonisation was a welcome contribution but must not be imposed. However, the latter perspective of possible imposition has seen powerful and continued discourse given to opposing the decolonising the curriculum movement, seeing this as a threat by accusing it of igniting culture wars through 'woke' ideology (Bekhradnia, 2023) with UK universities consumed by a racial moral panic (Stokes, 2023). The use of Critical Race Theory in schools was claimed by UK government (Conservative) ministers as breaking of the law in teaching white pupils about white privilege and inherited racial guilt (Murray, 2020; Warmington, 2024). However, this was a claim that aimed to quell the possibility of generating transformative anti-racist perspectives and approaches to critical curriculum teaching and learning and decolonising the curriculum. Persisting disparate notions of what decolonising the curriculum might mean ensures continuing disruption to progressing the level of discourse and real change.

Opportunities Ahead

Despite these charges held against decolonising the curriculum, the expert-led research contents as praxis shared by this BERA guide cannot be so easily suppressed.

In the introduction, this BERA guide shared some key aims:

To provide an overview of action being taken to decolonise the curriculum across key phases of compulsory and non-compulsory education in the UK.

While the sample of case studies within this guide is wide-ranging and diverse, the structure of each chapter affords the different examples of a uniformed starting point. This provides a framework for readers to compare and contrast different approaches and findings, as well as an opportunity to generate further questions and potential research foci for future investigation in the form of 'next steps'. As a result of this structure, this overview of decolonial praxis in action is not solely focused on the case studies themselves but also the theories, methods, and thinking processes that underpin this work. As an overview, this guide reveals similarities and differences, both within and across the key phases of education. As a collection, it reveals both depth and breadth in regard to decolonial praxis within the UK and also provides specific and research-informed suggestions for opportunities ahead.

To provide contextual international comparative approaches to decolonising the curriculum.

It is noticeable that the full range of references given across this BERA guide is written in the English language. As editors, we also recognise that the international communication of decolonising the curriculum is of far greater scope than the collective samples presented in this BERA guide from Burundi, Canada, South Africa, Trinidad and Tobago, the USA, and the four countries of the UK. Still, what is evident from these examples given is that the discourses around race, racialised identities, and coloniality shaped by the situated context of each contribution point to common themes. For example, Osivwemu (Chapter 7) writes about how educators in Johannesburg and London both shared an understanding of education as a transformative social justice tool and challenged tokenistic 'diversity' approaches. Taylor and colleagues (Chapter 19) evaluate an intercultural buddying programme between social work students in Burundi and England and highlight the students' critical engagement and mutual learning within a context shaped by colonial injustices. While the colonial histories in Canada and Scotland are very distinct, the chapters by Abawi and Berman (Chapter 5), and Devarakonda and Kustatscher (Chapter 4), illustrate the shared challenges of decolonising early childhood education, shaped by particular constructions of childhood and by hegemonic whiteness within the workforce and pedagogical approaches. Bringing together small-scale, situated contributions, our volume does not seek to provide international generalisations in terms of what decolonisation 'should look like' in these different contexts, but instead points towards the value of making visible a range of diverse and embedded case studies. The international nature of the contributions enables our readers to deepen their understanding of how European colonialism continues to be a dominant epistemic power that permeates societies, and educational policy and practice, across the world, in intersection with racism, classism, and patriarchy (Moncrieffe, 2022), while, at the same time, providing practical examples of resistance against these very structures.

To share a wide range of decolonial theories and methodological approaches for decolonising the curriculum.

The contributions in this book show that theoretical, epistemological, and methodological perspectives and practices do not stand outside the decolonial discourse, but very much need to be re-evaluated and re-imagined as part of any decolonisation efforts. In her seminal work, Smith (2012) revealed the 'dirty history' of research as an imperialist project, steeped in colonial notions of 'discovery', 'originality', and exploitative, othering practices. While research methodologies are often portrayed as mainly procedural or technological, their role in legitimizing what counts as valuable knowledge (and what does not) cannot be overstated (Ndlovu-Gatsheni, 2019). As editors, we were also mindful of how citational politics contribute to the reproduction of such epistemic inequalities (Ahmed, 2013), and sought to encourage citations of knowledges by all genders, by people from the Global South, and those who do not squarely fall into what is generally considered 'academic' knowledge. This volume showcases a breadth of methodological approaches designed to achieve innovative educational practice. Davis and Olusola (Chapter 15), for example, draw on collective and reflective approaches to collaboratively analyse and deconstruct Welsh ITE curricula and to feed into the newly developed Welsh Government organisation DARPL (diversity and anti-racist professional learning). Richardson and colleagues (Chapter 12) utilise arts-based approaches drawing on visuals and artefacts to connect the broader aims of their research with the highly personalized interpretations and experiences of their participants and to transform their mindset into one of activism. Sattarzadeh (Chapter 18) draws on indigenous theoretical and conceptual frameworks to engage students in creative ways with the findings of archival research. Overall, the chapters highlight the importance of adapting methodological approaches to the contexts and topics of research, of taking critical, reflexive, embodied, and transformative approaches to decolonial work, while also acknowledging the limitations and resistances to this work within the context of our educational institutions.

To provide insights on the positive impact generated by teaching and learning a decolonised curriculum.

This BERA guide encapsulates possibilities for a positive impact generated by teaching and learning a decolonised curriculum at all levels. The decolonial praxis presented in early childhood and primary education demonstrates how the school curriculum can foster broader learning of historical and current events as well as lived experiences. Students' involvement in co-creating impactful learning experiences contributes to an enhanced sense of connection, inclusion, belonging, and racial awareness. The triage of continued and advanced professional development, culturally responsive pedagogy, and critical reflexivity are crucial for developing a decolonised praxis. The chapters in the secondary and tertiary education section illustrates the importance of subject and disciplinary knowledge, and the role that they play as key foundation stones for building a subject-specific decolonial approach. This afforded opportunities to co-create knowledge, thus enriching the learning experience for all. In higher education, for example, Akbar and Fakunle (Chapter 16) illustrate the role of the educator taking a conscious and deliberate stance in facilitating a decolonial approach in the internationalized classroom. This recognises the possibilities inherent in internationalized classrooms to draw on the strength in diversity represented by the class membership (Fakunle et al., 2022) within national contexts and collaborative learning across borders.

To offer next steps for advancing decolonial praxis across key phases of compulsory and non-compulsory education.

Critical reflexivity as a decolonial tool weaves through the narratives across different sections in the book. This addresses a key gap, given the observation by Hayes et al. (2021) that educators' lack of reflexivity of their 'epistemological situatedness' has ensured the reproduction of coloniality. The contributors to this BERA guide have shared how reflexivity helps maintain a consciousness of their power and positionality. This, in turn, informs action to challenge structural injustices in the classroom and to promote equity. Although related, we propose that a distinction between decolonial research and pedagogy through a decolonial lens is helpful to offer next steps for advancing decolonial praxis across key phases of compulsory and non-compulsory education. Decolonial research requires an ongoing examination and contestation of the continuing impact of colonialism on everyday coloniality. In other words, reflecting the observations by Maldonado-Torres (2007) the end of colonial administrations has not diminished the arrogation of supremacy of colonial knowledge reproduction systems enshrined in the tenets of modernity. Not all educators will be involved in decolonial research, and not all need to be. However, learning and teaching through a decolonial lens affords a pedagogical approach that seeks to uncover and to dismantle underpinning structures that sustain coloniality. As has been stressed by several authors (Bhambra et al., 2018; Mbembe, 2021), a multitude of approaches to decoloniality do not undermine its applicability to different contextual realities. This is echoed by this BERA guide by showing diversity in decolonial praxis that transcends geographical regions. Core elements for advancing decolonial praxis include problematising and resisting ideological whiteness, normalising difference, and action in fostering equity in the curriculum design and practice. This will involve an interrogation of how 'a heterogeneity of conceptual, strategic and practical approaches to taking up the decolonial project' (Hayes et al., 2021, p. 888) can underpin the design and delivery of a decolonised curriculum.

We conclude this BERA guide with some final reflective questions for consideration:

1. What possibilities does a decolonial lens open up for reenvisaging children and childhoods within and beyond our education institutions?

2. What would be the value of a reimagination of the purpose of higher education from an international and intercultural perspective?

3. How can decolonial praxis grow and evolve through deliberate and purposeful sharing and co-production among practitioners – developing activist mindsets and action?

References

Ahmed, S. (2013). Making feminist points. *feministkilljoys blog*. Retrieved March 25, 2024, from https://feministkilljoys.com/2013/09/11/making-feminist-points/

Bekhradnia, B. (2023, May 25). *Universities should stick to their guns in the face of culture war attacks – By Bahram Bekhradnia*. Higher Education Policy Institute (HEPI). https://www.hepi.ac.uk/2023/05/25/24039/

Bhambra, G. K., Gebrial, D., & Nişancıoğlu, K. (2018). *Decolonising the university*. Pluto Press.

Fakunle, O., Kalinga, C., & Lewis, V. (2022). Internationalization and decolonization in UK higher education: Are we there yet? *International Higher Education*, *110*, 1–3.

Hayes, A., Luckett, K., & Misiaszek, G. (2021). Possibilities and complexities of decolonising higher education: Critical perspectives on praxis. *Teaching in Higher Education*, *26*(7–8), 887–901.

Maldonado-Torres, N. (2007). On the coloniality of being: Contributions to the development of a concept. *Cultural Studies*, *21*(2–3), 240–270.

Mbembe, A. (2021). *Out of the dark night*. Columbia University Press. https://doi.org/10.7312/mbem16028-003

Moncrieffe, M. L. (2022). Why decolonising curriculum knowledge? In M. L. Moncrieffe (Ed.), *Decolonising curriculum knowledge: International perspectives & interdisciplinary approaches* (pp. 1–14). Palgrave Macmillan. https://doi.org/10.1007/978-3-031-13623-8_1

Moncrieffe, M. L. (2023). What a primary school history curriculum for teaching and learning aimed at valuing cultural diversity should consist of. *Journal of the Chartered College of Teaching*. https://wakelet.com/wake/tnFFt-4_ZEt1ytPWF__it

Murray, J. (2020, October 20). Teaching white privilege as uncontested fact is illegal, minister says. *The Guardian*. https://www.theguardian.com/world/2020/oct/20/teaching-white-privilege-is-a-fact-breaks-the-law-minister-says

Ndlovu-Gatsheni, S. J. (2019). Provisional notes on decolonizing research methodology and undoing its dirty history. *Journal of Developing Societies*, 35(4), 481–492. https://doi.org/10.1177/0169796X19880417

Smith, L. T. (2012). *Decolonizing methodologies: Research and indigenous peoples*. Zed Books.

Stokes, D. (2021, March 18). *Decolonisation is a welcome contribution, but must not be enforced*. Higher Education Policy Institute (HEPI). https://www.hepi.ac.uk/2021/03/18/doug-stokes-the-white-paper-is-vital-for-the-defence-of-academic-freedom/

Stokes, D. (2023). *Against decolonisation: Campus culture wars and the decline of the west*. John Wiley & Sons.

UK Parliament Committees. (2020). *Black history and cultural diversity in the curriculum*. Retrieved March 20, 2023, from https://committees.parliament.uk/work/739/Black-history-and-cultural-diversity-in-the-curriculum

Warmington, P. (2024). *Permanent racism. Race, class, and the myth of postracial Britain*. Policy Press.

Glossary of Key Terms

Anti-racism – a range of ideas and actions which are applied to counter racial prejudice, systemic racism, and the oppression of specific racial groups.

Black Lives Matter – a decentralised political and social movement that seeks to expose racism, discrimination, and racial equality experienced by Black people and promote anti-racism.

Curriculum – a prescribed course of study with selected knowledge content and criteria expectations for what students will be taught and assessed on.

Decolonising – the challenging and undoing of historical and present colonial (Eurocentric) influences of power and knowledge authority.

Eurocentrism – a worldview centred on European/white knowledge, being, and doing, as superior to all other ways.

Epistemic – knowledge in relation to its scope of influence and validation.

Equity – a measure of achievement, fairness, and opportunity in education when each individual receives what they need to be on equal terms with others in the same environment.

Inclusion – equal access and opportunities in education for all people irrespective of race, gender, disability, medical, or other need.

Practice – related to ideas and theories for carrying out tasks and skills.

Praxis – conscious reflection and action upon practice in order to transform it.

Index

A level biology curriculum, 124
Academia/academic community, 69, 181–182
Academic knowledge, 228
Action research, 87–88, 125–126, 151, 179
Activism, 193
Activist, 89, 138, 203
African, 105, 203, 215
African American, 202, 207
Afro-feminism, 192
Afrocentric education, 73
Agency, 116, 137, 184
Anglo-American theory, 218
Anglo-centric/Eurocentric/western-centric, 92, 104, 178–179
Anglocentrism, 5
Anti-Blackness, 6
Anti-colonial curriculum, 190–191
Anti-indigeneity, 200
Anti-racism, 42, 53
   anti-racism/anti-racist, 52–53, 217
   protests, 170
Anti-racism framework (ARF), 160–161, 165–166
   analysis and findings, 162–164
   characteristics of effective anti-racist pedagogy in ITE/T, 163
   imagined case study, 165–167
   impact and next steps, 164–165
   literature, 160–161
   objectives and methods, 161–162
   research context, 160
   strengths and limitations, 164
Anti-racist pedagogy, 161

Anti-racist Wales Action Plan, 157, 170
Archival absences, 202
Archives/archival records, 106, 200
Arts-based approach, 133, 136, 229
Arts-based methodology, 133
Asset-based approach, 16
Asylum-seeking, 191

Banking concept of education, 77
Belfast/Good Friday Agreement (1998), 32
Belonging, 118
BERA guide, 4, 6, 8–9, 226, 229
Bias-free approaches, 56
Bilingual learners, 191
Bilingualism, 216
Biology, 123
   teachers, 124
   teaching, 124
Birth to 5 Matters, 64–65
Black, 42, 53
Black and Asian British history, 96
Black and Global Majority (BAGM), 160–161
Black Asian Minority Ethnic (BAME), 64–66, 69, 162
Black decoloniality, 203
Black diaspora, 202–203
Black digital archivists, 206
Black feminisms, 201
Black feminist decoloniality, 203
Black history, 94, 204
Black learner voice, 79
Black learners, 72, 74, 77–78
Black Lives Matter anti-racism movement (2020), 94, 123

Black Lives Matter anti-racism protests, 94, 226
Black Lives Matter anti-racism public protests, 4
Black Lives Matter anti-racist protests (2020), 42
Black Lives Matter movement, 20
Black radical paradigm, 73
Black Student Association, 199
Black women, 198–199
Black-British histories, 74
Blackness, 202, 204, 206
Britain, 77, 92, 105
British educators, 78
British Empire, 112
British history, 10, 21, 92
Buddying
 programme, 158
 scheme, 214
Burundi, 212, 215

Canada, 52, 55, 57
Capitalist/capitalism, 43, 46, 202
Caribbean, 135
Caribbean families, 63
Chartered College for Teaching, The, 20, 29
Childhood education, 43
Children, 9, 16, 33, 43, 63, 108
Christian moral principles, 34
Christianity, 32, 35
Co-creation/co-production/collaboration, 73, 75, 78, 88, 181, 213
Co-designing, 208
Coalition Government, 92
College of Early Childhood Educators, 54
Collegiality, 173–174
Colonial 'Western rationality', 73
Colonial epistemic dominance, 72
Colonial projects, 170
Colonialism, 4–5, 55, 170, 171, 228
Coloniality, 132
Colour-blindness, 56

Colourblind approach, 54
Common European Framework of Reference (CEFR), 181–182
Communities, 7, 10, 189, 200
Community archives, 200
Comparative critical review of course content, 62
Conceptual frameworks, 204, 229
Confucianism, 182
Conservative UK government, 160
Contemporary decolonisation movements, 33
Contextually relevant taxonomies, 182
Continued and advanced professional development (CAAPD), 15–16, 87
Continuous professional development (CPD), 20
Core Content Framework (CCF), 160
Core Syllabus, 35
Counter stories, 206
Counternarratives, 207
Course development, 165
Course enhancement questionnaire (CEQ), 181
Covid-19 pandemic, 20
Critical, 5, 7, 19, 63, 144, 229
Critical literacies, 206
Critical race theory, 53, 172, 226
Critical reflection, 142, 151, 182
Critical reflexive practice, 83
Critical reflexivity, 230
Criticality/critical thinking, 78, 146–148
Critically reflexive research-informed practitioners, 16–17
Cross-cultural collaboration, 212
Cultural diversity, 178
Cultural exclusion, 173
Cultural identities, 184
Culturally relevant pedagogy, 72, 77

Culturally responsive pedagogy (CRP), 16, 229
Culture/cultural, 16, 34, 125, 158, 182
Curricular choices, 99
Curriculum, 76, 190, 192
  approaches to decolonising and diversifying, 26–27
  changes and stimulus, 97–98
  decolonising, 72–74
  initiatives, 93
  knowledge, 21
  movement, 226

Data collection, 74
De-centre Christianity, 38
Decolonial 'archive'
  analysis and findings, 205–207
  archive, 200
  black feminisms, 201
  on decolonisation and decoloniality, 200–201
  impact and next steps, 207–208
  literature, 200
  objectives and methods, 201–205
  research context, 198–199
  sample NRU scavenger hunt clues and questions, 205
  strengths and limitations, 207
Decolonial agenda, 221
Decolonial curricula, 76
Decolonial education
  analysis and findings, 55
  impact and next steps, 57
  literature, 53–54
  objectives and methods, 54
  opportunities ahead, 226
  opposition and challenges, 225–226
  research context, 52–53
  strengths and limitations, 56
Decolonial epistemologies, 53
Decolonial practice, 46, 75
Decolonial praxis, 6–7, 15, 47, 73, 83, 171, 229–230
  analysis and findings, 173
  impact and next steps, 174
  objectives and methods, 171–173
  research context, 170
  strengths and limitations, 173
Decolonial process, 221
Decolonial research, 230
  interventions, 52
Decolonial theories, 3, 225
Decolonialised approach, 212
Decolonialism, 53
Decolonisation, 24–25, 42–43, 73, 104, 132, 135, 170, 180, 200–201
Decolonisation process, 135, 157, 172–174
Decolonisation/decolonising/decoloniality, 5, 7, 200–201
  analysis and findings, 126–127
  of curriculum knowledge, 42
  in further education, 122
  in higher education, 178
  impact and next steps, 128
  literature, 123
  objective and methods, 123–126
  research context, 122–123
  strengths and limitations, 127–128
Decolonised curriculum, 173, 225
Decolonising curriculum, 4–5, 93
  analysis and findings, 75, 180
  approaches to, 26–27
  arresting epistemic violence, 6
  background, 4
  contents, 9–11
  deconstruction, 180–182
  educator understandings and practice, 75–76
  empowerment, 182–183
  equity and inclusion, 7–8
  fostering decolonial praxis, 6–7
  impact and next steps, 79, 184
  learner perceptions, 77–78
  literature, 72–74, 178–179

objective and aims, 8
objectives and methods, 74–75, 179–180
reflection, 183
research context, 72, 178
strengths and limitations, 78–79, 183–184
Decolonising early childhood education, 43
Decolonising education, 5
Decolonising language teaching
  analysis and findings, 134–136
  impact and next steps, 137–138
  literature, 132–133
  objectives and methods, 133–134
  research context, 132
  strengths and limitations, 136–137
Decolonising of curricula, 87
Decolonising process, 143
Decolonising teaching and research
  analysis and findings, 214–216
  impact and next steps, 217–218
  literature, 212–213
  objectives and methods, 213–214
  research context, 212
  strengths and limitations, 216–217
Deconstruction, 180–182
  activities, 182
Department of Education, The, 37
Deracialised, 160
Developmentalism, 53
Dialogue, 72
Digitised texts, 200
Disability/disabilities/disabled, 29
Disciplinary knowledge, 88
Discomfort, 8, 172, 221
Discrimination/discriminatory, 46
Diversity, 104, 179
  anti-racist practice, 157
  of historical narratives, 115
  wind, 157
Diversity and anti-racist professional learning (DARPL), 174, 229

Diversity/diversifying
  approaches to, 26–27
  curriculum, 93, 178
Documents, 200
Domain of consequence, 113, 116
Domain of practice, 115
Dominant narratives
  analysis and findings, 107–108
  impact and next steps, 109
  literature, 104–105
  objectives and methods, 105
  research context, 104
  strengths and limitations, 108–109

Early childhood education, 15, 43, 47, 69, 83
  analysis and findings, 45–46
  impact and next steps, 47–48
  literature, 43
  model of awareness of diversity, 45
  objectives and methods, 43–45
  research context, 42–43
  spaces, 46
  strengths and limitations, 46–47
Early Childhood Education and Cares (ECEC), 9–10, 52
Early childhood practice
  advancing intercultural learning, 63–64
  analysis and findings, 67–68
  impact and next steps, 69–70
  international comparative perspectives, 62–63
  literature, 64–66
  objectives and methods, 66–67
  parent–practitioner relationship, 69
  participants' successful strategies for developing a trusting parent–practitioner relationship, 68
  participants' successful strategies for reflection on parent–practitioner relationship, 68

research context, 62
strengths and limitations, 68
Early childhood practitioners, 46, 56
Early childhood students, 69
Early childhood studies, 64
Early childhood teacher trainer, 63
Early years foundation stage (EYFS), 65
'Early years' student–practitioners' feedback, 66
Education, 33, 74
Educational policy, 52
Educational theories, 21
Educators, 76
  conceptualizations, 78
  understandings and practice, 75–76
Embedded approach, 163
Empire, 112
Empower/empowerment, 182–183
Engagement, 28, 65, 133
England, 3, 42, 62, 164
English context, 62
English language, The, 188
English language teaching programme (ELT programme), 188, 190–191
English National Primary Curriculum, 72
Enquiry, 116
Epistemic injustice, 32–33
Epistemic power /injustice / violence, 6
Epistemologies, 142, 181, 184, 202
Equality, diversity, and inclusion (EDI), 171
Equity, 7–8, 158
Ethical dilemmas, 79
Ethical global issues pedagogy (EGIP) resource
  resource, 142
  teacher resource, 142, 144
Ethnically diverse student body, 122
Ethnicity, 42

Euro-American knowledge production, 123
Eurocentric curriculum discourse, 21
Eurocentric developmentalism, 54
Eurocentric developmentalist discourses, 46
Eurocentrism, 5
European colonialism, 228
European Convention on Human Rights, 37
Evidence-informed education, 21
External domain, 113, 115–117

Families, 62
  modular content, 63
#FeesMustFall movement (2015), 73
Formal assessments for placement-learning modules, 69
Freire, 6, 72, 77
French, 132, 135, 214, 216
Further education, 122, 192

Global concept, 206
Global knowledges, 172, 174
Global literature, 161, 164
Global North, 201
Global South, 212
Good Friday Agreement, 192
Government policymakers, 226
Grassroot /grassroots, 16, 57, 84
Growth, 116

HAU students, 216–217
Hegemonic whiteness, 10, 228
Hegemony, 147
Hegemony, Ethnocentrism, Ahistoricism, Depoliticisation, Salvationism, Uncomplicated Solutions, Paternalism (HEADSUP), 142
  analysis and findings, 144–148
  impact and next steps, 148–149
  literature, 142

objectives and methods, 143–144
research context, 142
resources, 143, 147
strengths and limitations, 148
Hermeneutical injustice, 33
Heterogeneity, 192
High Court judicial review, 37
Higher education (HE), 10–11, 157, 198, 212, 226
  curriculum in Northern Ireland, 188
  transformation, 204
Higher education institutions (HEIs), 198, 204
Historical Association, 93–94, 112
History curriculum, 92, 98
  analysis and findings, 95
  impact and next steps, 98–99
  literature, 93–94
  objectives and methods, 94–95
  recent curriculum changes and stimulus, 97–98
  research context, 92
  teaching of specific topics, 95–97
History-making process, 106

Identity/identities, 52–53, 75, 79, 136, 166
'Idle No More' movement, 4
Ikibiri, 212–213
Imperialism, 114, 122
Impression, 97
Inclusion, 7–8, 158
  policy, 8
Inclusive engagement strategies, 62
Inclusivity/inclusive, 75, 115, 137, 184
Indigenous, 52, 56, 115, 190
Indigenous language learning, 193
Indigenous values, 158, 212, 217
Inequality, 62, 170
Inequities, 21, 52, 160, 166, 208
Initial Teacher Education (ITE), 171
  curriculum, 157

initial Teacher Education/Training for England, 160
ITE/T, 160–161
Initial teacher training, 22, 157
Injustice, 33, 35
Institutional racism, 162
Institutional structures, 73, 93
Intentional processes, 181
Intercultural teaching and learning, 63–64
International buddying programme, 214
International comparative perspectives, 62–63
International students, 158, 178, 183, 188, 190, 199
Interpretative paradigm, 74
Intersectional, 75, 136
Interviews, 35

Johannesburg case-study context, 76

Key Stage 3 (KS3), 92, 104
  curriculum at Park View School, 109
Key Stage two (KS2) Black learners, 74
King's Language Centre (KLC), 132, 134
Knowledge, 32
  knowledge-rich curricula, 92
  levels, 24

Language, 10, 64
Language education
  analysis and findings, 191
  curriculum, 192
  in higher education, 188
  impact and next steps, 192–193
  literature, 189
  objectives and methods, 190–191
  research context, 188–189
  strengths and limitations, 191–192

Language learning, 189
Language reclamation, 189, 191
Language teaching, 136
Leader/leaders/leadership, 16, 20, 23, 28
Learner perceptions, 77–78
Learning, 55, 64–65, 208
  module, 67
  process, 180, 192
  themes, 151
LGBTQ+ enquiry, 106, 108
LGBTQ+ unit, 105
Linguistic conformity of higher education, 190
Literature review, 164
Lived experience, 16, 29

Marginalised people, 76, 124, 126
Marginalised/marginalisation, 35
Masculinisation, 206
Methodological tools, 172
Methodology/methodologies, 208
Migration, 112
  histories, 104, 109
Minority, 34
Minority Ethnic groups, 42
Minority-serving institution (MSI), 204
Model of awareness of diversity, 44, 46
Model of diversity typology, 17
Modern foreign language (MFL), 87
Modern society, 4
Modules, motivation and knowledge levels before undertaking, 23–24
Multidisciplinary theoretical approaches, 53

Namibia, 213
Narratives, 114–116
National Association of School-Based Teacher Trainers (NASBTT), 162
National conference, 165

National Curriculum for History, 104
Neutrality, 56
New Labour Government, 21
Newly Qualified Teacher Survey, The, 42
NI Core Syllabus, 32
Noble Raile University (NRU), 198–199
Non-Eurocentric epistemologies, 6
North, 188, 221
Northern Ireland (NI), 32, 188, 190
  institution in, 189
Nuffield Foundation, 33

Observation, 108, 177
Official language, 188
Ojibwemowin, 189
Online buddying programme, 213
Online learning modules, 20
Online modules, 22
  of learning, 23
Online survey, 162
Onto-epistemological shift, 43
Oppression, 5, 22, 73, 172
Oral history, 106
  interviews, 107
Oral/aural approach, 108
Orientalism, 133

Parent-practitioner relationships, 62–63, 66
Parents as partners guidance, 65
Parent–teacher relationships, 67
Participants, 78, 147
Participation/participatory, 134
Patchwork methodology, 172
Patriarchy, 73, 201
Pedagogical intervention, 63
Pedagogy/pedagogies, 8, 53
Peer debriefing, 173
Peer reviewing, 22
People of colour, 122, 124
Personal domain, 113, 115–117
Policy, 8–10
Policy context, 164

Policy development, 178
Political campaigns, 112
Positionality, 17, 76, 174
Post-16 education, 122
Post-16 institution, 124
Post-graduate programme, 188
Post-learning surveys, 27
Post-session survey data, 55
Poverty, 62
Power dynamics, 217
Power relations, 43, 46
Practical approaches, 67
Practice/practitioner, 6–7, 10
Praxis, 3
Pre-session surveys, 55
Pre-survey data, 114
Predominantly white institutions (PWIs), 198
Predominantly white university, 198, 202
Prejudice, 44
Preservice teachers/PGCE students, 144
Primary curriculum
  analysis and findings, 34–37
  impact and next steps, 37–38
  literature, 32–33
  objective and methods, 33
  research context, 32
  strengths and limitations, 37
Primary education, 3, 8
Primary objective, 133
Primary school curriculum, 15
  analysis and findings, 23
  approaches to decolonising and diversifying curriculum, 26–27
  conversations about race, 27
  decolonisation, 24–25
  decolonise and diversify curriculum, 26
  histories, 25–26
  impact and next steps, 28–29
  literature, 20–22
  literature, 27
  motivation and knowledge levels before undertaking modules, 23–24
  objective and methods, 22–23
  research context, 20
  strengths and limitations, 27–28
Primary school education, 9–10
Primary school students, 15
Problematic normalised assumptions, 56
Professional development, 149
  analysis and findings, 114
  impact and next steps, 118
  initiatives, 57
  literature, 112
  migration and empire, 112
  model of professional growth, 112–114
  objectives and methods, 112
  programmes, 57
  reflecting on enquiry, 116
  reflecting on narratives, 114–116
  reflecting on sources, 116–117
  research context, 112
  strengths and limitations, 117–118
Professional dialogue, 15
Professional learning, 157
Professional placement module, 62
Public activism, 4

Qualitative research, 134
Queering, 206

Race, conversations about, 27
Racial, 4, 20
Racial abuse, 160
Racial literacy, 171
Racialisation, 46
Racially diverse, 162
Racism, 161, 166
Racist, 46
Racist incidents, 160
Radical approach, 76
Re-learning process, 143
Reconceptualist scholarship, 53
Reflection, 68, 172
  and enaction, 113
  on practitioners beliefs, 67

Reflective approach, 64, 134
Reflective practice, 172
Reflective thematic analysis (RTA), 144
Reflexive practice, 87–88, 151
Reflexivity, 16
Refugee, 191
Refugee and asylum-seeking (RAS), 191
Regional-level policy, 34
Regressive approach, 21
Relational language reclamation approach, 158
Relationality, 192
Relationships, 10, 53
Religious diversity, 32
Religious education (RE), 32
Research, 3, 7
Research collective, 171–172
Research-informed practice, 16
Resources, 16, 22
Revised learning outcomes, 67
Revolutionary approaches, 73
Rhodes Must Fall movement, 4
Runnymede Trust, The, 113

Salvationism, 147
Scavenger hunt, 202, 204
Scholars, 33
School of Education, Communication and Society (School of ECS), 132
School-level policy, 34
Schools History Project (SHP), 109
Schoolteachers, 135, 136
Science/scientific, 122
Scotland, 3, 42, 44
Scottish Government's anti-racism in education programme, 42
Secondary education, 87
Secondary school education, 10
Self–reflexivity, 173
Semi-structured educator interviews, 74

Settler-colonial, 52
Small-scale research project, 136, 142
Social work education, 210, 218
Sources, 116–117
South Africa, 3–4, 73, 78
South African educators, 78
Strengths-based approach, 64
Structural, 17, 73
Student body, 124
Student feedback, 107
Student researchers, 134
Student teachers, 138, 148
Student voice activities, 126
Student voice inclusion, 137
Student-led research, 134
Students, 191, 205
'Students' counternarratives, 206
Subject/subject knowledge, 88
Subversive thinking and action, 88–89
Surveys, 55
Sustainable Development Goals, 212

Tape Letters, 106
  enquiry, 107–108
Teacher as learner/re-learning/re-education, 114
Teacher education research, 21
Teacher standards, 160
Teacher/teaching, 95, 113, 135
Teaching approaches, 62
Teaching module, 67
Teaching themes, 151
Teaching to transgress, 73
Tertiary education, 10, 87
Testimonial injustice, 33
Theoretical framework, 65, 172
Tokenisation, 202, 205
TRACTION, 118
Training sessions, 56
Translanguaging, 180
Triangular trade, 95

Trinidad and Tobago, 62–63
Trust, 21, 64, 78

Ubuntu, 73, 212–213
   Questionnaire, 215
Unconscious bias, 68
Under-representation, 93
United Kingdom /UK, 42
United States /USA, 52, 161, 189
Universal history, 105
University colleagues, 136
University College London, 118
University of Liverpool TIDE project, 113
University of Oxford, 118
Unlearning, 55, 143

Voice/voices, 16, 124

Wales, 3, 170
Welsh education system, 171
Welsh government, 170
Western developmentalism epistemic norms, 53
Western paradigms, 182
White Eurocentric curriculum, 73
White-centric epistemic dominance, 72
Whiteness, 5, 45
Whitewashing, 200
World Forum Early Childhood Conference (2022), 66
Worldviews, 16, 33, 38

Young children, 53